Praise for

GET A FINANCIAL LIFE

"This is a must read for anyone in their twenties or thirties hoping to have a shot at using their hard-earned money to get ahead financially. It will give you an easy-to-use framework for managing your money, along with countless lessons for avoiding costly mistakes and saving money. Best of all, it's easy reading."
—Matt Fellowes, founder of HelloWallet

"This is the book I *wish* I'd read when I was just out of college. Filled with life-altering financial lessons, this new edition of *Get a Financial Life* reinvents the money guide for a new generation."
—Farnoosh Torabi, financial expert and host
of the award-winning podcast *So Money*

"Kobliner provides concise but comprehensive solutions to the biggest financial issues facing young people today. This guide is just what millennials need to fix their finances, especially since personal finance is a subject far too many schools fail to teach."
—Scott Gamm, correspondent for TheStreet.com
and author of *More Money, Please*

"One of the best guides to help young people get a handle on money matters."
—Burton G. Malkiel, Chemical Bank Chairman's
Professor of Economics Emeritus, Princeton University;
author of *A Random Walk Down Wall Street*

"Beth Kobliner's book provides a much-needed and sensible guide."
—Paul A. Volcker, former chairman, Federal Reserve Board

"Beth's book packs a punch of practical advice. It speaks the language of young professionals and students without dumbing down crucial concepts. Definitely a must read for any young person looking to get an edge on life."
—Ted Gonder, cofounder and CEO of Moneythink

"A highly readable and substantial guide to the grown-up worlds of money and business. . . . Backed up by bibliographies, source lists, and useful phone numbers, this book could be tucked into one of those ubiquitous backpacks to guide novices through the thickets of apartment rentals, mortgage applications, taxes, and more. Its strength is in explaining both the principles and the practicalities involved in each chunk of the landscape."

—*The New York Times*

"If you're saddled with student loan debt from years in college and want tips on how to pay it down effectively, need to understand the basics of things like health insurance and why you get bills even though your insurer pays for other things, and don't see how it's at all possible to save for a home of your own someday, this book is for you."

—Lifehacker.com

"Shaw said youth is wasted on the young. I suspect the Kobliner financial wisdoms will work out well at all our ages."

—Paul A. Samuelson, Institute Professor Emeritus, MIT; Nobel laureate in economics

"Kobliner's done it again! *Get a Financial Life* gives clear and straightforward advice on how to manage your money—even in a financial meltdown. A must read for twenty- and thirty-somethings who want to be fiscally smart and financially secure."

—Soledad O'Brien, TV news anchor

"*Get a Financial Life* gives you the essential information you need to get your finances in order as you're starting your career. The rest is up to you. Educate yourself, get motivated, and get your finances in shape now by reading this book."

—Sharon Epperson, personal finance correspondent, CNBC

"Smart, thorough—a tremendously useful guide to all the essentials of sound personal finance."

—*Fortune*

"A daring book . . . A life's worth of smart financial advice."

—*Newsweek*

"With numerous insights, this fine book demonstrates that, through discipline and enterprise, anyone can win their financial independence."

—Tom Gardner, cofounder of The Motley Fool

"Beth Kobliner is telling you it's time to smell the latte. In *Get a Financial Life*, Kobliner serves a rich, smooth brew of common sense on everything from paying off your student loans to saving for (gasp) your future. The advice is thoughtful, precise, and up-to-date. But the simple, step-by-step explanations make getting a financial life easier than steaming the perfect froth on a cappuccino."

—Saul Hansell, business reporter, *The New York Times*

"An eminently digestible resource. Buying this book right now is probably one of the best—and cheapest—investments."

—*Time Out New York*

"Get it. Read it. Reference it often."

—*Kiplinger's*

"*Get a Financial Life* is a great option for a young, analytical, and thoughtful person—it doesn't just cram a conclusion down your throat, but explains options in a clear and reasonable way."

—TheSimpleDollar.com

"This was the book I had been waiting for; everything you need to know about saving, budgeting, credit cards, debt, insurance, owning a home, and much more is in this book."

—Cara Newman, YoungMoney.com

"Sometimes the very best books are the simplest. And that's the beauty of *Get a Financial Life*. . . . It offers the fundamental ABCs of how to manage your money. . . . Kobliner's book is a gentle guide, carefully walking her money neophytes through the nuts and bolts of personal finance. There's no magic formula for taking control of your financial life here, but rather frank meat-and-potatoes money-management moves that have stood the test of time."

—*USA Today*

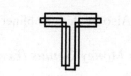

Also by Beth Kobliner

Make Your Kid a Money Genius (Even If You're Not)

Also by Beth Kobliner

Make Your Kid a Money Genius (Even If You're Not)

GET A
FINANCIAL
LIFE

PERSONAL
FINANCE

IN YOUR TWENTIES AND THIRTIES

BETH KOBLINER

TOUCHSTONE

New York   London   Toronto   Sydney   New Delhi

Touchstone
An Imprint of Simon & Schuster, Inc.
1230 Avenue of the Americas
New York, NY 10020

This Touchstone trade paperback edition March 2017

TOUCHSTONE and colophon are registered trademarks of Simon & Schuster, Inc.

For information about special discounts for bulk purchases, please contact Simon & Schuster Special Sales at 1-866-506-1949 or business@simonandschuster.com.

The Simon & Schuster Speakers Bureau can bring authors to your live event. For more information or to book an event, contact the Simon & Schuster Speakers Bureau at 1-866-248-3049 or visit our website at www.simonspeakers.com.

Cover design by Pentagram

Manufactured in the United States of America

10 9 8 7 6 5 4 3 2 1

Library of Congress Cataloging-in-Publication Data
Names: Kobliner, Beth, author.
Title: Get a financial life : personal finance in your twenties and thirties / Beth Kobliner.
Description: New York : Touchstone, 2017. | Includes index.
Identifiers: LCCN 2016005360 | ISBN 9781476782386 (paperback)
Subjects: LCSH: Finance, Personal. | Young adults—Finance, Personal. | BISAC: BUSINESS & ECONOMICS / Personal Finance / Budgeting. | BUSINESS & ECONOMICS / Personal Finance / Money Management. | BUSINESS & ECONOMICS / Personal Finance / Investing.
Classification: LCC HG179 .K59 2017 | DDC 332.0240084/2—dc23 LC record available at http://lccn.loc.gov/2016005360

ISBN 978-1-4767-8238-6
ISBN 978-1-4767-8239-3 (ebook)

To my parents, Harold and Shirley Kobliner,
who taught me how to handle money,
and to Sylvia Porter,
who gave me the opportunity to write about it.

CONTENTS

Chapter 10: Making the Most of Military Benefits 279

Know What You Deserve If You Serve

Further Reading 289

Special Acknowledgments 293

Acknowledgments 297

Index 315

INTRODUCTION

IF YOU'RE LIKE most people in their twenties and thirties, you worry about money.

And who can blame you?

The job market is rough. Salaries are flatlining. Student debt loads are at an all-time high. And housing costs—whether you rent or buy—are eating up a bigger chunk of paychecks than ever before. So while the idea of reading a book about money may not be high on your bucket list, it should be.

The good news? Getting your financial life in order is very doable if you start now. All you need is a modest amount of knowledge—much less than you'd think—plus a little effort. This book is your guide.

What makes me so sure? That one's easy: I've seen it happen, again and again. Since *Get a Financial Life* was first published twenty years ago, more than half a million readers have used this book to help them get out of debt, start to save, and begin to invest. This edition has been entirely updated and completely revised for the financial challenges you face today. I've re-reported, reexamined, and rewritten it from cover to cover. I've updated facts and links. I've also rethought every table, worksheet, and bullet point to help you take control of your finances—whether you're climbing the corporate ladder or doing your own thing as an entrepreneur, whether you earn $20,000 or $200,000, whether you're single or married, whether you're financially inclined or fiscally challenged.

Though many of the details have changed, the guiding principle of *Get a Financial Life* is the same: It focuses exclusively on what you need to know, and leaves out everything else.

You'll come away with strategies to help you save, even if you are barely scraping by. You'll get clear advice on paying down your debts—whether you have student loans, credit cards, or both—and learn how to shop for everything from auto loans to mortgages. You'll discover the best reasons (and the best ways) to save in 401(k)s and IRAs. You'll find clear guidelines on how to choose the right investments for you, and figure out what kind of bank you need. You'll get the scoop on whether you should borrow for grad school—and if so, how. You'll uncover tips based on the latest research on reining in spending, and learn how to avoid fees that eat into your savings. You'll pick up tax strategies that can easily save you hundreds if not thousands of dollars. You'll read unbiased advice about what insurance you need—and what insurance you should avoid.

You'll also get answers to specific questions, including: How can I fix my credit score? When is it smart to rent a place rather than buy? Should I invest in the stock market—and if so, how? Is there a safe place to put my money and earn a decent return? Plus, if you or someone you know is in the military or is a veteran, you'll get the rundown on available benefits.

Of course, the thought of reading an entire book on personal finance may still feel like pure drudgery. But don't despair. Start with Chapter 1, which is the "Crib Notes" version of what you need to know. Then peruse the end of each chapter, where you'll find "Financial Cramming" review sections that spell out the key concepts and online resources for you. And, I promise you, if you do decide to take the plunge and read the full book, you will discover that the details of getting a financial life are actually easier than you think. Especially since you have one major advantage on your side: time.

1

CRIB NOTES

A Cheat Sheet for
Time-Pressed Readers
Who Need Help Now

IF YOU'RE OVERWHELMED by the idea of diving into a whole book on personal finance, this chapter is for you. It cuts to the chase and sets you on the path to a solid financial life. No kidding around: Adopting even one or two of these strategies will put you ahead of the game and—I promise—make a big difference sooner than you think.

Of course, as someone's mother once said, cheaters only cheat themselves. And while this chapter is a good launching pad, ignoring the remaining nine chapters is a little like relying on the SparkNotes version of *Hamlet*: You'll get the basic plotline but never understand what all the fuss is about. That said, the following crib notes will give you the "need to know" basics. I've tried to list the advice in rough order of importance, but your priorities will depend on your own situation, of course.

1. Insure yourself against financial ruin.

You need health insurance. Period. As of this writing, the law requires that you have it. Even more important: It'll help protect you if you have an accident or illness, and guarantee that you don't bankrupt yourself—or your family—if you run into any serious medical problems. For these reasons, health insurance should be considered your number one financial priority.

If you work for a company that offers its employees health insurance, you're lucky; participating in a plan at work will almost always cost you much less than buying a policy on your own because your employer pays for part of it. Your company may offer more than one type of plan; make sure you consider not only the price but also the extent of the coverage. You'll want to find out exactly how much you'll be expected to pay out of pocket before insurance kicks in (this is known as the **deductible**), the rules for seeing specialists, and what happens if you want to visit a doctor who doesn't participate in the plan.

If your job doesn't offer coverage, you work for yourself, or you're looking for a job, you'll have to pay for it on your own. First, see if you can get coverage through a family member. Federal rules say you can be covered by your parents' insurance until you turn 26; some states will let you stay on even longer. If you're married and your spouse is insured through work, see about being added to that policy. Many companies also cover unmarried domestic partners.

If all else fails, you'll need to purchase a policy on your own. As of this writing, you can comparison shop at Healthcare.gov, sites like eHealth.com, or go directly to individual insurance companies.

For additional tips on the insurance that you need—and the kinds you should avoid—see Chapter 8.

2. Pay off your debt the smart way.

One of the smartest financial moves you can make is to take any savings you have (above and beyond money you need for essentials like rent, food, and health insurance) and pay off your high-rate loans. The reason is simple: You usually can "earn" more by paying off a loan than you can by saving and investing. That's because paying off a credit card or high-rate loan that has a 15% interest rate is equivalent to earning 15% on an investment, *guaranteed*—an extremely attractive rate of return. If you want a full explanation of this concept, turn to p. 31. Otherwise, take my word for it.

The first step in attacking high-rate debt is to try to reduce your interest rate. Start by simply calling your credit card company and asking for a lower rate. (Seriously, this often works.) Next, see if you can qualify for one of the lower-rate cards listed on sites like CreditCards.com and CardHub.com, and then transfer your remaining balance to it.

If you have several different types of debt—say, a balance on a credit card with a 15% interest rate, another credit card balance with a 12% rate, and a student loan with a 4% rate—pay off the loan with the highest interest rate first. One way to make this easier is to ask your federal student loan servicer to stretch out your payments for longer than the standard ten years by switching to a different repayment plan. This will reduce your monthly student loan payment, leaving you with extra cash, which you can use to pay off your credit card balances faster. Once you've gotten rid of your 15% card balance, increase the payments on your 12% balance. After you wipe out that one, increase your student loan payments to at least their initial levels.

The only time it doesn't make sense to kill your debt is when the interest rate you're being charged is *lower* than the rate you can receive on an investment. If, for example, you have a student loan with only a 3% rate and no other debt, you'd be better off maintaining your usual payment schedule on the loan and putting your cash into an investment that pays you an after-tax rate greater than 3%, assuming you can find it. One such place would be a 401(k) with matching contributions, which is coming up in the next point.

For detailed information on credit cards, auto loans, and student loans, see Chapter 3.

3. Start contributing to a tax-favored retirement savings plan.

This one might strike you as nuts at first. Why would you think about retirement now? But here's the reality: Saving money in a retirement plan is one of the smartest (and easiest) things you can do when you're young. If you're fortunate enough to work for a company that offers a retirement savings plan like a 401(k), you should take advantage of it. The big attraction here is that many employers will match a portion of the amount you put into such a plan. That means the company contributes a set amount—say, 50 cents or a dollar—for every dollar you contribute, up to a specified percentage of your salary. That's free money, equivalent to an immediate 50% or 100% return. There's nowhere you can beat this! (In fact, if your company offers such a fabulous matching deal, you should probably contribute to the plan even before paying off your high-rate debt.) In addition, the federal government allows the money to grow tax-free. (See p. 135 for an explanation of how this saves you even more money.)

It may seem crazy to lock up your money in a retirement savings plan. Ignore that feeling. While it's true that you won't be able to withdraw your money from a 401(k) until you reach age 59½ without facing a penalty, the benefits of matching and tax-advantaged growth are so huge that this is still the best deal out there. If you switch jobs, you may be able to move your 401(k) money into your new employer's plan (or transfer it into something called an IRA; see below). Also, most plans allow employees to borrow against their retirement savings in an emergency. As of 2017, the maximum you can contribute annually is $18,000, which may be more than you can manage, but try to at least contribute the maximum amount for which you're eligible to receive matching funds.

If you don't work for an employer who offers a 401(k) or a similar retirement plan, you should start investing in an **individual retirement account (IRA)**. The most you can contribute to an IRA as of 2017 is $5,500 annually; if at all possible, contribute the maximum amount every year.

IRAs don't provide matching contributions, so putting money in one is somewhat less pressing than enrolling in a company-sponsored plan that offers a match. That said, certain IRAs known as Roth IRAs do offer one special benefit: There's no penalty for withdrawing the money you contribute to them at any time. You're not allowed to freely withdraw the interest you earned on the money you contributed until after you turn 59½. (Note that there's also something called a Roth 401(k); see p. 135.)

Bottom line: Max out your company's 401(k) up to the matching limit if you have one. If that's not an option, go with an IRA.

For all your questions on tax-favored retirement savings plans, see Chapter 6.

4. Build an emergency cushion using an automatic savings plan.

If you find it nearly impossible to save money, you're not alone. But once you've gotten rid of your high-rate debt, taken care of health insurance, and started saving for retirement, it's time to begin stashing away three to six months' worth of living expenses.

Your safest choice is to have money automatically withdrawn from each paycheck and funneled into an old-school savings account. That's a relatively painless way to force yourself to accumulate a cushion. The downside to all that safety? Interest rates on savings accounts are generally low, though Internet-only banks tend to offer slightly better rates.

At various times, a type of investment called a **money market fund,** aka a money fund, which is considered almost as safe as a traditional bank savings account, has tended to pay higher interest rates. To comparison shop for the best rates on money funds, check out iMoneyNet.com and Cranedata.com. You can set up an automatic transfer from your checking account once or twice a month so it's as easy as saving in a bank savings account. (For more on money market funds, see Chapter 5.)

No matter what type of automatic savings plan you choose, focus on your goal of accumulating that emergency cushion. To figure out how much you need to save, use the worksheet (Figure 2–2) on p. 16.

5. Consider investing in stock and bond funds.

Once you have your savings cushion in a low-risk bank account or money market fund, it's time to get more aggressive with your investments. The advantage of stocks and bonds is that they've tended to earn more for investors over long periods of time, yielding higher returns that stay ahead of inflation. (For a discussion of inflation and why you need to worry about it, see Chapter 5.)

The downside of stocks and bonds is that they're riskier than savings accounts or money market funds. Translation: You can lose money by investing in them. So for money that you absolutely need to be there—say you've set it aside for a down payment on a home in a couple of years—don't invest it in stocks or bonds.

Only you can decide how much risk you're willing to accept, but there's an old rule of thumb that you subtract your age from 100, and that's the percentage of your investment money that should be in stocks; the rest should be in bonds and money market funds. Like any generalization, this one has to be tailored to your specific situation, but it can be a useful starting point.

If you do decide to put some of your money in stocks and bonds, invest it in **funds**, a type of investment that pools together the money of thousands of people. Here are some general rules: Avoid investing in funds with a **load**, which is the commission that some companies charge each time you put money into or take money out of a fund. They don't perform any better on average than no-load funds, so there's no point in paying extra for them. I also recommend that you consider only funds with low **expenses**, the annual fees charged by the fund that can take a huge bite out of your investment returns if you're not careful.

Although stock funds are considered somewhat riskier than bond funds (see below), they have also performed somewhat better over long periods of time. If you decide to invest in a stock fund, I like low-cost **stock index funds** and **exchange-traded funds (ETFs)**. (To find out exactly what these are, you'll need to read Chapter 5.)

Two companies that offer a large selection of low-cost index funds are Charles Schwab (Schwab.com) and Vanguard (Vanguard .com). You'll generally need to commit $1,000 to $3,000 to open an account if you want to invest in their stock index funds. If you don't have a lot of money, for about $100 you can start investing in a Vanguard ETF. (See p. 124 for more details.)

Holding bonds as well as stocks will help to diversify your investments, reducing your overall risk. Vanguard also offers low-cost bond funds. While there are several different types of bond funds, a reasonable approach would be to choose a **bond index fund** that invests in government securities or highly rated corporations.

To learn more about stocks, bonds, index funds, ETFs, and investing in general—you guessed it—you'll have to read Chapter 5.

6. Find out your credit score and improve it.

A **credit score** is the number that tells lenders whether or not you're a good risk. The score is based on information about you kept by the three major credit bureaus: Equifax, TransUnion, and Experian. These records, which include information received by the bureaus from your various lenders, are called your **credit reports**. You're legally entitled to one free report from each of the bureaus every year from AnnualCreditReport.com. It's smart to check your credit reports to make sure all the information included about you is accurate.

You can think of your credit score as the GPA of your financial abilities, a numerical representation of how appealing you are to lenders. Unlike your GPA, however, your credit score is being recalculated all the time. If you want to qualify for a low-rate credit card, car loan, or home loan; rent an apartment; or get insurance, your credit score will matter. You can get a free version of your credit score at CreditKarma.com, which also offers unlimited access to the information in your credit reports from Equifax and TransUnion. Before you apply for a loan, it may make sense to get your "official" credit scores from all three bureaus (they often vary) at myFICO.com for about $60. (See Chapter 3 for details.)

The better your credit score, the better the loan deals you'll get. For that reason, it's important to take steps to make sure your score is as good as it can be. The biggest component of your credit score is your track record for making on-time payments, followed by the amount of credit you're using and the length of your credit history. One of the easiest, most foolproof ways to keep your score in good shape is to pay all of your bills automatically online. That way, you'll be much less likely to miss a payment. For more on your credit—including how to fix and prevent identity theft—see p. 60.

7. Think hard before buying a house or apartment.

At some point in the next few years you may start to feel that it's time to purchase a home of your own. The decision about whether to switch from renter to owner involves more than simply comparing your monthly rent to the mortgage payments you'd make as an owner. A range of financial factors should enter into your decision, including the tax break you'll get from buying, the fees you'll pay when you buy, and how long you plan to live in the new home. For a discussion of how to analyze your own situation, see Chapter 7.

If you do decide that it's time to buy, you'll need to apply for a home loan, or a **mortgage**. One of the obstacles for first-time home buyers is coming up with the down payment required by the lender. You will likely need to have an amount equal to at least 10% (and ideally 20%) of the purchase price of the home. In addition, you will need a good credit score. You will also have to prove that your salary is high enough—and your other outstanding debts low enough—to make the monthly mortgage payments.

To shop for the best mortgage deal, you'll want to look at sites like HSH.com, Zillow.com, and Bankrate.com. It's also a smart idea to check with your local bank or credit union—sometimes the best home loan deals are right in your own backyard.

But what if you're eager to buy and can't come up with the full down payment or don't have great credit? All is not lost. For several alternative loan options—as well as caveats to make sure you don't get in over your head—see p. 172.

If you don't qualify for a mortgage (and still want to buy), don't give up. Make it your goal to spend the next one to two years improving your credit score (pay those bills on time!) and saving up for a down payment. You'll be surprised how quickly you can build your credit record (and increase your savings) if you follow the steps in this book.

For more housing-related tips for renters as well as buyers, see Chapter 7.

8. Get smart about income tax.

Nobody likes paying taxes. One way to decrease the portion of your paycheck that goes to Uncle Sam is to take as many tax **deductions** as you're eligible for. Deductions are specific expenses that the government allows you to subtract from your income before calculating the amount of tax you owe.

You can take deductions in either of two distinct ways. The easiest approach is to take the **standard deduction**, which is simply a fixed dollar amount ($6,350 for singles or $12,700 for couples in 2017) that you subtract from your income. Although all taxpayers are permitted to take the standard deduction, depending on your circumstances you may wind up owing even less if you **itemize** your deductions instead. Itemizing means listing separately the specific items that are deductible under the tax laws and then subtracting their total cost from your income.

If you do itemize, you'll file a tax form called a 1040 and list your deductions. (You can use a simpler form known as the 1040EZ if you don't itemize.) Among the expenses you may be allowed to deduct on the 1040 are state and local income taxes (or sales taxes) you've paid, charitable donations, housing costs like mortgage interest and property taxes, and some medical costs. (The list of deductions begins on p. 252.)

Say you earn very little, or have children or educational expenses. You may also qualify for valuable tax **credits**, which subtract money directly from the amount you owe the government. (For a list of tax credits to consider, including help with your health insurance premiums, see p. 260.) For other ways to cut your tax bill, see Chapter 9.

When the time comes to submit your tax return to the IRS, if you earn less than $64,000, you can use irs.gov/freefile to file online without any charge. Otherwise, try the tax prep software at TurboTax.com, HRBlock.com, or TaxAct.com, which may cost about $100 if you have a complicated return. Based on the answers to a few questions, this software will also help you determine whether you will save money by itemizing, as well as all the deductions and credits available to you.

If you've read this far—it wasn't that bad, was it?—you've already done yourself some good. But why stop now? The next eight chapters go more in-depth on all of the above topics, while Chapter 10 offers information tailored to military service members, veterans, and their families.

2

TAKING STOCK OF
YOUR FINANCIAL LIFE

Figuring Out Where You Are
and Where You Want to Go

IF YOU'RE LIKE a lot of people, you're not sure where your money goes. After you pay for basics such as rent, food, and utilities, most of what's left just . . . disappears. The concept of setting aside any money for the future seems like a cruel joke.

But hey, you're still young. There's plenty of time to get your financial life in order, you keep telling yourself. You'll get control once you start earning some real money, right?

Well, unfortunately, there's no guarantee it'll get any easier. Unlike, say, a fancy bottle of wine, financial management skills do not necessarily improve with age. Although your paycheck will increase as you get older (let's hope!), your financial obligations will also grow.

The good news is that if you start paying attention to your finances today, you can set in motion habits that will pay off for the rest of your life. And even better, you don't have to spend forever tracking every penny or poring over the *Wall Street Journal*. But you do have to put in a little effort up front, starting now. This chapter is the one that will help you get organized.

PUTTING A PRICE TAG
ON YOUR GOALS

Like most of us, you probably have one or two specific financial dreams that you'd love to realize within the next few years. You may want to buy a car by the time you're 25. You may long to own a house (or a condo) by age 30. You may imagine the day that you're free at last from credit card debt—or that you've paid off all of your student loans. Or you may simply want to move out of your parents' basement as soon as humanly possible.

The first step toward turning your financial desires into achievable goals is calculating the dollar value of your dreams. (Yes, it may seem unromantic, but even dreams have a price tag.) If you're not sure what that figure is, use the following guidelines:

- *A home.* The median-priced home for first-time buyers is about $170,000. (Obviously, home prices can vary widely depending on where you buy.) Ideally, you'll put down 20%, but to qualify for a home loan, you usually need a down payment of at least 10% of the total price. You'll also need to pay 2% to 5% of the house price to the bank for "closing costs." So for a $170,000 home, you would need to have saved at least $20,000. And again, these figures could be higher or lower depending on the mortgage deal you get. (For details, see Chapter 7.)

- *A car.* Down payments vary, but you should aim to pay about 20% of the total price to the dealer up front. To buy a $25,000 new car, figure you'll need $5,000 in cash; for a $15,000 used car (which I recommend over a new one, especially at this stage in your life), you would need about $3,000 for the down payment. (For more on car loans, see p. 54.)

- *A livable plan to tackle your student loans.* College graduates who borrowed for school owe about $37,000 on average in student debt. No matter the amount, you're typically expected to keep up with a ten-year repayment plan starting just a few months after you leave school.

- *A zero balance on your credit card.* If you owe $5,000 on a credit card with an interest rate of 17%, and you make only the minimum payment each month, it'll end up costing you $6,500 in interest (that's *in addition* to the $5,000 balance) by the time you pay it off—about 22 years later.

- *A financial emergency cushion.* Although saving for a car, a home, or any other tangible item is a lot more exciting, accumulating enough for a financial emergency cushion is a real necessity. An acceptable savings cushion is equal to at least three months' worth of living expenses—six months is even better. This safety net will help you if, for example, you lose your job, have a long stretch between freelance assignments, or incur a major expense like a car repair.

LEARNING HOW TO REACH YOUR GOALS

Okay, you've figured out your goals. Now it's time to build a road map to reach them. To start, use the table in Figure 2–1 on p. 14. It gives you a rough idea of how much you'll need to put aside each month to end up with a specific dollar amount in a set number of years. For example, to have $1,000 saved three years from now, you need to sock away $28 a month.

If you tend to be a good saver, you may not be fazed by the amount you'll need to save each month. If you're like most people, though, you'll probably have to set aside more than you think you can spare. Don't get discouraged. The next part of this chapter will help you figure out how to extract this money from your current income. Though you still may ultimately decide to adjust your planned goal—or the amount of time it takes for you to reach it—at least you'll be on your way to making it happen.

Figure 2–1

HOW MUCH DO YOU NEED TO SAVE EACH MONTH TO MEET YOUR GOAL?

Look across the top row and find the dollar amount that corresponds to your goal. Now look down the far-left column and locate the number of years in which you hope to achieve your goal. The point at which your goal and the number of years intersect is the amount you need to save each month.* The table assumes that inflation will be 1% and your money will earn an interest rate of 2%. [No one can know what will happen to inflation and interest rates in the future, but these are reasonable estimates to work with.] It also assumes that your combined federal, state, and local tax rate is 30% for the next ten years. The table factors in tax rates because you'll have to pay taxes each year on the earnings you receive on certain investments.

YOUR SAVINGS GOAL

Years to Reach Your Goal	$1,000	$2,000	$3,000	$5,000	$7,000	$10,000	$20,000	$30,000	$50,000	$70,000	$100,000
1	$84	$168	$251	$418	$585	$836	$1,671	$2,506	$4,177	$5,848	$8,354
2	42	84	126	210	294	419	838	1,257	2,095	2,933	4,190
3	28	57	85	141	197	281	561	841	1,401	1,961	2,802
4	22	43	64	106	148	211	422	633	1,054	1,475	2,107
5	17	34	51	85	119	170	339	508	846	1,184	1,691
6	15	29	43	71	99	142	283	424	707	990	1,413
7	13	25	37	61	86	122	243	365	608	851	1,215
8	11	22	32	54	75	107	214	320	533	747	1,066
9	10	19	29	48	67	96	191	286	476	666	951
10	9	18	26	43	61	86	172	258	429	601	858

* The goals listed across the top row of the table are in constant dollars. This means that if your goal is to buy a car in five years that's equivalent to a $20,000 car today, you need to set aside $339 every month in a sum that has the right purchasing power. ($20,000 today is equal to roughly $19,029 five years from now.) In other words, you don't have to worry about keeping track of inflation eroding the value of the $20,000; the table factors it in for you.

WHERE DOES YOUR MONEY GO?

Saving isn't easy for most people, and the idea of setting aside money each month can seem like an impossible task—especially when you're living from paycheck to paycheck, as many in their twenties and even thirties do. But the fact is you probably *can* save, even if you think you're barely making ends meet now.

It's easy to automate your savings so you don't even have to think about it. (See p. 26 to learn how.) But the big hurdle is convincing yourself that there's any money there to save at all. And that begins with understanding your current spending habits so that you can make choices about where to trim costs and make saving a reality. This section will help you do the necessary financial soul-searching it often takes to turn saving into a priority.

The best way to gain control of your money is to be mindful. You don't need to head out to a meditation retreat or find a mantra. But you do need to keep a detailed spending diary for just one month so that you can become conscious of exactly where your cash goes. There are good apps available for tracking and analyzing your spending and tackling other personal finance tasks, and I recommend some on p. 28. But before you try one, I'm asking you, as an experiment, to keep an old-school spending diary for four weeks. That's because the very act of writing down each and every expense in a little notebook or the notes function of your phone forces you to actively pay attention each time you buy something (a pack of gum, a tank of gas). Use this diary all the time—whether you are paying with cash, credit, or debit.

If you do this for only one month, you'll have a pretty clear picture of exactly where all your money goes. The next step is to use that information to fill out the worksheet in Figure 2–2, which will help you adjust your spending according to your priorities. (See p. 16. To do this online go to bethkobliner.com/budgetcalculator.)

It's not necessary to be insanely precise when you fill out Figure 2–2. Use your pay stubs and your bank statements to come up with reasonable estimates in the income section. For the outflow

Figure 2–2

WORKSHEET:
A MONTH IN YOUR FINANCIAL LIFE

INCOME (what you take in each month)

Salary and bonuses (before tax)   _____

Additional income (before tax)   _____

Financial aid/scholarships   _____

Parental support   _____

TOTAL MONTHLY INCOME (BEFORE TAX)   _____

OUTFLOW (what you pay out each month)

Taxes

Federal, state, and local income tax and FICA
   (get this figure from your pay stubs)   _____

Tax on investment income*   _____

Savings

Emergency savings   _____

Retirement savings (401(k)/IRA contributions)   _____

Living Expenses

Car (gas, maintenance, parking)   _____

Cell phone   _____

Groceries/basic supplies   _____

Home maintenance/repair   _____

Internet service   _____

Laundry   _____

Mortgage or rent   _____

Public transportation (bus, train, taxi) _____

Utilities (gas/electric)   _____

Debt

Car loan payments   _____

Credit card payments/fees   _____

Student loan payments   _____

Insurance

Auto insurance   _____

Disability insurance   _____

Health insurance   _____

Homeowners/renters insurance   _____

The Rest

Cable/satellite   _____

Child care   _____

Clothes and shoes   _____

Dry cleaning   _____

Eating out (including morning coffee, snacks,
  lunch)   _____

Entertainment (concerts, movies, theater)   _____

Furniture/home decorating   _____

Gifts/charity   _____

Gym   _____

Hobbies   _____

Medical/dental expenses not covered by insurance   _____

Nights out   _____

Personal care (haircuts, toiletries, cosmetics)   _____

Pet care   _____

Subscriptions (news, music, streaming video)   _____

Travel (flights, lodging, entertainment)   _____

Tuition   _____

Miscellaneous   _____

TOTAL MONTHLY OUTFLOW   _____

TOTAL MONTHLY INCOME (BEFORE TAX)   _____

minus TOTAL MONTHLY OUTFLOW   _____

equals your MONTHLY CASH FLOW   _____

* If you've held this investment for more than a year, multiply the investment income by 0.15
to get a rough idea. If you've held it for less than a year, multiply the investment income by
your tax bracket—if you don't know your tax bracket, multiply the income by 0.25.

section, look at the data from your spending diary. Don't forget that my worksheet helps you examine your *monthly* expenses. For large and one-off expenses (like tuition, insurance, travel, and furniture), come up with monthly estimates. For expenses that vary from month to month (such as car repairs, clothing, and entertainment), take an average of your last four or five months' worth of spending in that category. If possible, choose a month from each season so you can calculate a more accurate average.

Once you complete the worksheet, subtract your total monthly outflow from your total monthly income. If you come up with a negative number, you're spending more than you're taking in (obviously a problem, but you're not alone). You'll need to think about your priorities and make some tough choices. Would you be able to save by cooking at home more often? Do you spend as much on clothes as you do on rent? Could you switch to a cheaper cell phone plan or a less expensive gym? Are you overspending when shopping online or Venmo-ing like crazy after a night out? When you make a purchase, could you get a better deal by using an app like RetailMeNot or a browser extension like Honey? If these changes don't yield a big enough payoff or you don't want to nickel-and-dime yourself, consider making a larger lifestyle change—like selling your car and taking public transportation to work (if feasible), taking in a roommate, or moving to a less-trendy neighborhood where rents are cheaper.

Now go over your outflow section again to see where you can cut back—and by how much. While you are doing this, star those items that are absolute necessities, like mortgage or rent, groceries, Internet service, cell phone, gas/electric, health insurance, and student loan payments—although even here, you probably could reduce some costs. (Note that you can multiply this monthly outflow for necessities by three to calculate your bare-bones three-month financial emergency cushion.) Next, subtract your outflow for necessities from your total monthly income. The answer (which is a positive figure, hopefully) is the amount of discretionary income you have left.

Now divide your discretionary income into two parts: the amount you'll save to meet your goals (like buying a car or a home or saving for retirement) and the amount you'll spend on things that aren't necessities (like movies, clothes you don't really need, and so on). At this point, it should become clear whether you need

WHEN A SPENDER MARRIES A SAVER

Anne and Marc moved in together in June and started to plan a March wedding. Anne's parents said they'd be willing to contribute $20,000 for the event, so the couple figured out that they'd need to pitch in $10,000 of their own to have the wedding of their dreams.

The problem was coming up with the cash. Anne, who is frugal and likes being debt-free, felt that with some careful planning, they could accumulate the money. After all, they each earned about $55,000. Marc, however, thought that raising that kind of cash was out of the question. He already *owed* more than $4,000 to various credit card companies and didn't see how he could possibly save the money. Why couldn't they just wait and see how much cash they received as wedding presents, and then charge the rest?

After two weeks of discussion (actually, arguments), the couple decided to list their income and expenses and see if they could work out the problem. By writing things down, Marc quickly realized that if he cut out expensive lunches (he spent four times as much as Anne did) and put off buying clothes for work until the spring (turns out, Marc was a bit of a clothes-horse), he could come up with a good chunk of change. He also acknowledged that having Anne as his roommate would actually make saving much easier; it cut his rent and utilities in half. The compromise: Anne and Marc would each set aside $260 every two weeks in a joint bank account earmarked for wedding expenses only, enough to reach their $10,000 goal in nine months.

The point is, by setting their goal, figuring out where they could cut with a spending diary, and sticking to a consistent savings plan, they were able to have the celebration they both wanted.

to adjust the size of your goal or the number of years in which you can realistically hope to attain it.

Of course it's hard to spend less, but this exercise will only work if you're ready to commit to putting limits on your spending. Can you cut $25 a week from eating out and entertainment? Is it worth it to forgo the latest phone upgrade or pair of boots for your long-term goal? Once you start paying attention to your cash flow, it's easier than you'd think.

THREE FINANCIAL RULES OF THUMB

To help you evaluate whether your current spending and saving habits are right on track, wildly off base, or somewhere in between, I've listed a few financial rules. Realistically, these targets may not always be possible to hit, but it's good to aim high. Use the worksheet you filled out in Figure 2–2 on p. 16 to help with your calculations.

1.   **The Debt Rule: Your debt payments (not including your mortgage) should be less than 20% of your monthly take-home pay.** To see if you meet this standard, list all the monthly payments you make on your student loans, credit cards, car loan, and any other lines of credit, and add them up. If your total monthly payments exceed 20% of your monthly take-home pay, don't panic—yet. Chapter 3 has tips on reducing debt, and as you adjust your spending, you'll free up more money to pay off debt faster.

But this often-quoted rule is a bit tricky. For instance, it's possible that your monthly payments are artificially low—say you pay the absolute minimums on your credit cards—so the 20% rule could mask a dangerous amount of debt. For example, if you earn $50,000 a year (taking home around $3,000 a month) and you owe

$20,000 in credit card debt, your minimum monthly payment could be about $450, which is less than 15% of your take-home pay. So while on paper you meet this rule of thumb, the reality is that you're drowning in debt. When you pay only the minimum amount due on a credit card, you drag out the amount of time it will take to pay off the debt, which means you will end up paying a lot more in interest. In this example, it would take more than thirty years to pay off the entire bill, and the total interest payments would be nearly $25,000 on top of the $20,000 you owe.

So in addition to the above rule, try this one as well: If the unpaid *balance* on your so-called consumer debt (that's your credit cards, car loans, and other lines of credit that aren't student loans or home loans) exceeds 20% of your *annual* take-home pay, you are probably carrying too big of a debt load. (Of course, the percentage to shoot for in both cases is zero.)

2. **The Housing Rule: Spend no more than 30% of your monthly take-home pay on rent or mortgage payments.** This policy may be impossible in major cities like New York City, San Francisco, or Washington, D.C., unless you have roommates. But if you're in a small town or a relatively affordable city like St. Louis or Houston, it's

THE REAL COST OF SHOPPING

Things cost more than you think. Here's what I mean: Want to buy a $75 sweater? If you are in the 25% tax bracket (you're making about $50,000), you actually had to earn $100 in order to pay for it. That's because $100 taxed at 25% is $75. Keep this in mind on your next shopping spree.

reasonable. No matter where you are, it's something to try for—and if you can get away with spending even less, great.

3.   **The Savings Rule: Save at least 15% of your take-home pay each month.** It's critical to think of your savings as a fixed monthly expense that's part of your budget, just like your car payment and your rent. While there's no magical reason to save exactly 15%, it's a good target to aim for. Include in that 15% the money you set aside to meet your short-term goals as well as the money you put in a retirement plan.

GETTING YOUR FINANCIAL LIFE IN ORDER

It's easier to gain control of your finances if you're organized. But if you're like most people, when it comes to your financial files, you're baffled by what to keep and what to toss. Some people solve the problem by holding on to absolutely *everything*—from to-do lists scribbled in 2006 to crumpled receipts from late-night cab rides (because, hey, you never know what the IRS might need at tax time).

If you want a better plan for organizing your financial flotsam, check out Figure 2–3 on p. 24. As for how to save these docs, that's entirely up to you; you can keep either hard copy *or* electronic versions of them. Some documents, such as pay stubs and credit card statements, are easily accessible via company websites, meaning that you don't need to keep your own copies as well. Just know that there can be a cost or delay when retrieving older records. (One tip: If you're saving your files in electronic form, make sure you back them up securely in the cloud. Dropbox and Google Drive are great for this.) But when it comes to those vital personal docs like birth certificates and such? Keep a hard copy *and* save an electronic version, just to be safe.

WHEN YOU NEED THOSE PAPERS

Jacob was on a road trip to visit friends in Boston when his car skidded on some winter ice and slammed into a curb. No one was hurt, but a local repair shop told him it would cost $2,500 to fix the damage. Jacob knew that his car was worth only about $7,000. (A recent transplant to New York City, he had decided it was too expensive to own a car there and had already looked up his car's value.) So he decided to skip the repair and just sell the damaged car in Boston. When he contacted a car dealer, he was asked for the certificate of title. His girlfriend back in New York was able to retrieve the document from his files and overnight it to the Boston car dealer. Within a week, Jacob received a check for $4,500 and successfully avoided a huge hassle.

Moral of the story: Save and file your key documents. You never know when you'll need them.

KEEPING TRACK OF MONEY COMING IN AND GOING OUT

Below are some ways to help you organize your payments and track your spending. It doesn't matter which system you use—the point is to choose one that works for you so you'll stick with it.

- **Automate all of your bill payments for simplicity—and to eliminate late fees.** Most banks provide a free way to pay your bills electronically. (If your bank charges for this, consider the advice on finding a new one on p. 79.) When a bill comes in, the bank will alert you by text, email, or whatever way you set it up. You then have two options for paying: manual and automatic. With the manual option, you need

Figure 2–3
YOUR FINANCIAL FILING SYSTEM

What to save *How long to save*

BROKERAGE AND MUTUAL FUND ACCOUNTS

- Statements that show purchases and sales of investments — Forever
- Year-end statements — Forever

CAR

- Certificate of title — As long as you have the car
- Loan agreement — Until you pay off the loan
- Loan payoff documentation — Forever
- Purchase agreement — As long as you have the car, or seven years, whichever is longer
- Receipts from repair work — As long as you have the car

CREDIT CARDS

- Credit card agreement (the original, plus updates) — As long as you have the card

HOME

- Closing documents — Forever
- Home improvement receipts — Seven years after you sell (for tax purposes; see Chapter 9)
- Home inventory — Forever (keep it updated for insurance purposes; see Chapter 8)
- Mortgage payoff documentation — Forever
- Mortgage statements — Seven years
- Property tax and real estate tax statements — Seven years
- Receipts and warranties for major purchases (furniture, appliances, etc.) — As long as you own the items, or seven years after you claim them as a tax deduction, whichever is longer
- Rental agreement — As long as you're renting

INSURANCE

- Life, health, car, home, renters, and disability policies, including claims, police reports, and reimbursement statements

While the policy is in effect, or seven years for tax-deductible expenses. Save proof of health coverage going back seven years.

PERSONAL DOCUMENTS

- Adoption papers, birth certificate, college transcripts, diplomas, divorce decree and property agreement, driver's license (current one and previous one), marriage certificate, military discharge papers, passport (current one and previous one), Social Security card, and will (original copy)

Forever

RETIREMENT ACCOUNTS

- Annual statements from IRAs or 401(k)s

Forever

- Tax-related forms for IRAs or 401(k)s

Forever

STUDENT LOANS

- Annual statements

Until you pay off the loan, or seven years after you claim a tax deduction, whichever is longer

- Loan agreement

Until you pay off the loan

- Loan payoff documentation

Forever

TAXES

(For more details, see p. 271.)

- Copies of your tax returns and tax-related forms

Forever

- W-2s you receive from your employer and 1099s from employers, banks, fund companies, and other sources

Forever

• Business-related expenses and medical expenses (unreimbursed), child care/ dependent care expenses	Seven years
WORK	
• Bonus and profit-sharing plan documentation	Seven years
• Job evaluations	Forever
• Pay stubs	One year

to authorize the bank to make the payment for you each time. This is a good choice for bills that vary from month to month—like credit card bills—since you'll want to make sure all the charges are accurate before you press "pay." Just make sure you don't procrastinate and forget to authorize the bank to send the payment.

With automatic, you still get a chance to look over your bill when it comes in, but the bank is going to make the payment for you in a few days unless you tell it not to. The automatic system is a particularly good way to pay those bills that are the same each month, like your rent or your car payments. One caveat: With automatic payment, you need to always have enough money in your account to cover the bills— otherwise your payment won't go through and you could be hit with fees and penalties from the merchant. You also might get hit with overdraft fees from your bank, so see p. 81 in Chapter 4 for details on how to avoid this costly problem.

• **Have *savings* automatically deducted from your paycheck or bank account.** People can talk till they are blue in the face about the virtues of saving, but in the end, the only system that definitely works is one that doesn't require you to think about it. That's why automatic savings is so brilliant: You don't see the money that's being set aside, and before long you don't even miss it. (I promise.)

There are a couple of ways to do this. Ask your company's payroll office if you can have a fixed sum taken from each paycheck—say, $50 a pay period—and funneled directly into your savings account before you even get your paycheck. Or, if your employer doesn't provide this automatic savings option, you can go to your bank's website and arrange it so that every month or pay period, money is transferred from your checking account into a savings account. If you had $50 siphoned into savings every two weeks, at the end of the year you'd have $1,300—plus interest.

Studies show that once people establish an automatic savings plan, inertia sets in—in a good way—and they

MAKE MORE, SAVE MORE

While most of the tips in this chapter involve learning to spend less (and smarter), there's another way to beef up your savings: Make more money. Might sound obvious, but bear with me.

Even if you already have a full-time job, there are still plenty of ways to bring in extra cash: babysitting (it's not just for college students—ask around in the office!); freelancing (writing, editing, graphic design, baking, you name it); pet- and even house-sitting; waiting tables or bartending on the weekends; and manning someone's stall at a festival, flea market, or farmers market. You get the idea. Not only will you earn extra money, you'll also make connections. Who knows? A part-time or freelance gig could morph into a passion that turns into a career. It happens. Just be sure to pay the required taxes on this additional income. (See p. 241.)

If your situation allows, once you have that money in hand, view it as "found money" that should go directly into your savings account.

stick with it. Research also suggests that labeling a savings account with a goal—"new car," "down payment"—actually results in people adding even more money to their savings pot. (See p. 92 for more automatic-saving details for bank customers.)

- **Use online budgeting tools to help control and monitor spending.** You probably need to take a look at your checking account through the bank's website or app only once or twice a week to keep track of your balance and make sure that no erroneous charges appear. But if you are interested in figuring out *where* you're spending your money, free apps like Mint and Prosper Daily make it easy for you to calculate what portion of your income goes to various categories, such as "housing," "clothes," and "dining out." Similarly, HelloWallet is a great tool that's free if your employer provides it; otherwise, it will cost you $100 a year.

  At the end of a few months you can see how much you spent in each category, and you might learn something useful. (I know one friend who prided herself on not buying new clothes but was astonished one month to see that she spent almost 25% of her take-home pay on going out to eat.) And if you and your partner fight about money, these tools can be especially helpful because they offer an objective way to see where the money is actually going. Mint, for example, gives you an easy-to-understand snapshot of your entire financial picture: credit cards, bank accounts, retirement funds, and investments.

FINANCIAL CRAMMING

- To calculate how much you need to save each month to reach specific financial goals, look at Figure 2–1 on p. 14. It will give you a rough idea of how much money you'll need to set aside.

- Keep a spending diary for one month. By forcing yourself to write down everything you spend money on, you'll get a better sense of where it's going and where you might be able to trim so you can free up money to put toward your savings goals. (See bethkobliner.com/budgetcalculator.)

- Automate your savings by having a certain amount siphoned from your paycheck each month and put into a savings account. See p. 26.

- Consider these guidelines when evaluating your financial fitness: Spend no more than 30% of your monthly take-home pay on housing, and dedicate at least 15% of your take-home pay to savings. Also, don't allow your monthly debt payments (not including your mortgage) to exceed 20% of your monthly take-home pay—or your *total* debt (not including your mortgage or student loans) to exceed 20% of your *annual* take-home pay.

- Gain control of your finances by setting up a filing system and developing regular bill-paying habits. Use tools like Mint and Prosper Daily to help control your spending, and set up alerts through your bank to make sure you pay your bills on time.

3

DEALING WITH DEBT

Finding the Cheapest Loans and
Getting Yourself Out of Hock

GET THIS: YOU'RE 30 years old and you owe $5,000 on your credit card. The interest rate on your card is 15%. If you regularly make only the minimum payment required by the credit card issuer—and you never make another purchase on the card— when will you have paid it off? (Drum roll, please.) The answer is ... when you're 52 years old. By then, you would have paid $5,729 in interest, *plus* the $5,000 you borrowed—a grand total of $10,729, more than double the amount of your original loan!

The point of this example: Carrying a lot of debt—*any* type of debt—can be hazardous to your long-term financial health.

Chances are, you know this already. But you also know that there are times when debt is unavoidable—be it a loan to pay for college or a home or a car. This chapter will help you manage all your debt—whether showing you how to avoid the pitfalls of credit cards, how to find low-cost car loans, or how to repay your student loans the smart way. It also gives you an inside look at how your bill-paying habits affect your credit score, which is arguably the most important number in your financial life. I'll even show you how to achieve a good score and why doing so can make you eligible for the very best loans—which can save you literally tens of thousands of dollars. (For everything you need to know about home loans, aka mortgages, see Chapter 7.)

FOUR POINTERS FOR ANYONE WITH DEBT OF ANY KIND

Before we plunge into the nitty-gritty of credit cards, student loans, and auto loans, there are four basic principles you should know:

- **If you have savings, use it to pay off your high-interest-rate debt.** In most cases, the best investment you can possibly make is to pay off your credit cards and other high-rate debt. This is because the interest rates on such debt are higher than the rates you can expect to receive from almost any investment. Paying off a loan with a 15% interest rate, for instance, is in effect paying yourself 15% interest, guaranteed and *tax-free*. That's a great return.

  To better understand this, consider the following situation. Say you owe $1,000 on a credit card that charges an annual interest rate of 15%. You also have $1,000 in the bank—earning interest at a rate of 1%. If you keep the $1,000 in the bank for a year, you'll *earn* $10 in interest on it while *paying* $150 in interest on the credit card, ending up with a $140 loss. With me so far?

  But if you take that money out of the savings account and pay off the credit card debt completely, you'll earn no interest—but you will also *pay* no interest. Clearly, it's better to break even than to pay $140 in interest.

- **Transfer debt from high-rate loans to lower-rate loans.** This is known as **refinancing**. Obviously, it's better to pay 8% to borrow money than it is to pay 18%. So if you currently have credit card debt that you can't pay off right away, consider applying for a low-rate card that allows you to transfer your current debt to it—but doesn't charge a huge fee for doing so. (I'll explain this more later in the chapter, so stay tuned.)

- **Pay on time.** Lenders, landlords, and sometimes potential employers have the ability to look at your credit history to get a sense of how responsible you are when it comes to making monthly payments. (For more on this, see p. 60.) The number one factor that goes into determining your credit score is your record of paying bills on time. People who have trouble making on-time payments get charged higher interest rates on everything from credit cards to car loans to home loans. (They are also more likely to get turned down as a renter—or even as an employee.)

  You can't change your past, but you can make a huge difference in your future by paying your bills punctually from now on. (For more on why you should never pay late, see the box on p. 68.)

- **Call your lender.** Email may be easier, but picking up the phone is often a better way to state your case and make yourself more than just another account number. If you have a debt-related issue (or even if you're just trying to get a better deal), talk to your lender and explain your situation. Ask (in a polite way) to speak directly with a supervisor. You may find that he or she is willing to waive a late fee, refund a month of interest charges, or even lower the interest rate on your credit card.

CREDIT CARDS

If you don't already have a credit card, at some point you will. That's why it's important to know the steps you can take to reduce your costs. I'll dive into the details in a minute, but first let's talk about three simple points that are among the most important lessons in this book.

- **Using a credit card is like taking out a loan.** For some this may be obvious; for others it can be a life-changing revelation. The issue isn't just semantic. Turns out lots of smart people mistakenly view credit cards as just one more account to tap when they need cash. But think about it: When you borrow money to buy a car or to go to college, it's obvious that you're taking out a loan. Using a credit card is basically the same thing. You're borrowing money—whether it's for a fancy juice, a pair of jeans, or a new iPad. If you don't have the money to pay your bill in full each month, you'll owe interest. By any definition, that's a loan.

- **Credit card debt is never good.** When times are tough, you may feel you need to use a card to pay for essentials like food, housing, or clothes. But here's the thing: If you commit to the rule that you'll use your card to buy only those items that you can afford to pay for in cash, you'll be happier in the long run. That's because research suggests people who aren't weighed down by credit card debt have less stress—and more financial freedom.

- **You don't need to have credit card debt to build a credit history.** Although there is a whole section on credit reports and credit scores coming up (spoiler alert!), I want to make this point. Ignore people who say you need to carry a balance from month to month to build credit. They are wrong. Using your credit card for convenience—buying items with it instead of carrying a wad of bills—and then paying it off immediately will count toward building your credit history, too. And you'll pay no interest.

How to Find the Best Card for You

Although there are hundreds of different credit cards available, most of us don't need more than two. Here's how to choose the right ones for you.

Despite what the ads say, whether your card has a Visa seal or MasterCard logo is not that important. These are just membership organizations. It's the bank or company that *issues* the card—such as Citibank or Bank of America—that matters. These issuers control the rates, fees, and other factors that are critical to you.

Look for a credit card that suits your personal spending habits. If you always pay off your balance in full every month, the interest rate doesn't matter. Your priority is to find a card that doesn't charge an annual fee—or charges a very low one and offers you points, frequent-flyer miles, or cash back that you actually use. If you usually carry a balance from month to month, don't think about anything other than getting the lowest interest rate—technically called the **annual percentage rate**, or **APR**—you can.

How to Get a Low-Rate Credit Card

If you owe money on your credit cards but don't have enough cash to pay them off, you'll want to find a new card with the lowest interest rate you can qualify for and transfer your debts to it. The details vary from card to card, though, so you need to read the fine print before signing up. For example, many cards charge a hefty fee of 3% or 4% of the total amount transferred, but other cards allow you to transfer your balance without paying a fee. However, it may be worth paying these fees if you reap big savings from new lower interest in the end. Use a balance transfer calculator such as the one at bankrate.com/calculators/credit-cards/credit-card-balance -transfer-calculator.aspx to see if it makes sense for you.

In general, there are two kinds of low-rate cards: those with low rates that last, and **balance transfer cards**, which offer low introductory rates, also known as **teasers**. While cards with long-lasting low rates may have somewhat higher interest rates than teaser cards do, the rates are far more stable. For cards with teasers, rates can be as low as 0% but only last from six months to up to a year and a half. After that, the rate often increases dramatically. While the low teaser rate is in effect, however, it can save you a lot of money. Transferring a $3,000 balance from a 19% card to one with a 0% teaser rate, for example, would save you about $278 in interest over six months. Even if you were charged a 4% balance transfer fee— $120 in this example—you would still come out ahead by $158. So

THE TRICKY TEASER

Rebecca is a dedicated credit card surfer who prides herself on her ability to pay the lowest possible interest rates on the $3,000 balance she tends to carry from month to month. Because she has a good credit history, she gets solicitations from card companies almost daily, offering her extra-low introductory rates. Every few months, she switches cards and gets a new teaser rate, so she never ends up paying more than 5% on her debt. Clever, right?

Well, recently Rebecca transferred her balance to a card with a six-month teaser rate of 0%. Then she used the card to buy hundreds of dollars' worth of books and clothes. When she got her credit card statement at the end of the month, she was shocked to see that while the balance she had transferred from her old card was indeed running up zero interest, the new money she had spent on books and clothes was being hit for 18.9%! What Rebecca hadn't noticed was that the teaser rate on her card only applied to the balance she brought over from her *previous* card—not to any new purchases she made.

The obvious moral of the story: You should read all the fine print before you rush to switch cards. While many cards will give you that low teaser rate for both balance transfers and new purchases for a certain amount of time, others offer a low teaser rate for balance transfers and (surprise!) a higher rate for new purchases.

The hidden moral: Rebecca, like all card surfers, should stop wasting her time and pay off her debt once and for all.

if you know for sure that you can pay off the whole card before that teaser rate runs out, you're golden.

Naturally, the card issuer hopes that you won't be able to meet such a short deadline to pay off your entire balance—and most people can't. If that's your situation, you may be able to get another low rate by going "credit card surfing"—transferring your balance to a new teaser-rate card whenever your old teaser rate runs out. But you'll need to factor in any transfer fees to determine if surfing makes sense. Warning: Many surfers fall into the bad habit of shuffling their cards without actually making much headway on the balance—a game you'll want to avoid, since you aren't reducing your debt. Finally, be especially careful to avoid a late payment since some cards punish tardiness by hiking up the APR.

For the most comprehensive list of long-lasting low-rate and teaser deals, go to CreditCards.com or CardHub.com. In addition, Mint.com, Bankrate.com, and NerdWallet.com have a mix of advice and card offers. If you belong to a credit union, national association, or labor union, you might be able to get a card with a relatively low rate through one of those organizations. Also investigate local banks, which sometimes offer lower rates on cards than national institutions do.

Tips If You Carry a Balance

While your goal is to pay off your credit card debt entirely, until you can, take note of these suggestions:

- **Never miss a payment.** If you can't afford to pay your bill in full, pay at least the minimum (and ideally more) by the due date. Otherwise, you will be charged a late fee of as much as $25 for a first offense; if it's your second late payment within six months, it could be even more. Worse, more and more card issuers punish payers who are late by 60 days or more by not only slapping on fees but also jacking up their interest rates to "penalty rates" of up to 30%. And don't forget: Even if you have a credit card that doesn't charge a late fee, these tardy payments go on your credit report and affect your credit score.

If you are socked with a penalty rate for a late payment, by law the credit card company must reset your account to your old rate after six straight on-time monthly payments. (Check with the issuer to make sure they do.) One tip: If you're transferring a balance from a high-rate card to a low-rate one, keep making at least the minimum payment on your old accounts until you have confirmation that the transfer has gone through, so that you avoid any late fees or penalty rates. If your old issuer ends up owing you money, just request a refund.

- **Know how interest is calculated.** Most lenders calculate interest using a system known as the **average daily balance method including new purchases**. Here's how it works. The issuer divides the year into roughly 30-day periods known as billing cycles. At the end of each billing cycle, the issuer posts your statement online. If you pay the entire amount by the due date, you won't pay any interest. But if you leave even just $1 unpaid, it will have a negative impact on your next bill. (To see how this works in real life, see "A Nasty Card Surprise" on p. 38.)

- **Pay more than the monthly minimum, and resist skip-a-payment offers.** Many issuers calculate your monthly minimum as 1% to 2% of your outstanding balance plus interest and fees. If you pay just the minimum it will take you a long time to rid yourself of debt—and will cost you a lot in interest. (See Figure 3–1 on p. 40 to calculate how long it will take to pay off your balance.) Even paying just $10 more than the minimum a month can save you hundreds if not thousands of dollars in interest. Also, resist the skip-a-payment deals offered by some issuers. What they often don't make clear is that you'll still be charged interest on your outstanding balance for that month. (There's no *interest*-skipping involved.)

If You Can't Get a Regular Credit Card, Try a Secured Card

If you've never had any credit, you've defaulted on a loan within the last few years, or you just don't meet lenders' requirements, you may find it difficult to get a credit card. One option to consider is a **secured credit card**. With a secured card, the issuer requires you to provide collateral by depositing money into a special savings account. The issuer usually allows you to charge up to the amount you have on deposit. You can't withdraw the money from the savings account while you have the card.

Most secured cards show up on your credit record, so using them helps you build up (or rebuild) a track record of managing credit responsibly. Once you've demonstrated that you can handle a secured card, issuers will be more willing to take a chance on giving you a regular credit card.

Be aware, though, that secured cards often charge higher interest rates than traditional credit cards, and most have annual fees

A NASTY CARD SURPRISE

Kathy and Michael went on a honeymoon to Hawaii and charged all their expenses on a credit card with an 18% interest rate. A week after they got home, the $5,000 credit card bill arrived. They had enough money to pay the whole bill, but Michael decided to pay it over the course of two months so he wouldn't fall below the minimum balance he needed to maintain free checking at his bank. He submitted a payment for $4,900 by the due date. When the next credit card bill came, Michael was shocked to discover that although he owed only $100 from the previous balance, he also owed $63 in interest. Because he didn't pay off his balance entirely, he was charged interest for the average daily balance—in this case, about $4,180—of the billing cycle. The lesson: Don't carry a balance if you can help it.

that range from $25 to $50. And though some issuers pay interest on the required savings account, most do not. That's why you should shop around. Sites like CreditCards.com and Bankrate.com provide lists of secured card options and let you compare them side by side.

Some Final Tips on Credit Cards

Whether you carry a balance or not, here are a few more pointers that will save you some money:

- **Ask your current card company for a better deal.** Seriously. Many cardholders who ask for a lower rate get one, but you'll have to speak to an actual human being to do it. First, research low-rate offers from other credit card companies on sites like CreditCards.com and CardHub.com. Then, call the toll-free number on the back of your card and ask for the "retention" department. Ask for a manager or supervisor right away; the first customer service rep you speak with may not have the authority to change your rate. Once you're on the phone with a higher-up, say that you'd like a lower interest rate. (Have a target APR in mind, in case you're asked for a specific number.) Explain that you're a good customer (if this is true) but you're thinking of canceling your card because of the high interest rate. Even if you've messed up in the past, it doesn't hurt to ask. If that doesn't work, mention those low-rate offers that you found (be prepared for the manager to ask you to name companies), and sweetly say that you're considering switching to one of those cards unless your rate is reduced.

- **Don't use your credit card for cash advances.** Most credit cards can be used to obtain cash from an ATM. But when you do this, you're borrowing money from the credit card company in an even more expensive way. That's because many issuers charge higher interest rates on cash advances

Figure 3-1

HOW MANY MONTHLY PAYMENTS
YOU'LL NEED TO KILL YOUR DEBT

This table can help you get a rough sense of how long it will take you to get rid of your credit card debt entirely, regardless of how much you owe.

Here's how it works: Look down the far-left column and ask yourself what percentage of your debt you can comfortably commit to paying off each month. If, for example, you have $1,000 in debt, you may decide that you can pay off 3% of $1,000, or $30, every month until the balance is completely wiped out. Now look across the top row and find the annual interest rate charged by your credit card. Say it's 18%. The point at which 3% intersects with 18% is the number of months it will take you to pay off your debt. In this case, the answer is 47 months. But as you'll see from the table, if you're able to refinance that debt with a credit card that charges only a 10% annual rate, the number of monthly payments you'll make will drop to 40.

If you want to do the math using your own numbers, you'll find a credit card calculator at credit.com/tools/credit-card-payoff-calculator.

| Payment as a % of Initial Debt | ANNUAL INTEREST RATE | | | | | |
	3%	7%	10%	14%	16%	18%
2%	54	60	65	76	83	94
3%	35	38	40	43	45	47
4%	26	28	29	30	31	32
5%	21	22	22	23	24	24
10%	11	11	11	11	11	11
15%	7	7	7	7	8	8
20%	6	6	6	6	6	6
25%	5	5	5	5	5	5

(24% is typical) than they do on purchases. And even worse, most cash advances don't have a grace period; interest begins accruing the moment you get the cash. On top of the interest, you may also have to pay a one-time fee of $10, or 5% of the amount you withdraw, whichever is greater.

- **Evaluate rewards cards carefully.** We all know people who are obsessed with amassing points toward frequent-flyer miles, hotel stays, and gift cards. But this "free stuff" isn't a good deal if you carry a balance, because the interest rates that rewards cards charge are often higher than those of other cards. It's also not worth paying an annual fee for a rewards card if you don't charge enough overall to earn the points (and perks) that would outweigh the fee. Look for a fee-free rewards card at CreditCards.com or CreditKarma.com.

- **If you travel internationally a lot, look for a card that doesn't charge extra fees.** Many credit and debit cards tack on **foreign transaction fees** of 2% to 3% for every purchase you make outside the United States. To avoid them, check your card policies before you leave home and stick with the cards that don't charge them. To find such a card, check CardHub.com or NerdWallet.com.

- **Stay within your credit limit.** Credit card issuers try to encourage customers to sign up for overlimit "protection," which basically is permission for you to charge something even if you've exceeded your credit limit. While this might protect your ego in that you won't be embarrassed by having your credit card charge denied, it's expensive: Your card issuer can charge you a hefty fee (of up to $35) per overlimit transaction. So don't sign up for it. Besides, if you're close to maxing out your credit limit, you probably shouldn't be charging anything to your card anyway.

- **Be careful when you pay with your phone.** Using your phone to pay for stuff—with Apple Pay or Google Wallet, for example—is convenient, but know that it could still put your personal info at risk. In case your phone gets stolen, you should know how to go online and disable your mobile payment system, just to be safe.

- **Stay away from store credit cards.** Salespeople in department stores and other retailers will often ask you that

CREDIT AND DEBIT CARD FRAUD

If your card info is stolen—whether your credit card or debit card gets lost and falls into a thief's clutches or, say, there's a data breach at the bank or a store where you shopped—someone out there could be running up bills under your name, with or without your card. Fortunately, there are some protections in place.

In cases of credit card fraud, federal law limits your liability to $50—and most credit card companies won't ask you to pay anything at all. But be proactive. If you notice a strange purchase, call the number on the back of your card, and ask that the card company remove the charge. You may not even have to have a new card issued. Also, get into the habit of checking your account online a few times a week to make sure recent charges are legit. Free apps like Mint and Prosper Daily also enable you to keep tabs on your charges. (See p. 28 for more details on personal finance apps.)

Fraud protection is less clear-cut with debit cards. The law says that if you report a debit card stolen or missing before someone uses it on a shopping spree, you won't be held responsible for the fraudulent transactions. But if a crook actually uses your debit card and you report the theft within 48 hours, your liability is $50; if you take longer than two days to report it, however, you could be liable for up to $500. Take longer than 60 days and you could be on the hook for the whole amount. The good news is that in practice most banks offer protection that goes beyond what federal law requires. Check your debit card's rules.

Most debit and credit cards have an EMV chip. This technology makes it tougher for thieves to steal your card information when you use it in a store. If your debit or credit card doesn't have a chip, see if your issuer can replace it with one that does.

enticing question, "Would you like to open a store credit account? You'll get a 10% discount on your entire purchase." Don't do it. Interest rates on store cards, including those from online outfits, are generally 20% or more—higher than the national average for ordinary credit cards. If you spend $500 on a store card to get the 10% off, and then pay only the minimum on your bill each month, you could end up paying nearly $200 in interest. That's one costly $50 discount. The exception: If it's a place where you shop regularly, you may save money with a store credit card—but only if you pay it off in full each month.

STUDENT LOANS

The average student with debt graduates from college with about $37,000 in student loans. (The median amount—what most students owe—is less than half that.) So it's not surprising you'll need some guidance. This section can help.

First, a quick review of the basics. Most student loans are from the federal government. The most common type are **Federal Direct Loans** (aka Federal Stafford Loans), which are for both undergraduate and graduate students. You may also have **Federal Perkins Loans. Federal PLUS Loans** are made to undergrad students' parents and to graduate students. Some students also have **private loans**, which are offered by banks, credit unions, and some schools.

There are two key differences between federal loans and private loans. First, federal loans tend to offer lower, fixed rates, recently as low as 3.76% for Direct Loans. Private student loans can charge interest rates of 18% or even more. Second, federal loans offer a number of different ways to pay your loans, which can be really helpful; private loans generally don't. So stick with federal loans whenever possible.

The companies to whom you send your payments are called **loan servicers**. Throughout this section, I'll be using the term "servicer" to refer to the company that actually deals with you when you're paying off your student loans.

How to Reduce the Cost of Your Student Loans

Here are three strategies to consider for both federal loans and private loans:

- **Sign up for automatic payments so you pay on time.** If you agree to make electronic payments from your checking account automatically each month, there's a good chance your federal loan servicer may reduce your interest rate by a quarter of a percentage point, and some private servicers will lower it by as much as half a percentage point. Some servicers even reward you for good behavior and give a small discount if you make, say, 12 or more consecutive on-time payments or graduate on time. Regardless, automating your payments will ensure that you'll get them in on time as well as avoid missing one altogether. If you don't pay on time, you will be hit with late fees—and you'll hurt your credit score. (See p. 60 for more on credit reports and credit scores.)

- **Prepay your student loans.** If you're not weighed down by other high-rate loans or credit card debt, consider paying back your student loans faster than you're required to under your current payment schedule. (If you do have credit card debt, see the box on p. 53.) Paying off a student loan more quickly will save you interest in the long run. Say you have $37,000 in loans with an interest rate of 3.76%. Assuming the interest rate remains the same and you pay back your loans over ten years, your monthly payment under the standard plan will be $370. If you can add just $50 extra per month to that amount, you'll pay off your loans in eight years and eight months—and save over $1,000 in interest. But remember: Prepayment makes sense only if the interest rates on your loans are higher than the rates you can earn on investments.

- **Deduct your interest payments.** The government gives students a tax break: You may be able to deduct *interest* payments on your federal and private student loans, up to a maximum of $2,500 a year. For example, if you're in the 25% tax bracket and you paid $1,500 in interest this year on your student loans, you'll get to cut roughly $375 off your tax bill this year. For more details, see Chapter 9.

Getting Your Federal Loans Organized

Most people who have student loans have federal loans. And they're a great deal. But that doesn't mean you won't get overwhelmed when it's time to start paying them back. The first thing you need to do is locate all of your student loans. If you're not sure where they are, either because you've changed your contact information, your lender has given your loan to a different loan servicer, or you just can't remember, there's good news: The National Student Loan Data System (nslds.ed.gov) can help you find all your federal loans and the servicers who are handling them.

This site lists the type of federal loan, when you took it out, and the interest rate for each. Since you were likely issued a new loan each semester, you'll see quite a few—maybe some you didn't even remember you had. For instance, if you took out Direct Loans (aka Staffords), you may see two types listed—**subsidized**, for which the government pays the interest for the years while you're in school and continues to do so for six months after you leave, and **unsubsidized**, for which you're responsible for the interest from day one.

Choosing the Right Federal Loan Repayment Plan for You

You are automatically enrolled in the **Standard Repayment** plan, which requires making the same payment every month for ten years. It's the best option if you can swing it because you pay your loans off faster, so you'll pay less interest.

But what if the monthly payments with the standard plan are too high for you to afford on your entry-level salary? Here's the beauty of federal loans: There are several repayment plans that can make paying back your loans more manageable.

One quick note: Although the idea of lowering your monthly payment sounds tempting, the downside is that you'll almost always be *increasing* the total amount of interest you pay in the long run. So even if you choose a plan with a lower monthly payment, you should switch back to the standard plan once you can afford it.

The best way to compare your choices, which change often, is to use a handy government tool called the Repayment Estimator at studentaid.gov/repayment-estimator. Keep in mind that you'll need to requalify for some of the plans each year.

Here are some common choices:

- **Graduated Repayment:** The payoff period is ten years, the same as for the Standard plan. But payments start extremely low and then increase every two years until the loan is paid off.

  Pro: Good if you can't afford the monthly payments under the Standard plan but are fairly certain your income will increase over the next few years.

  Con: You'll pay more interest than you would with the Standard plan.

- **Extended Repayment:** If you owe more than $30,000 in federal student loans, you can stretch out your payments over a period of up to 25 years. Those payments can either be fixed or graduated (rising every two years).

  Pro: Your monthly payments are lower than with the Standard or Graduated plans.

  Con: You will pay much more interest over the long haul than with Standard or Graduated.

- **Income-driven repayment plans:** These plans take into account how much you owe and how much you *earn*, and your income has to be low enough to qualify. Your monthly payments will be low, and if you stay on an income-driven repayment plan for a set number of years, the government will forgive the remainder of what you owe. Here are some of the income-driven options as of this writing:

> » *Pay as You Earn (PAYE)* has the lowest monthly payment. Qualifying for it is more difficult than any other plan, but after 20 years your remaining debt is forgiven.

> » *Revised Pay as You Earn (REPAYE)* has generally higher monthly payments than PAYE but less strict eligibility requirements. It will also forgive your debt after 20 years.

> » *Income-Based Repayment (IBR)* is another plan for which eligibility is easier than PAYE, and it forgives debt after 25 years.

Pro: All income-driven plans can be a good temporary option when you're young and not making much money. As your salary grows, you'll probably want to switch back to Standard Repayment so that you can pay off your debt faster.

Con: The government may forgive, but it doesn't forget. You'll likely have to pay tax on any debt that's being forgiven. For more details, check out IBRinfo.org.

Special Breaks If You Can't Make Your Federal Loan Payments at All

Most federal loans require you to start paying them back six months after graduating or leaving school. But if you can't make the payments at that point, you may qualify for a **deferment,** in which the government lets you off the hook from paying back your loans for up to three years.

Your servicer may grant you a deferment if you're unemployed, a part-time or full-time student, experiencing economic hardship, a Peace Corps volunteer, or a recipient of an approved graduate fellowship. During deferment periods, the government pays the interest for subsidized loans. With unsubsidized federal student loans, you'll eventually have to pay the interest that accrues during the deferment period.

If you don't qualify for a deferment, all hope is not lost. Loan servicers can also offer time off from paying through a process known as **forbearance,** which can be granted for a variety of reasons, many of which are up to the servicer. Forbearance allows you to reduce or stop making payments for up to 12 months at a time. You'll be responsible for the interest that accrues on any type of loan during that period. You can learn more about federal student loan deferment and forbearance at studentaid.gov/deferment-forbearance or by contacting your loan servicer.

Getting an official stay is important because when you miss a payment without one, your loan becomes **delinquent**. After 90 days without payment, your credit score will take a serious hit. What you want to avoid at all costs is **defaulting,** since there are serious repercussions. Default happens when you don't make your loan payments for at least 270 days (nine months). You may have to pay hefty penalty fees and collection charges. In addition, the government could withhold your tax refund, for instance, or even take money directly out of your paycheck. A default is also going to make a complete mess of your credit score.

If you've fallen down the default rabbit hole, you can make your way out. But it'll take work. You need to contact the Department of Education and tell them you would like to **rehabilitate** your loans. Get the process started at Myeddebt.ed.gov or call the department's Default Resolution Group at 800-621-3115. Under loan rehabilitation, you make nine full, on-time monthly payments over 10 months—allowing you to miss one if you must—to get back on track. These payments are capped at a small percentage of your income. (You can calculate the payment at asa.org/calculators /rehab.)

For ongoing problems with the servicer of your federal student loan, contact the Federal Student Aid Ombudsman (studentaid .gov/ombudsman). If you're having trouble with your private loan servicer—say, you're seeing erroneous late fees on your account— and the servicer is not responding, contact the Consumer Financial Protection Bureau, or CFPB, either online (cfpb.gov/complaint) or by calling 855-411-2372. The CFPB will forward your complaint to the loan servicer and then work to get a response. All but the most complicated cases are usually closed within 60 days.

One note: It's very difficult to rid yourself of student loans by declaring bankruptcy. Only in extreme cases is it possible, and you'd need to prove that paying back your student loans would cause you severe financial distress for a long time. So consider that option off the table.

Special Breaks on Federal Loans for Those Who Help Out

There are a number of **forgiveness** programs geared toward people who want to devote themselves to helping others. These programs can wipe your federal student loan debt clean after a certain period of time. For more information go to studentaid.gov/forgiveness.

A terrific program called **Public Service Loan Forgiveness** is a break that can save you a lot of money for doing good. If you're a full-time teacher, librarian, nurse, military service member, police officer, or government or nonprofit worker (and that's just a partial list) and you make ten years of on-time monthly payments, you could have the remainder of your federal student loan debt wiped away. What's especially great is that you will not owe tax on the debt you did not have to pay back.

Here's an example: Ben owes $30,000 in federal student loans out of college. He gets a job teaching junior high school in a rural town, with a starting salary of $35,000 a year. If Ben signs up for Public Service Loan Forgiveness and keeps teaching, he could pay about $24,000 over ten years and then have the balance of about $16,000 (that's his remaining loan plus accumulated interest) completely forgiven.

To maximize the amount you're forgiven, select the repayment plan that gives you the lowest possible monthly payment during the ten years (probably Pay as You Earn). You must have Federal Direct Loans or a Direct Consolidation Loan in order to take advantage of this deal. For details, see studentaid.gov/publicservice.

If you don't meet the criteria for Public Service Loan Forgiveness, you may be eligible for other forgiveness programs if:

- **You teach.** Teachers who work in a school designated as "low income" by the government may be able to have as much as $17,500 of Federal Direct Loans forgiven. For more information, consult the American Federation of Teachers (aft.org/benefits). There are also specific benefits for people who join the AmeriCorps teaching and community service program (nationalservice.gov/programs/ameri corps), including Teach for America (Teachforamerica.org).

- **You join the Peace Corps.** Volunteers may apply for deferment of Direct Loans and Perkins Loans as well as partial *cancellation* of Perkins Loans (up to a total of 70%).

- **You work in health care.** Doctors and nurses who are willing to work for two years in regions that are remote or economically depressed can have their federal loans partially forgiven through the National Health Service Corps (nhsc .hrsa.gov) and the Nurse Corps Loan Repayment Program (hrsa.gov/loanscholarships/repayment/nursing).

- **You enlist.** If you sign up to join the Army or Navy, you may qualify to have up to $65,000 of your federal student loan debt paid through the Student Loan Repayment Program. (Learn more at military.com/education/money-for-school /student-loan-repayment.html.) If you join the Air Force, the program will pay your federal student loan debts up to a maximum amount of $10,000 (if you qualify). (Currently, the Marines don't have a college loan repayment program.) Perkins, Direct, PLUS, and Consolidation loans are included in this perk. Don't assume that enlisting automatically means that your loans will be forgiven, though. For more on military benefits, see Chapter 10.

Understand the Pitfalls of Private Loans

If you had to take out private loans to pay for college, you're not alone. Increasingly, students and their families have had to turn to pricey options offered by banks and financial institutions when federal loans weren't enough. The problem is that not only are private loan interest rates often much higher than those of federal loans, but the rates are usually variable, meaning they can rise to unpredictably high levels. (Some are capped at 18%, but others can go even higher than that.) Nevertheless, a few private student loans may offer fixed rates that are competitive with federal loans, if the borrower (or the parent) has very good or excellent credit. Here are some important factors to keep in mind about paying back your private loans:

- **Know what you owe and to whom.** You may have been making payments on your private loans while you were still in school, but often private lenders allow you to wait until you're no longer a student. (Don't think they are being charitable; you'll have to pay the interest that accrues while you're in school, unlike with federal subsidized loans.) Although you likely will be contacted by your private lenders when it's time to start paying your loans back, if you haven't heard from them by the time you graduate, make sure to reach out. If you've lost track, check your credit reports (see p. 63 for details) or contact your school's financial aid office. Otherwise, you could be considered delinquent when you didn't even know you were supposed to be making payments. This is particularly important with private loans, whose repayment terms are much less flexible than those of federal loans. And private loans do not offer forgiveness for public service.

- **Find out if your parents are on the hook, too.** Chances are, your parents had to cosign your private student loans when you took them out. The borrower and the cosigner are *equally* responsible for paying back the loan—so if you're late on a payment, the parent's credit score can nosedive. Once you've graduated and made a certain number of on-time payments, your lender may allow you to request that your cosigner be released from his or her loan obligations. Though this can be complicated to do, and not always successful, you should try if you can afford to. Your parents will love you (even more) for it.

- **Consider a consolidation loan.** Sometimes you may be able to fold all of your private loans into one new loan with one monthly payment and a lower interest rate, particularly if your credit score is better today than it was when you first took out the loan. You can do it through a bank, a credit union, or an online lender like SoFi or CommonBond. In order to get these low-rate private consolidation loans, you'll need a very high credit score and a job. To see what private loan consolidation options might work for you, go to PrivateStudentLoans.guru. Beware of companies that offer you the chance to consolidate your federal loans into a private loan. This is usually a bad deal. It can turn your relatively low fixed rate into a variable one, which can rise over time, and make you ineligible for federal loan repayment and relief programs.

If You're Thinking of Going to Grad School

Although the unemployment rate for people with graduate degrees is lower than that for people with bachelor's degrees, that doesn't always mean that grad school is a wise investment. Here are a few questions you should ask yourself:

- **Will that advanced degree really help you advance?** The earnings premium for grad degrees is different for every field—and the difference can be drastic. Engineering majors or computer scientists who go on to get advanced degrees in their field, not surprisingly, will likely see a big bump in their earnings. For English and philosophy majors, the salary outlook is more uncertain. To get an idea of how much a grad degree in your field is worth, check out the stats from Georgetown's Center on Education and the Workforce at cew.georgetown.edu/valueofcollegemajors.

- **How much debt are you willing to take on?** Of course, any money you borrow for grad school gets added to the debt

IF YOU HAVE CREDIT CARD AND STUDENT LOAN DEBT

The interest rates on your student loans are probably lower than the interest rates on your credit cards. If this is the case, you should pay off your credit card debt faster than you pay off your student loans. By choosing a repayment plan that extends the number of years over which you pay back your student loans, you can reduce monthly student loan payments and free up some cash to pay down your debt more quickly. (Of course you'll need to resist the temptation to spend this cash instead.) Once you've wiped out your credit card debt, increase your student loan payments to at least their original levels.

But what if you don't have any high-rate credit card debt to worry about? In that case, does it make sense to prepay student loans? The answer is almost always yes. But again, you'll want to compare interest rates—only this time it's the rate you have to *pay* on your student loans versus the rate you could *earn* if you put your money into, say, some sort of savings or investment account.

from your undergraduate years. There are two kinds of federal loans available to grad students. The Direct Loan program allows graduate students to borrow up to $20,500 in loans each year, or $40,500 for medical school (with a cumulative limit of $138,500, including all the federal loans you took out as an undergrad).

If that's not enough, you can consider a **Grad PLUS Loan**. The program's loans can be used to fund the entire cost of your education (tuition, books, and living expenses) minus whatever other financial aid you receive. You need to have had no recent major credit problems in order to qualify. The downside of Grad PLUS Loans is that they come with higher interest rates than Direct Loans. Still, they'll probably beat a high-rate private loan.

- **Will your employer chip in for you to go back to school?** Many employers offer programs to help out with grad school costs. Often, employers will only pay for a program related to your job, and/or you might be required to stay with the company for a certain number of years after you get your degree. Talk to whoever handles benefits at your company.

- **Can you get a tax break for learning?** If you want to enroll in a graduate program (or even just take classes for your own enrichment), you may be eligible for the Lifetime Learning Credit from the feds. There's no limit on the number of years you can claim it on your return, and you can get a break of up to $2,000 a year. For more information, see p. 261.

CAR LOANS

Most people know it's smart to negotiate a car's price with the dealer before buying. You know you should google the make and model and shop around to see what local deals are being offered. That way, you'll be armed with information when you stride onto the lot to haggle your way to a discount. Maybe you'll even manage to get $1,000 knocked off the price (or free floor mats).

At that point, the salesperson will no doubt offer you financing. Eager to get the deal done, you'll sign on the dotted line and drive away feeling like one smart cookie.

But here's the problem: While you saved yourself money off the sticker price, you may be surprised to learn that the financing a dealer sells with the car is more profitable to him than the actual car sale. If you didn't shop around on the financing, you may have signed off on a car loan that will eat up all that savings—and then some.

Once you get a car loan with a high interest rate, you're probably stuck with it. It's difficult to find a lender who will refinance an auto loan to a lower rate. That's why you need to research not only the price of a car, but also where you can find the best loan deals. For instance, a 2% rate versus a 4% rate on a $25,000 five-year loan would save you about $1,300 in interest.

To get a sense of what rates you might qualify for, go to the loan savings calculator at myfico.com/crediteducation/calculators /loanrates.aspx. The better your credit score, the lower the rate you can get. You'll generally need a credit score of at least 720 to qualify for the best rates. This section will offer advice on finding the right car loan for you.

How to Get a Good Deal

You're going to need to do some legwork. Here are some pointers:

- **Check out the rates from at least one bank and one credit union.** In addition to going through a dealer, you can get a car loan from a bank or a credit union, or online. So before you step foot in a dealership, do some research. Consult Bankrate.com for options. Credit unions tend to charge lower rates on car loans, so if you don't belong to one visit Asmarterchoice.org or MyCreditUnion.gov to search for one you may be able to join. See if a bank is willing to give you a break if you have your payments deducted automatically from your account—most banks will knock off 0.15% to 0.25%, but a handful will give you a discount of as much as 1%. Also, ask a lender with a good rate if you can get preapproved for an auto loan. They will look at your income, debts, and other financial information to determine what rates you may qualify for and how large a loan you can handle, and preapprove you for that amount. When a seller knows you're preapproved, you're in a better position to negotiate.

- **Settle on the exact price of the car before you discuss financing.** Often the first question a car dealer will ask is how much you can afford to spend on monthly payments.

Although you should have a rough idea of the answer (see Figure 3–2 on p. 57), don't share that information. The reason: Once the dealer knows, he can adjust the terms—say, by extending the length of time you'll repay the loan or the interest rate you're charged—to make himself more money, while still matching your monthly payment figure. (Dealers can be a tricky lot!) Instead, simply say that you want to check out the different cars you're interested in and settle on the price before you discuss financing.

Haggling is an expected part of buying a car. In general, the sticker price is about 5% to 10% higher than what the dealer paid for it (known as the **factory invoice price**). For all but the hottest models, you should never pay the sticker price. To get the factory invoice price, go to Edmunds.com and KBB.com (Kelley Blue Book). You should aim to pay no more than 5% above that.

- **Weigh low-rate versus rebate.** A few car dealers offer rebates to entice potential buyers. Others offer really low-rate loans as incentives. If you have a choice, do the math to see which deal makes the most sense. There are good calculators available at Bankrate.com. If you have very good credit, you might be able to qualify for 0% financing, but the term of your loan could be unusually short—as little as three years—so be sure you can handle the high monthly payment.

- **Steer clear of low-down-payment auto loans.** The lower the down payment, the bigger loan you need and the more interest you'll end up paying. If you can afford it and don't have other high-rate debt, the best move is to pay the entire cost of the car up front. If not, try to put down at least 20%. If you can't afford that, get a cheaper car.

- **In general, go with the shortest-term loan you can afford.** The average term on new auto loans is about five years (up from four years not long ago). Although it may seem appealing to pay off a loan over a longer period since it'll

Figure 3-2

HOW MUCH YOU'LL PAY EACH MONTH WITH AN AUTO LOAN

This table can help you get a sense of what your monthly car payments will be, given a specific term and interest rate on a $24,000 auto loan. Although your monthly payments are lower with a longer-term loan, the total amount you'll pay is higher. To figure out the total cost of the car loan, multiply the monthly figure by the number of months it will take you to pay it off. So, for example, if you're paying 4% on a five-year loan (the national average as of this writing), you can expect to pay about $442 every month, adding up to $26,520 over the course of five years. Go to bankrate.com/calculators/auto/auto-loan-calculator.aspx to plug in your specific numbers and get your monthly payment.

Term (Months)	INTEREST RATE								
	3%	4%	5%	6%	7%	8%	9%	10%	11%
24	$1,032	$1,042	$1,053	$1,064	$1,075	$1,085	$1,096	$1,107	$1,119
36	698	709	719	730	741	752	763	774	786
48	531	542	553	564	575	586	597	609	620
60	431	442	453	464	475	487	498	509	522
72	365	375	387	398	409	421	433	445	457

mean that you have lower monthly payments, the problem is that you'll be paying more interest overall. Many owners end up owing more than the car is worth by the time they sell it or trade it in. Get a loan with a term of four years or fewer.

- **Beware subprime auto loans.** Subprime lending is when a bank or other lender extends credit to you even if you have a lower credit score (about 640 or below), meaning you have a history of missed or late payments. Subprime loans tend to have very high interest rates (often double or triple what you'd pay if you had decent credit). Some unscrupulous lenders will even ignore or adjust your income and employment history so that you can "qualify"—which means you could get saddled with a big loan that you can't really afford.

- **Buy a used car.** You'll pay about half as much for a used car as you will for a new one. That means that your auto loan will likely be smaller. And although the risk of getting a clunker is higher than it is when you're buying a new car, you can minimize that risk by doing some homework. If you're buying from a dealer, browse the dealer's website and ask if the car you want has a Carfax report, which uses a car's VIN (vehicle identification number) to gather important info about its service and inspection history; whether it has been in major accidents; estimated mileage; title info; and more. Many used car dealers will provide you with the Carfax report for free if you're interested in a car. (If they don't or you're buying from a private owner, you can get it yourself at Carfax.com for $40.) You should also search the free recall database from the government at vinrcl.safercar .gov. If it's a private sale through an online listing, call the seller directly to make sure it's not a scam. Never buy a car without evaluating it in person and taking a test drive. Finally, pay a trusted independent mechanic to inspect a used car before you purchase it.

Many dealers sell what are known as certified pre-owned (CPO) vehicles. A car with this designation is used but has been carefully inspected by the dealer. Certified pre-owned vehicles are usually under six years old and have lower mileage than many used cars. Most important, when you buy a certified pre-owned car it generally includes a manufacturer-backed warranty that is often just as good as the ones that come with new cars. That said, make sure you read the terms so you know exactly what is and isn't covered by this warranty.

Steer Clear of Leasing

If you've been shopping for a car, you may have found that some dealers are pushing leasing instead of buying. You may find the low down payment and low monthly payments enticing. But it's in your financial interest to resist.

When you lease, you're essentially renting a car for a fixed amount of time, typically three years. Although it's most common to lease a car through a dealership, a dealer is actually just a middleman who works on behalf of a leasing company. As a leasing customer, you pay for the amount the vehicle **depreciates**, or loses value, during the lease period (plus interest on this amount). Your monthly payments are based on the price of the car, the interest rate you're charged, the number of years in the leasing period, and the car's expected resale value at the end of the lease. If all this sounds confusing, it is, which is why many people end up shelling out more money than they should for the privilege of driving a new-looking car.

But here's the catch: When you *buy* a car that has, say, a four-year loan, at the end of the term you own the car free and clear. Not so with a lease. After the leasing period is up, all you have is the *option* of buying the car you've been leasing.

The bottom line: Leasing really only makes sense for people who want to drive a new or almost-new car at all times. (Not exactly a priority at this point in your life.) It's a particularly bad deal for people who drive a lot or aren't great about upkeep, because you have to pay for damages and extra mileage when your leasing contract is up. Even if you buy a car with a three- or four-year loan, you will likely be able to drive it for many more years after the loan is completely paid off. If you keep leasing a car every three years, however, you're always making a monthly car payment.

If you're still undecided about whether to buy or lease, take some time to crunch the numbers at Bankrate.com. Another helpful website for leasing options is LeaseCompare.com. The Federal Reserve publishes a useful guide called *Keys to Vehicle Leasing*, which you can get at federalreserve.gov/pubs/leasing. Also search for "Leasing vs. Buying a Car" at ConsumerReports.com.

CREDIT SCORES AND CREDIT REPORTS

Throughout this chapter, I've mentioned your credit score and credit report, and now is the time to tell you everything you need to know. Your **credit score** is a number lenders use to judge your ability to pay them back, and is one of the most important factors in your financial life. A good score will enable you to get the best deals on everything from credit cards to car loans to home loans; a bad one could cost you tens of thousands of dollars. This section will tell you what you need to know about your credit score, including the details of how it's determined, how to track it, and how you can make sure it's good.

In order to understand credit scores, you first need to understand **credit reports,** since your score is based on the financial information contained in these reports. Companies called **credit bureaus** (also known as credit reporting agencies) create credit reports by gathering information from a range of credit card companies, lenders, and merchants with whom you have done business. Included in your credit report is the date you opened each account, how much you owe, the maximum amount you can borrow, and your payment history. The credit report also has some basic personal information about you—your age, birth date, Social Security number, current

BORROWING FROM FRIENDS AND RELATIVES

James wanted to pay off the $3,000 balance he owed on his credit card, which charged an interest rate of 15%. His parents were willing to lend him the money to do it. Even with the best of intentions, this can get messy. Here are the steps to make the transaction as painless as possible:

- **Make sure the deal is good for both parties.** James agreed to pay his parents back with interest, and they settled on a rate of 5%. Not only was this a good deal for James, but it was also beneficial to his parents, whose money had been sitting in a bank savings account earning just 1%.

- **Put everything in writing.** James's parents wrote up an agreement that included the interest rate charged and the dates payments were due. It might sound formal, but this helped avoid confusion. You can download sample contracts and get advice from Nolo.com.

- **Make sure there aren't any negative tax consequences.** Bizarre as it may seem, the IRS sets a minimum interest rate—the **applicable federal rate (AFR)**—that family members and friends are required to charge on certain types of loans. Even if your parents, for example, want to lend you money without charging you interest, they may owe tax on the interest they would have received had they charged you the AFR. If you borrow less than $10,000 to buy an item like a car or to pay off debts (as James did), you don't have to worry about these rules. But if you borrow the money to purchase assets like stocks and bonds, or if you borrow more than $10,000 for any purchase, your parents, friends, or relatives may be expected to charge you interest.

and previous addresses, and sometimes your current and previous jobs. Your report will indicate whether you've ever had major financial problems, like defaulting on a loan or declaring bankruptcy. It also shows recent requests for your credit history by third parties like landlords, employers, and lenders.

All this information from your credit report is plugged into a complex mathematical formula to create your credit score. Every time you apply for a new loan or credit card, credit bureaus supply that company with your credit report or credit score, and sometimes both. Landlords and employers can also request credit information and use it to evaluate whether you reliably pay your bills on time, among other particulars of your financial life. (Employers cannot request your scores, only a stripped-down version of your credit report.)

How Your Credit Score Is Calculated

The type of credit score most commonly used by lenders to evaluate customers is called the FICO score, named for the Fair Isaac Corporation, which created it. There are five factors that determine your FICO credit score. Most important is your payment history, which accounts for 35% of your score. How much you owe counts for another 30%, and the length of your credit history represents 15%. The last two factors—the different kinds of credit you're managing (people with top scores tend to have a mix of student loans, credit cards, and auto loans, for instance) and the number of new credit applications you have—account for 10% each.

Most FICO scores range from 300 to 850—the higher, the better. (The average score hovers around 700.) For a sense of how your score can help you or hurt you, see Figure 3–3, "The Cost of a Weak Credit Score," on p. 63.

Figure 3-3

THE COST OF A WEAK CREDIT SCORE

The lower your credit score, the greater the interest you will pay. These figures are for a 30-year, fixed-rate, $200,000 mortgage. (See Chapter 7 for more on home buying.)

SCORE	INTEREST RATE (NATIONAL AVERAGE)	MONTHLY PAYMENT	TOTAL COST (MORTGAGE PLUS INTEREST)
760–850	3.80%	$ 931	$335,325
700–759	4.02%	$ 957	$344,487
680–699	4.20%	$ 977	$351,882
660–679	4.41%	$1,003	$360,931
640–659	4.84%	$1,054	$379,458
620–639	5.39%	$1,121	$403,628

Source: myFICO.com

Get Copies of Your Credit Reports and Credit Scores

There are three major credit bureaus that maintain your credit reports—Equifax, Experian, and TransUnion. You are legally entitled to one free credit report within a 12-month period from *each*. You're also entitled to an additional free report from each bureau if you're turned down for credit or unemployed and job hunting (so you have an idea of what potential employers might be seeing). You can access your free annual reports by filling out the request form at AnnualCreditReport.com. If you want to check the information in your credit reports more frequently, you can do so for free at any time at CreditKarma.com, which draws your data from TransUnion and Equifax.

Each of the three bureaus maintains its own credit score for you based on the information in your report. In theory there shouldn't be much variation among the scores since all the bureaus should have the same information about you in their credit reports. But errors do occur, so you should get a score from all three bureaus periodically, especially before you apply for a car loan or a home loan. If there is a significant difference among your scores at the different bureaus, there's probably something you need to correct on your credit reports. (See p. 66 for how to fix these mistakes.)

While you can get one free credit *report* from each bureau every year, that's not the case with your credit *scores*. You can get your score for about $20 from each of the three bureaus at myFICO .com. Some credit card companies have special arrangements that allow you to view your FICO score from one of the bureaus on your monthly statement. You can also get a free score at Credit Karma.com. While the score you see there won't be identical to the credit scores you get from the bureaus, it will give you a good sense of how your credit score measures up against other people's, and it can help you monitor your credit for unusual changes.

Tips on Improving Your Credit Score

As I've said, the better your credit score, the easier it is to qualify for a loan or credit card with a low interest rate, and the more money you'll save. Figure 3–3 on p. 63 shows how your credit score would affect your monthly payments and ultimately how much you will pay over the life of the loan.

Here are some tips to help raise your score:

- **Automate your payments.** You need to do whatever it takes to pay your bills on time. The surest way to do this is to automate your payments through your credit card or checking account.

- **Owe much less than you're allowed to borrow.** Your **utilization ratio** is the amount you borrow compared to the amount you can *potentially* borrow and is a significant factor in determining your credit score. Lenders like to see that you're using only a small percentage of your potential credit. Say you have four credit cards, each with a $1,000 limit, and you owe a total of $2,000 spread across all four. Your total credit limit is $4,000, so your utilization ratio is 50%. (If you owed $4,000, your utilization ratio would be 100%.) Keeping your utilization ratio under 20% is a good idea—under 10% is even better.

- **Once you pay off your debt, don't close your accounts.** If you close a credit card (thinking you are being responsible), you lower the amount of credit available to you, and that could bump up your utilization ratio. Take my example from above with the four credit cards on which you owe $2,000. Say you close one card. You still owe $2,000, but your total available limit shrinks from $4,000 to $3,000, and your utilization ratio jumps from 50% to 67%. Not good, in the eyes of lenders. For this reason, it's smart to keep open old credit cards that you've paid off—unless you're having to pay a big annual fee to do so. But don't backslide and use them.

- **Have different kinds of accounts.** Having a variety of account types—credit cards, student loans, auto loans, maybe a mortgage—can have a positive impact on your credit score. If you don't have a mortgage, see if you can get the company managing your rental to submit a record of your on-time payments to the credit bureaus. Sometimes large property management companies will do this, and having that information on your credit report could be a positive for your credit score.

- **Don't be a serial credit applicant.** Every time you apply for a credit card or loan, it is noted on your credit report as an inquiry. There are two types of inquiries when it comes to your credit report. A "soft" inquiry is when someone (such as an employer) looks at your credit report as part of a background check or when you check your own report. A "hard" inquiry is when a lender such as a bank or a credit card issuer checks your credit report in response to your application to decide whether or not to give you a loan or a card. Soft inquiries don't affect your credit score, but hard inquiries tend to cause a slight, temporary dip. You want to avoid multiple hard inquiries, which lenders may interpret as a sign that you are in financial distress. That said, there are times when you need to make multiple inquiries—like when you are shopping for a mortgage or car loan. The good news is, the scoring models will view a group of hard credit inquiries within a short amount of time (say, two weeks for a car loan and four weeks for a mortgage) as essentially one inquiry.

Credit Score and Credit Report FAQs

Q: What should I do if I find a mistake in my credit report?
A: Credit bureaus, unfortunately, make mistakes. Sometimes it's simply misspelling your name or giving a wrong address, but other times it's an error that could potentially damage your credit score, such as incorrectly indicating that you've defaulted on a loan.

If you find a mistake, contact the credit bureau right away to dispute it. (Go to equifax.com/dispute, experian.com/dispute, and transunion.com/dispute.) Be specific about your concerns and be prepared to send supporting documents like a paid bill or a letter from your lender that explains the error. If the bureau can't verify the details that you've disputed within 30 days, it is legally required to delete the incorrect info from your report. If this happens, you can ask that copies of the corrected report be sent to any lender who has seen the report within the past six months or any potential employer who has seen it within the past two years. Another tip: If you've initiated a credit dispute and your report has changed as a result of it, the bureaus are required to provide you with an additional copy of your report for free if you request it.

If you don't agree with the outcome of the investigation, write a short statement (100 words or fewer) and send it to the credit bureau to include in your credit report. (For information on how to handle identity theft, see p. 69.) And if the bureaus aren't being responsive, submit a complaint at cfpb.gov/complaint. The Consumer Financial Protection Bureau will follow up on it.

Q: Can an employer find out about my credit problems?
A: Federal law says that credit bureaus can disclose information about you to any person or organization with a "permissible purpose" for seeing the information. That can include a lender, an insurance company, or a landlord who wants to find out about your past financial habits. When it comes to employers (and potential employers), federal rules say they cannot get credit scores but may review your credit report. However, they must first get your written permission. Note that many cities, including New York, and some states have limited this practice, so check with your local consumer protection office to see whether it's legal for an employer to check your credit. Your credit report will show who has made inquiries about you in the past two years.

Q: If I'm turned down for a loan, do I get to find out why?
A: Yes. The Equal Credit Opportunity Act says that if your application for credit is denied, the lender must either give you an explanation for the rejection or inform you how you can get an explanation. Explanations should be fairly specific—for example, you earn too little money or you haven't worked long enough.

Under the Fair Credit Reporting Act, if the denial was due to something in your credit report, the lender must tell you the name and address of the credit bureau that provided it. If you're denied credit, credit bureaus are also required by law to send you a free credit report if you request it within 60 days. The same is true if you've been turned down for a job or an apartment because of your credit history. (Unfortunately, you usually aren't entitled to get a free copy of your credit score.)

Q: How long will my credit report show my misdeeds?
A: Most negative information will be deleted from your report after seven years. If you ever file for bankruptcy, it could take as long as ten years before your credit report will be clean. This doesn't mean you won't be able to get credit before then. Your behavior in the last two years or so counts the most.

THE $63,000 LATE PAYMENT

Although she'd never been late on a credit card payment before, when Anna went on a two-week vacation, she lost track of time and ended up paying her bill a month past its due date. Anna paid the interest and the $35 penalty and assumed it was all behind her. But it wasn't. When she started shopping around for a home loan a few months later, she was shocked. Although people with great credit were qualifying for 3.8% interest rates at the time, her one late payment had lowered her credit score so much that she could only qualify for a rate of 4.8%. That didn't sound like a big difference, but she did the math and discovered that 1% meant she'd pay $63,000 extra in interest over the life of her 30-year loan. After consulting a few more lenders, Anna learned she could build up her score again by reestablishing her old pattern of paying all her bills on time. She decided to wait, and over the next three years her score slowly but steadily climbed back to where it was in the first place.

Q: I keep hearing of companies that'll protect or fix my credit reports and scores. Are their services worth it?

A: No. These services are advertised online, on TV, and just about everywhere else—and are offered by banks, credit card issuers, and other companies. They promise to protect your credit by monitoring your credit reports for activity and by scanning public databases to see if your name pops up anywhere strange (such as court records or in a change-of-address record for someplace you've never lived). If they find any signs of unusual or fraudulent activity, they alert you. But they're expensive and usually not necessary, especially since you can sign up for free credit monitoring through sites like CreditKarma.com. More importantly, don't waste your money on firms that promise to fix credit reports. At best, these companies work the legal fine print to trip up the credit bureaus and force them to remove negative information. But most of the time, they do nothing for you. For tips on avoiding credit repair scams, see cfpb.gov/askcfpb/1343/how-can-i-recognize-credit-repair-scam.html.

Q: *I'm married. Does that mean my spouse and I have the same credit report and credit score?*
A: No. But if you have a joint credit card or loan, this account will be noted on both your individual credit reports. When you apply for credit together, the lender will generally look at both of your credit histories and make a judgment based on the lower score. Keep in mind that whenever you share a card or cosign a loan, you're liable for each other's debts. It's important for you to keep at least one loan or credit card in your own name and for your spouse to do the same, so that each of you establishes a separate credit history. If you don't, you'll have trouble getting credit if you get divorced or if your spouse dies.

IDENTITY THEFT

Identity theft is the fastest-growing crime in the country. Odds are, if it hasn't already happened to you, it's happened to someone you know. It's easier than ever for thieves and con artists to get hold of your personal information, including your Social Security number, driver's license number, and even your PIN codes. Using this information, they can set up accounts in your name, run up huge bills, and leave you to clean up the mess. Federal law often saves you from having to pay these fraudulent charges, but your credit report and score could be wrecked for a long time.

One problem is that it's often difficult to know if your identity has been stolen. In fact, sometimes you're alerted to the problem long after someone has taken out credit in your name. Maybe a debt collector calls you asking about unpaid accounts that you never opened. Maybe your credit card statement has a bunch of small charges you don't recognize. (These could be from a hacker testing the waters.) Maybe your card company calls to ask if you just tried to charge $600 at a Foot Locker a thousand miles from where you live. (You didn't.) Or you may get a notification from your bank alerting you that there's been a data breach and your information may be at risk. The aftermath in each of these scenarios may require a great deal of time, effort, and perseverance to fix. This section will show you how to do it.

Fixing Identity Theft

The first step to take after discovering that your identity has been stolen is to contact the fraud departments of the three major credit bureaus and request that an initial **fraud alert** be placed on your files at Equifax (alerts.equifax.com, 800-525-6285), Experian (experian .com/fraud/center.html, 888-397-3742), and TransUnion (transunion .com/fraud, 800-680-7289). (While in theory a fraud alert on one will be shared by all three, it's good to contact each bureau just to be sure.) A fraud alert is simply a written warning on your credit report stating that your identity has been stolen and that potential creditors should take extra precautions (such as requesting ID) to verify your identity before approving a credit request in your name.

The alert will stay on your file for at least 90 days. Once the alert is on your account, you're entitled to a free copy of all three of your credit reports; get them directly from the credit bureaus. (These reports are in addition to the annual free reports you can get on AnnualCreditReport.com.) If you find fraud, you will have to do some annoying legwork before the bureaus will remove it.

You'll need to create an **Identity Theft Victim's Complaint and Affidavit** with the Federal Trade Commission at IdentityTheft.gov. Fill it out online, print it out, and then take a copy of it to your local police station—you really need to do this in person—where you'll fill out an official police report. Then send a copy of the police report, along with a copy of your identity theft affidavit and a letter explaining why you're disputing the information on your credit report, to the fraud department of each of the credit bureaus, as well as any businesses where the thief used your information. Okay, still with me?

Once you have the police report and the identity theft affidavit, you can have the credit bureaus place an **extended fraud alert** on your credit report. It lasts for seven years, and it instructs your lenders to make sure that any requests for credit using your info are actually coming from you.

You can upload and submit the documents via the bureaus' websites. The credit bureaus have 15 days from the time they receive your material to ask for any additional information; if they don't, by law they're accepting your version of what happened and must remove the disputed information from your credit report.

Preventing Identity Theft

Clearly, this process is something of a nightmare that takes weeks if not months to sort out, so it's best to do what you can to avoid having your identity stolen in the first place. Here are a few precautionary habits that could help:

- **Check your credit card and bank accounts once or twice a week.** Consider setting up push notifications on your phone from your bank and credit card companies for big purchases (say, $100 or more).

- **Never give out personal information over the phone or online to anyone you don't know.** This includes your street address, birth date, phone number, email, PINs, online passwords, Social Security number, and, of course, your bank account and credit card numbers.

- **Beware of phishing scammers.** They pose as everything from IRS bureaucrats to eBay account managers in order to nab your personal information by sending you attachments and links. Dead giveaways are poorly spelled or ungrammatical requests for personal info (like passwords or bank account numbers). A link that doesn't match up with the purported website is another. Never click on any of the links in a suspicious message. Instead, search online for the name and contact info of the company that is requesting the information, and call or email to ask if someone from there indeed emailed you.

- **Tear up or, better yet, shred personal documents (including junk mail) before throwing them in the garbage or recycling bin.**

- **Check your credit reports for free at least once a year.** (See p. 63 for details.)

- **Don't get lured in by scammers on Twitter, Facebook, and other social media.**

- **Create a nonobvious password (no pet names, not "abcdefg," not "trustnoone," not "password") and change your online passwords once a year.** If you have trouble keeping track of them, you can download an app (LastPass is good) that stores your passwords or helps you update them securely.

For more information on identity theft, visit IdentityTheft .gov or check out the nonprofit Identity Theft Resource Center (IDtheftcenter.org), which offers free assistance from advisors at 888-400-5530.

A Stronger Defense Against Identity Theft

If you've had your identity stolen, or you're really worried about this happening, you should consider a **credit freeze** (also known as a security freeze).

With a credit freeze, only companies with which you already have a relationship can access your credit report and credit score. This restriction makes it very hard for thieves to open up new accounts with any lenders that require a credit check. But there's a downside: Credit freezes can be a hassle if *you* want to open a new account or get a loan.

To put freezes on your credit reports, go to each of the credit bureaus' websites (freeze.transunion.com, experian.com/freeze, and freeze.equifax.com) and submit a request. The cost varies by state, but it's generally around $10. If you've been a victim of identity theft, the fee is generally waived. You can temporarily lift (or "thaw") the freeze using a customized PIN code if you need to apply for new credit. If possible, ask the lender which bureau's report it'll be pulling so that you need to contact only one agency.

IF YOU'RE IN SERIOUS DEBT

You may be having trouble paying your bills for any number of reasons. Maybe you've lost your job or had a health crisis. Or maybe you've just run up a bunch of debts. Whatever the case, the first thing you should do is go straight to your lenders and explain your situation. You may be surprised to find some are willing to work with you to come up with a more flexible schedule that will reduce your monthly payments. After all, they have a vested interest in making it possible for you to pay them back. But others may not be so accommodating.

If your creditor has hired a debt collector to force you to pay up, know your rights. Debt collectors can contact you by phone, email, mail, fax, or in person, but they must contact you during reasonable hours (not before 8 a.m. or after 9 p.m.). They can't harass you or repeatedly phone you with the intent to annoy you. Under the Fair Debt Collection Practices Act, the collection agency must stop contacting you at your written request, except to notify you of plans to bring legal action against you. Debt collectors are forbidden to contact you at your workplace once you tell them your boss doesn't allow it. It's also illegal for them to discuss your debt with your boss or fellow employees.

If you need help negotiating with lenders to lower your monthly payments and possibly reduce the interest rates on your loans, the next step is to contact a nonprofit credit counselor. Your initial consultation should be free, but you may be charged a small fee for follow-up sessions. Before your appointment, be sure to ask what kind of documents you need to have handy. These might include current credit card statements, pay stubs, any correspondence from collection agencies or the IRS, and a breakdown of your monthly living expenses and income sources. During the session, your counselor should be able to give you your FICO credit score (for free) and info about what steps to take next. Try the Financial Counseling Association of America (FCAA.org or 866-694-7253) and the National Foundation for Credit Counseling (NFCC.org or 800-388-2227). Some colleges and credit unions also offer help, and you might be able to get a referral from a local bank or consumer protection office. Be aware that some credit counselors are incentivized to downplay bankruptcy as an option, so stick with counselors certified by the FCAA or NFCC. For more information, go to consumer.ftc.gov/topics/dealing-debt.

Avoid debt settlement firms that claim to help you pay off your bills for a fraction of what you owe. These companies (you may have noticed their ads) promise to settle all your debts for pennies on the dollar, but in reality they often don't deliver—leaving you with those unpaid debts, a ruined credit score, and the fees you paid for their "services."

WHEN TO CONSIDER BANKRUPTCY

At first blush, declaring bankruptcy, especially the type known as Chapter 7, can seem appealing if you're drowning in debt. You have to fill out some paperwork, pay a fee ($335 as of this writing), and probably find a bankruptcy lawyer to help make your case. But if your petition for bankruptcy is accepted, your debts will be "discharged," meaning you'll be absolved of responsibility for the money you owe to creditors such as your landlord, doctors, and credit card companies. Some of your assets can be seized to pay off

SKIP PAYDAY LOANS

One loan you should avoid at all costs is a payday loan. This wildly expensive way to borrow money is meant to tide you over until your paycheck clears. Here's how it works: A lender loans you money as an advance on what you have coming from your job. But this will cost you $15 to $25 for every $100 that you borrow for a period of two weeks. Paying a $15 charge every two weeks for an entire year would be like having a credit card with an Annual Percentage Rate of 391%! Frequently, payday borrowers get caught in a cycle of debt, borrowing again and again.

People desperate for money often turn to payday lenders in order to avoid asking family or friends for a loan. But the sad reality is that to get out of hock, you may have to ask your loved ones for money anyway. Why not cut out the middleman and avoid all those fees? (For more information on borrowing from friends and relatives, see the box on p. 61.) As an alternative, some employers will allow you to borrow from your own paycheck—for either a small fee or even nothing at all.

these creditors, but depending on which state you live in, you may be able to work out a deal where you get to keep your car, home, and household possessions. And it may not be long before you can start borrowing again. Sounds pretty good, right?

Not so fast. For starters, there's a long list of debts that can't be discharged. Student loans, for instance, usually can't be wiped out. What's more, Chapter 7 bankruptcy is noted on your credit report for ten years. (Chapter 13, which I'll explain in a moment, sticks for seven years.) True, you may be able to get some form of credit sooner, but you probably won't be eligible for low-rate credit cards or other attractive loan deals for a long, long time. Finally, keep in mind that prospective employers may learn from your credit report that you declared bankruptcy. You may have trouble changing jobs, especially if you're trying to get a position that requires you to deal with money, even handling a cash register at a store.

It's hard for people with relatively high incomes to declare Chapter 7. If you make more than your state's median income, you'll need to pass a means test to figure out whether you qualify. If the test determines you have enough disposable income to make debt payments, you'll have to file for Chapter 13 instead.

With Chapter 13, you'll pay a slightly lower filing fee, but your debts won't be wiped clean. The court will instead set up a repayment plan that will make it easier for you to pay off all or part of what you owe creditors. It's not, however, all that simple. Chapter 13 filers with incomes above the median in their state, for example, have to hand over all of their income above and beyond what the IRS determines they need for living expenses.

Consider bankruptcy only as a last resort. If you're in deep trouble and have no choice, do some research at sites like TheBankruptcySite.org or Bankruptcyresources.org.

- Take any savings you have and pay off your high-rate credit card debt. Paying off a balance on a credit card that charges 15% is the equivalent of earning 15% interest on your money (after taxes). This is a great investment.

- If you have a decent credit history and you can't pay off your high-rate credit card debt immediately, try to get a low-rate card and transfer your debt to it (but beware of transfer fees). You can find listings of low-rate cards at CreditCards.com and CardHub.com.

- If you're having trouble paying off your federal student loans, find a repayment plan that works better for you at studentaid .gov/repayment-estimator. See p. 45 for details.

- Before you visit a car dealership, shop around to get an idea of current auto loan rates and car pricing information. Then, once you find the car you want, negotiate an exact price before you discuss financing.

- Get free copies of your credit reports from AnnualCreditReport .com and CreditKarma.com and purchase credit scores from myFICO.com (if you can't get your score for free from your credit card company).

- If you've been a victim of identity theft, start by calling the credit bureaus' fraud departments to have a 90-day fraud alert placed on your file, then see p. 70 for the next steps.

4

BASIC BANKING

How to Keep Your Costs Low
and Your Money Safe

NOT SO LONG ago, people's financial lives revolved around their local bank. They kept their savings there (recorded in a nifty little "passbook"). They obtained their first credit card there. They got their mortgage there. And they might have even gotten their toaster there as a bonus for opening a checking account.

But today, just about all of the services that were once the domain of your local bank branch can be handled elsewhere. For instance, you probably got your credit card or shopped for a car loan online.

So do you still need a bank? The answer is yes. Banks offer two services that are still difficult to get elsewhere: a safe, all-purpose checking account and easy access to your cash through ATMs. But you don't want to settle for just any bank. Your goal is to find the one that gives you those things for the lowest fees and the least hassle.

This chapter will show you how to shop for a bank and how to manage the money you keep there. It will also give you tips on how to cut costs and maximize savings. And it will explain how you can keep your money safe.

A BANK BY
ANY OTHER NAME

For our purposes, it doesn't matter whether an institution calls itself a bank, a savings bank, or a savings and loan (S&L). These classifications only reflect the government agency that oversees the institution and have no impact on you whatsoever. A **credit union** is slightly different: a sort of not-for-profit bank formed by people who have something in common, such as their workplace or profession. Credit unions tend to offer lower-priced services than ordinary banks. (For details on the advantages of credit unions and how to join, see the box on p. 87.)

Nearly all banks, savings banks, and S&Ls in the United States are covered by something called federal deposit insurance, which guarantees that if the institution fails, the money in your account is protected. The government agency behind this is the Federal Deposit Insurance Corporation (FDIC), and it protects accounts up to $250,000. Check for "Member FDIC" on the website or on signs at banks that you're considering, or consult research.fdic .gov/bankfind. At credit unions, look for the NCUA sign, which indicates that accounts are protected up to $250,000 through the National Credit Union Administration. If you don't see "NCUA" on the website, or on a sign or sticker at your institution, ask or go to mapping.ncua.gov.

For simplicity, I'm going to stick with the term "bank" when discussing all these financial institutions.

WHAT TO LOOK FOR
IN A BANK

Whether you just moved to a new city and need to find a bank or you're simply thinking about switching to a new one, here's what you want:

- **Free checking.** Many banks offer this—you just have to wade through the options and sign up for the right account. But be careful: Some banks require you to either maintain a minimum balance (usually anywhere from $500 to $1,500) or have a regular paycheck automatically deposited into your account through **direct deposit** in order for the bank to waive its monthly fee.

  Sometimes banks will allow you to combine the amounts in your savings and checking accounts in order to meet the minimum balance requirement for free checking. Be sure to pay attention to how the bank calculates that minimum balance.

  Try to avoid institutions that use what is called the **minimum daily balance method.** This system requires you to maintain the minimum balance *every single day* in order to avoid fees. If your balance drops below the minimum for even one day, you will be charged a fee. Instead, look for a bank that uses the **average daily balance method,** which means the bank adds up your daily balances and then divides that total by the number of days in the billing cycle. So if your bank's balance requirement is $1,000 and your account dips below that a couple of times a billing cycle, you won't be penalized as long as your *average* balance is at least $1,000.

- **Free nearby ATM access.** Banks generally don't charge you for using their own machines, but you most certainly will be charged for using other banks' ATMs. Make sure you open a checking account at a bank with ATM locations near your work and home—or find one that reimburses you for using an ATM not affiliated with it.

- **Online and mobile banking.** If you're not doing it already, online banking is a great way to monitor your accounts. You'll spot any bank errors much faster if you check your accounts once or twice a week using your bank's app or website instead of waiting for your monthly account statements. Features to look for include free online bill paying, an app that allows you to deposit your checks by snapping pictures of them with your smartphone, and customized auto alerts that let you know if, say, you're bumping up against your minimum balance requirement or a large withdrawal has been made from your account.

MANAGING YOUR CHECKING ACCOUNT

Make sure you're on top of your checking account. If you aren't handling it wisely, you could find yourself paying hundreds of dollars in fees each year. These fees are big business for banks. Here are some tips that will help you avoid some hefty charges:

- **Monitor your checking account balance.** You should check your balance at least once a week to ensure that you have the money you need and to spot anything that isn't right. For example, I know someone whose account mysteriously showed her balance to be *minus* $600, even though she knew she had $400 in the account. If she hadn't checked, she would have missed what turned out to be a $1,000 bank error.

- **Be wary of overdraft protection.** For years, banks got a bad rap for charging as much as $30 for each bounced check. On top of that, you'd have to pay $20 to $30 to the merchant who got stuck with the bad check. These days, most banks offer what they call **courtesy overdraft protection** to "protect" you from these fees and the inconvenience and embarrassment of a returned payment. But be careful. Sometimes, it's more expensive than the charges from which it allegedly shields you. Some courtesy.

    There are two kinds of overdraft protection your bank will offer—one for checks and bill payments, and one for debit transactions and ATM withdrawals.

With the first, if you overdraw your account by writing a check, paying a bill online through your bank, or making an automatic payment through a payee (such as a utility), the bank has the option to let the transaction go through. If it does, you'll be charged a flat fee (generally $25 to $35), and possibly additional charges for each day your balance remains below zero. While this isn't ideal, it's better than the hit you'll take on your credit report if your credit card or car payment doesn't go through due to lack of funds. And if you have a good track record with the bank and rarely if ever overdraw, you may be able to get the fee waived if you have a good explanation.

For these reasons, you're slightly better off opening an **overdraft line of credit**, which is essentially a loan that automatically covers you. Although the interest rate on the overdrawn amount can run an outrageous 18% or higher, and there's sometimes an annual or per-transaction fee, it's generally cheaper than the courtesy overdraft protection described above or bounced check fees. Plus, you avoid a black mark on your credit report from a missed payment.

There is a whole other set of rules when you attempt to use your debit card without adequate funds or try to make an ATM withdrawal for more than you have. When you open your bank account and receive a debit card, banks are obligated by law to ask if you want to opt in for debit card overdraft protection. Don't do it. Sure, there may be times when your debit card is declined at a store or you can't make an ATM withdrawal because you don't have enough in your account. But let's be real: That's the way it should be. If you don't have money, you shouldn't be spending it. Not to mention that this type of overdraft protection is costly.

- **Link your accounts.** The simplest and smartest way to avoid paying fees for being overdrawn or falling below minimum balance requirements is to ask the bank to link your checking account to your savings account. You can then transfer funds for free between your savings and checking accounts as needed, to prevent any shortfalls. In addition, you may be able to use the total balance of all of your linked accounts to meet the minimum balance requirement (if there is one) for your checking account, and avoid fees.

- **Avoid interest-bearing checking accounts.** Checking accounts that pay interest sound appealing, but they can be a bad deal. Some require you to keep thousands of dollars in your account while paying you next to nothing. At one major bank, for example, in order to earn a pitiful 0.01%, you have to maintain a minimum balance of $10,000. At that interest rate, you'll make $1 at the end of a year. And that's assuming your balance doesn't dip below the required minimum—in which case you'll be dinged with a $25 monthly fee. At the same time, by leaving your money in such a low-paying account, you're not keeping up with inflation, so you're actually losing purchasing power. (For more on beating inflation, see Chapter 5.) You're better off keeping enough in your checking account to avoid fees and finding a higher-paying savings account for overflows.

- **Pay your bills online.** As I wrote earlier, you should find a bank that provides an option for making bill payments online through your checking account, a free feature often called **bill pay.** You enter the names of merchants, the amounts you owe, and the date on which you want each payment to arrive, and then the bank makes a free electronic transfer. These may be recurring bills or one-time payments. (See Chapter 2 for details.)

- **Use direct deposit for your paycheck.** If you have a regular paycheck, ask your employer to electronically transfer it straight into your checking account. Many banks will waive

THE $33.50 PACK OF GUM

When Adam moved to New York City, he signed up for a checking account at a bank near his office and got a debit card linked to the account. He was told that if he wanted, he could get courtesy overdraft protection for his new debit card, and even if he didn't have enough money in his account, his purchases would still go through. All he had to do was sign a form to "opt in" to the courtesy overdraft plan. Sounded good. That Friday, Adam got his first paycheck, and he deposited it into his brand-new checking account. On Saturday, he began to use his debit card and bought the following things:

Purchase	Merchant	Charge
Gum	Pharmacy	$1.50
Cappuccino	Coffee shop	$4.50
Dinner	Pizzeria	$19.00
Groceries	Grocery store	$25.00
Total		$50.00

On Monday, Adam checked his account online, and was shocked to find that he'd been charged an extra $32 for *each* of the things he had purchased. So how did this happen? Despite the fact that Adam's check didn't clear until Monday and there was no money in his checking account, the overdraft protection had enabled him to buy things with his debit card. The total bill: $128 in "insufficient funds fees." Adam was understandably freaked out. Fortunately, he had the wherewithal to talk to the bank manager, who agreed to reverse all but one of the $32 fees. Adam also canceled the courtesy overdraft protection, vowing to keep a closer eye on his account balance from now on.

the minimum balance requirement—meaning you won't be charged a monthly fee for falling below it—if you sign up for direct deposit; some may even offer you a small cash bonus.

- **Pick up the phone.** Many banks waive fees if you contest them. If you find a fee on your statement, call the bank to explain why the fee occurred and why you think it should be erased. If it's your first offense—an overdraft mistake, for example—there's a good chance you can talk the service rep into removing it.

USING THE ATM WISELY

Unless you use your own bank's machines exclusively, you're likely to encounter ATM fees. In fact, people spend billions of dollars annually on them. Here's how I suggest you keep those ATM habits—and your spending—in check:

- **Use only ATMs owned by your bank or its network (unless your bank refunds ATM fees).** By doing this, you should never have to pay anything to access your cash.

- **Consider getting "cash back" rather than making an ATM withdrawal.** The next time you urgently need cash, think about going to a store (usually a grocery or drugstore) that offers cash back and making a small purchase of something you need (say, an energy bar). This is a much better deal than making a withdrawal from an out-of-network ATM, and you'll have something to show for it. (Just be aware that some stores levy a small fee to do this, so ask.)

- **Find out what your bank charges you to use another bank's ATM.** Banks charge you a fee (the average is close to $2) for using machines that are affiliated with other banks.

The amount of the fee will be disclosed when you open the account, but the ATM will not warn you about the fee at the time of the transaction. However, you will see it on your next statement. So stick with your own bank's ATMs whenever you can.

- **Find out what other banks charge.** It's the nasty one-two punch of ATM fees: In addition to the fees your own bank may charge you for using another bank's ATM, you will almost certainly also have to pay a **surcharge** (the average is nearly $3) to that other ATM owner. These surcharges can be especially high when you're dealing with ATMs in places like restaurants, bars, or the mall. Between this surcharge and the fee your own bank charges, you'll end up shelling out an average of close to five bucks per withdrawal. This fee must be disclosed on the ATM before you're locked into the transaction, so you will be warned!

- **Limit yourself to one ATM withdrawal per week.** Withdrawing $20 a day is a bad way to keep track of where your money goes. Use the worksheet you filled out in Chapter 2 to estimate how much cash you need each week. Then pick one day a week to withdraw cash from the machine—say, every Monday. Make a pact with yourself to make that cash last for the entire week. Promise yourself that once it runs out, you won't get more. This strategy will help you rein in your spending.

- **Count your cash.** It's rare, but occasionally there can be a malfunction at the ATM, so it's smart to take the extra few seconds to do this (as long as you're not alone in a desolate area at 3 a.m.). If you find a mistake, save your receipt and contact your bank immediately. You'll need to make your case and then fill out the necessary paperwork to get your money back.

CONSIDER A CREDIT UNION

Credit unions tend to charge lower rates on loans and pay higher rates on savings accounts than ordinary banks. And credit unions typically charge less for everything from money orders to bounced checks. As with your deposits in a traditional bank, the money you have in most credit unions is federally insured (up to $250,000).

But before you sign up with a credit union, be sure that it provides all the services you need. For instance, ask if it's a member of an ATM network that would allow you to use the ATMs of other banks for free. (Typically, credit unions don't have a lot of their own ATMs.) Also, since credit unions tend to lag behind big banks when it comes to technology, make sure that yours offers the kind of mobile apps and website features you want, such as account alerts and free online bill paying.

Still, if you like the idea of doing your banking with a lower-cost, nonprofit community outlet, look into credit unions. To find one you may be able to join, check Asmarterchoice.org or the Credit Union Locator at mycreditunion.gov/pages/mcu -map.aspx. If you work for almost any government employer, chances are there's a credit union available to you. Also, your church, synagogue, or alma mater may have one, or there may be a community credit union for people who live, work, or worship in your neighborhood. If you have a relative who belongs to a credit union, you might be eligible to enroll; some credit unions accept immediate family members only, while others allow members of the extended family to sign up. Some credit unions even allow you to join if you make a donation to a charity affiliated with them.

INTERNET-ONLY BANKS

You may choose to go with a bank that exists only online—called an **Internet-only bank**. These banks don't have branches, tellers, and ATMs like regular brick-and-mortar banks do; for that reason, they have lower costs and in turn can pay customers higher interest on savings accounts. Not surprisingly, more people are putting their savings in Internet-only banks.

But the decision to open an Internet-only bank *checking* account is not as clear-cut. Here are the pluses: An Internet-only bank checking account allows you to do many of the things that you can do at a traditional bank, like get a debit card for purchases at stores or cash withdrawals at ATMs, write paper checks, and make online bill payments. The Internet-only bank might also pay interest on the money in your checking account with no minimum balance.

But there are some negatives to Internet-only bank checking accounts. Customer service is generally limited to emails and phone calls, so you won't be able to meet in person with a bank rep. (Not a deal breaker for most people.) Internet-only banks may not have their own ATMs, so you may be charged a fee each time you use other banks' or independent ATMs. You also typically won't be able to deposit checks or cash at an ATM.

There are ways around some of these limitations. For instance, there are Internet-only banks that will reimburse you automatically for some or all of your ATM charges, or belong to a network of sur-charge-free ATMs. And some allow you to deposit checks by taking photos of your endorsed check and uploading them using the bank's app. Look for these features when shopping for an Internet-only bank.

One compromise: Keep your savings in an Internet-only bank, and open a checking account at a brick-and-mortar institution. Most Internet-only banks will allow you to transfer money between the two accounts for free, although it can take a couple of days to complete money transfers between different banks. Of course,

SKIP PREPAID DEBIT CARDS

Prepaid debit cards are a lot like store gift cards in that they come loaded with a specific dollar amount that decreases as you spend. And, at first glance, they can seem really convenient. For one thing, they're reloadable, meaning you can keep adding money to them. They're also easy to get, since you don't need a checking account to obtain a prepaid debit card as you would for an ordinary debit card.

So what's so bad about the prepaids? While there are a few cards that can be good deals, the problem is that most cards out there tend to charge a slew of fees—for activation, inactivity, monthly use, reloading, and so on—that can end up costing you a lot. Bottom line: Find a checking account with a regular debit card and low minimum balance requirements.

this arrangement makes sense only if you can still meet the minimum balance requirement to avoid monthly fees on your checking account at the brick-and-mortar bank.

Just one last note: As with a brick-and-mortar bank, it's important that your Internet-only bank is federally insured so that your money is safe. You can check by searching research.fdic.gov /bankfind.

WHAT TO DO WITH YOUR SAVINGS

Bank savings options don't offer the potential for phenomenal gains, but that's not what you're after here. In fact, in recent years, savings accounts have paid next to nothing. Still, when it comes to savings, safety and access are the goal. You'll make your big money elsewhere.

Banks offer good places to accumulate the three-to-six-month emergency cushion discussed in Chapter 2. Your goal is to find a risk-free account, with the best interest rate possible. And you'll also need an account that is **liquid**, meaning you can withdraw your cash whenever you want without any penalty. To find the best savings accounts, check Bankrate.com or DepositAccounts .com. Here are some details on the interest-paying accounts you'll encounter:

- **Traditional savings accounts.** This plain-vanilla type of account is the simplest way to keep money in the bank and earn interest on it. To avoid a monthly fee, many major banks require you to maintain a minimum balance (usually $300 to $500).

  Some banks may waive that minimum balance requirement if every month you transfer money from your checking account into your savings account, or if you sign up for direct deposit.

  The bummer about traditional savings accounts is that they tend to pay very low—almost negligible—interest. Traditionally, banks raise the rates on savings accounts when interest rates in the economy rise, though they are slow in doing this. But what savings accounts lack in return, they make up for in safety and liquidity.

- **Savings at Internet-only banks.** Rates on these accounts tend to be higher than those on traditional bank savings accounts. Internet-only banks are able to offer these better rates because their expenses are lower than those of brick-and-mortar banks. Generally you can open one of these savings accounts in less than five minutes with no minimum cash requirement (though it may take about a week for the money to appear in your new account). Although money in an Internet-only bank savings account is liquid, it may take you a couple of days to actually get the cash in hand when you make a withdrawal. (For the ins and outs of Internet-only banks, see p. 88.)

- **Money market accounts.** A money market account (MMA) is basically a savings account with a more complicated name. These accounts tend to pay slightly higher interest, but they usually have higher minimum balance requirements. Like savings accounts, MMAs are liquid and available from traditional banks and Internet-only banks alike. My advice: Consider an MMA only if (1) it pays a higher interest rate than your bank's savings account *and* (2) the minimum balance required to avoid the monthly fees isn't much higher than the minimum required in a savings account. Unless both these criteria are met, you might as well stick with a regular savings account. Note: MMAs are different from money market *funds*, which are nearly as safe, have paid slightly higher rates historically, and are also worth considering as a place to stash your emergency cushion. (You'll learn more about money market funds in Chapter 5.)

- **Certificates of deposit (CDs).** A certificate of deposit is a savings product that usually pays a fixed interest rate if you keep your money in it for a specified period of time (known as the **term**). A common term for a CD is one year. CDs almost always pay slightly better rates than savings or money market accounts. With a CD you make a one-time investment and earn interest until the CD's term is complete. You do not continually add money to a CD; if you want to invest more money, you can open a new CD.

  At many banks you need at least $1,000 to open a CD, but some banks don't have a minimum requirement. Basically, you're giving up the liquidity you have with a savings or money market account in exchange for the CD's higher rate. If you take out the money you've deposited before the CD's term is complete, you'll likely be hit with an early-withdrawal fee. In some cases, you could lose all your interest plus part of your initial investment. So CDs are best for money you know you won't need for a set amount of time.

THE BEAUTY OF SAVING AUTOMATICALLY

Although you're probably not going to keep your life savings in a bank forever, a bank savings account is a great place to start. If you haven't been able to accumulate much savings on your own, have it done *for* you. There are a couple of ways to do this: One is to ask your bank to transfer a specific amount from your checking account into your savings account each time your paycheck is deposited. Or you can ask your employer to have a fixed portion of your salary go directly into a savings account while the rest goes into your checking account, assuming you have direct deposit available to you. These automatic savings methods offer you an effortless way to build up your emergency financial cushion. Because you won't even see the money that's being set aside, before long you won't miss it. (For more details, see Chapter 2.)

There's another issue to consider before choosing a CD over a savings account. When you lock yourself into a CD, you're in effect placing a bet on the direction of interest rates. Here's why: Say you deposit money in a two-year CD that promises to pay you 2%. Now suppose six months later, interest rates in the economy increase dramatically, and banks are now paying 3% on two-year CDs. You're stuck with a 2% CD for another year and a half. Though you would like to get out of the 2% CD and into a 3% CD, the early-withdrawal penalty you'd have to pay might be so large that it wouldn't be worth it. You won't face this risk with a money market account or a savings account because the rate you receive will rise along with interest rates in the economy. Of course, this works in reverse, too. If interest rates fall and new CDs are paying 1%, you'd be a winner with your 2% CD.

Check Bankrate.com and DepositAccounts.com to find the best CD rates. Keep in mind that if you get a CD at the bank where you already have a checking account, you may be able to link the two, allowing the money in the CD to help you meet your bank's minimum balance requirement and avoid fees.

JOINT VERSUS SEPARATE ACCOUNTS

Before you open a joint account with anyone, give it serious thought. With a joint savings or checking account, either person has complete access to all the money. What's more, if you have a falling-out with that person, dividing up the money could get ugly.

Many people in serious relationships do decide, though, to open joint accounts both for the sake of convenience and to ensure that their partner has their money if anything happens to them. But this can be tricky. When you sign up for a joint account, most banks will automatically enroll you in what's called a **joint account with the right of survivorship**, which means that when one account holder dies, the other will become the sole owner of the account. Another type of joint account, called a **joint account with the right of convenience**, does not entitle one person to inherit all the money in the account if the other dies. With a convenience account, you should discuss what to do in case one of you dies, and specify those wishes in a will. (See p. 234.) Bottom line: Make sure you have the type of account that meshes with your intentions.

Even married couples should discuss the joint account question. If you favor separate accounts but your spouse wants a joint one, there's a way to compromise: Consider putting a certain percentage of each paycheck into your own accounts and keeping the rest in a joint savings account. This way you'll have the freedom to spend some of your money independently.

If you and your spouse or partner decide to have a joint account, you're going to need to develop a system for managing it so that you can avoid returned payments and overdraft fees. The

WHY IT PAYS TO KNOW YOUR BANK MANAGER

If you have an account at a brick-and-mortar bank, it's a good idea to introduce yourself to the local branch manager at some point, just to get acquainted. I know this may sound old-school—most of us think of banks as faceless institutions—but I'm telling you it might actually help you out someday.

Of course, emails and phone calls are how most people deal with banks. And that's certainly more convenient when you have a question or a small problem. But the people on the other end of the communication are mostly working off scripts and have limited leeway to cut you a break. If you have a bigger problem, the manager at your bank branch is more empowered to help, and may be more likely to do so if you're not just another multidigit account number. It may even make sense to add your bank manager to your holiday card list. (No need to go overboard and invite him to your wedding.)

When a bank teller charged a friend of mine $30 for two certified checks—an amount he felt was too high—he politely discussed it with the bank manager, who waived the fees for him. The fact is, bank managers often forgive fees for customers who speak up, especially customers who have clean banking records.

So don't wait for a problem to arise. The next time you're at the bank, make a point of saying hello.

reality is, with two people making ATM withdrawals, paying bills online, writing checks, and buying things with debit cards, it can get complicated. Many couples put one person in charge of bill paying—whether that's overseeing automatic payments, individual electronic payments, or check writing. Whatever you decide, establish a reasonable price limit for individual purchases and agree that you won't buy anything over that amount without consulting the other person. That's a helpful method to avoid overdrafts—not to mention money squabbles.

A WARNING ABOUT BANK-SOLD INVESTMENTS

Banks used to offer only federally insured savings options (savings accounts, MMAs, and CDs). Today they sell stocks, bonds, and an array of investment funds. Although I'll go more in depth on this in Chapter 5, I need to mention something right away: Investments sold in banks are *not* protected by federal deposit insurance. That means you *can* lose money that you put in them. Bank salespeople, who like to call themselves "financial counselors" or "financial advisors," are supposed to explain this; they sometimes "forget."

As a rule, you're almost certainly better off investing directly with a low-cost mutual fund company rather than with a bank. That's because banks tend to sell investments that charge higher commissions and expenses. So skip the investments at the bank no matter how persuasive the salesperson is. Chapter 5 will tell you all about where to invest.

BANKING SECURITY TIPS

Ah, cybercriminals: They keep coming up with creative new ways to steal our information. With so much of your personal and financial data stored with your bank, it's important that you be proactive and do what you can to protect yourself. Here are some basic pointers for safe banking:

- **Check your accounts once or twice a week.** Keeping on top of your account activity is the single best defense against fraud; this will help you notice anything unusual that you can then report to your bank.

- **Protect your information if your bank is hacked.** Your bank will let you know if a security breach has been detected. In general, banks have separate insurance that protects your money in case of a hack, so your account balance should be fine. Still, it can be disturbing to know that hackers may have gotten hold of some of your personal data including your name and Social Security number, not to mention your account information. If you have concerns that someone might try to use any personal information to then open new credit accounts, you can place a fraud alert or a freeze on your credit reports to help prevent that. (For a detailed explanation, see the steps outlined in the Identity Theft section on p. 69.)

- **Be smart about passwords.** If your bank does have a breach, change your online password. Even if your bank says you don't need to, it can't hurt. Visit Strong PasswordGenerator.com, which helps you come up with a safe, free, random password that includes numbers and special characters, instead of an easy-to-guess word.

- **Protect your PIN (personal identification number).** The four-digit PIN you enter into ATMs should be random, not based on other personal info like your birthday or your phone number. Also, never share your PIN with anyone, and don't write it down.

- **Take precautions if you deposit checks by using your smartphone.** Although this method is incredibly convenient, make sure to sign your name and write "For mobile deposit only" on the back of the check before you use your phone to take a photo of it and send it to the bank via the app. After the deposit is posted to your account, you should shred the paper check or write "deposited" across the front and back before throwing it out. These steps will prevent a fraudster from trying to cash it if it's left around—or you from accidentally attempting to deposit it again.

- Find a bank that has all the services you need: free checking and online bill pay; a full-service app; and conveniently located ATMs. Use Bankrate.com or DepositAccounts.com to compare the rates offered by different banks.

- Consider options other than your local banks. Internet-only banks may offer higher interest on your deposits but may not meet all your banking needs because they lack branches or their own ATMs. Credit unions are not-for-profit institutions that tend to offer cheaper services (check Asmarterchoice.org or MyCredit Union.gov). Examine your needs and choose wisely.

- A safe and easily accessible bank savings account can be a good place for your three-to-six-month emergency fund.

- Skip fee-packed prepaid debit cards and opt instead for a checking account with low minimum balance requirements and a normal debit card.

- It's smart to use your bank's app or website to set up alerts to notify you of any large transactions. Report any fraudulent activity to your bank immediately so you can get your funds restored.

- If you've been charged an outrageous fee for a bank service, complain. Being firm but polite will often help you persuade the customer service rep, bank teller, or manager to waive the charge.

- Resist buying stocks, bonds, or other investments from your bank. Instead, look into some of the investment options discussed in Chapter 5.

5

ALL YOU REALLY NEED TO KNOW ABOUT INVESTING

It's Time to Have Some Fun(ds)

IF YOU'RE LIKE a lot of people, you have most of your money sitting in a checking account. Maybe you have just enough to get by and investing doesn't seem realistic. Maybe you have some money set aside but have no idea where or how to grow it. Maybe you're simply terrified of making a bad investment and losing the little bit of money that you do have, especially after having heard about the dramatic stock market swings of the last decade or so. Whatever your own maybes may be, it's time to learn about investing. Fortunately, this is a lot easier than it sounds.

Instead of taking your life's savings and betting it all on some stock tip that promises to make you rich (but probably won't), you should be thinking about putting your money into investments known as funds. For now, you can consider funds your entire investment universe. This chapter will explain what a fund is, the different types of funds, why they are good for new investors, and how you can use them to meet the goals you formulated in Chapter 2. Later in the chapter, you'll get my specific fund suggestions.

TWO POINTERS
FOR NEW INVESTORS

Before we get into the details, I'd like to take a minute to acknowledge two sad truths about investing. Though these points may seem obvious, they're often lost on investors who should know better.

- **There's no easy way to pick a winner.** The fact that a given investment did well last year provides little or no information about how well it will do in future years. More generally, there's no proven investment strategy that will always beat the others. If people tell you otherwise, don't believe them—including the analyst from a major brokerage firm who appears on CNBC, the distinguished economist who is quoted regularly in the *Wall Street Journal*, or your favorite uncle on your mother's side who had the foresight to buy stock in Apple at the turn of the millennium.

- **In general, you don't get something for nothing.** Typically, the way to get an unusually high rate of return on your investments is to accept an unusually high level of risk. So if anyone promises you a very high return with "no risk," be skeptical.

FUND FUNDAMENTALS

Before we dive in, you'll need to know what a fund is. Simply put, a **fund** is an investment that pools together the money of many people, and then that money is invested by the fund's manager. At any given time, a fund is typically invested in dozens (and sometimes hundreds or even thousands) of different stocks, bonds, or money market instruments; these are called **securities**. (I'll explain what stocks, bonds, and money market instruments are later on.)

The great thing about investing in a fund is that you reduce your investment risk. That's because if you invested on your own, you might have enough money to purchase just one of these securities (for example, an individual stock), and your success or failure would depend solely on the performance of that one security. When you invest in a fund, though, you avoid putting all your eggs in one basket. So even if half the stocks in the fund lose value, for instance, you won't necessarily lose money; the other half may be profitable and may balance out the losses with offsetting gains. The term for this investing principle is **diversification**.

I'll be explaining many types of funds, but the most important kind for you to know about is called a **mutual fund**. (I will also talk about another type called an **exchange-traded fund,** or ETF, later on, but the difference is subtle and you don't have to worry about that now.)

One technical note: When you invest in a mutual fund, you are actually buying units known as **shares**. As a shareholder, you and thousands of other people are the owners of the fund. The mutual fund's share price—meaning the price at which you can buy or sell a share in the fund—is called the **net asset value (NAV)**. Remember this term. It will not only impress your friends when you use it at parties (okay, maybe), but it *will* come in handy later in the chapter.

MONEY MARKET FUNDS

The least risky type of mutual fund is called a **money market fund,** also sometimes called a money fund.

But don't let the name confuse you. Money market *funds* (MMFs) are not the same as federally insured bank money market *accounts* (MMAs), which you learned about in Chapter 4. It's rare for a money market fund to lose money—only two have done so since MMFs were first created in the early 1970s—but it can happen, although even in those cases the losses were very small.

Historically, money market funds have tended to pay interest rates that are higher than those paid by bank savings accounts. That hasn't been the case in recent years, though, and because of that money market funds have lost some of their appeal. Still, experts believe there's a good chance that money market fund rates will surpass bank savings accounts again in the future. At that point, once you have enough money in the bank to get free checking, you'll want to consider putting money that you want to be really secure—like your three-to-six-month emergency cushion (discussed in Chapter 2) or savings for a down payment on a home—into a money market fund.

One nice thing about money market funds is that, like bank savings accounts, they allow you to get at your cash whenever you want it, although some have a minimum starting balance of $1,000 or more.

To better understand money market funds, you'll need a basic knowledge of the securities that money funds invest in. When large companies or governments need money for very short periods of time, they issue **money market instruments** in exchange for the cash they need. These money market instruments are basically IOUs from reliable institutions like the federal government, various state governments, and big-name corporations that promise to repay these debts very quickly, and are considered quite safe.

How You Make Money from a Money Market Fund

As with any mutual fund, when you invest in a money market fund, you're actually purchasing shares of that fund. Money fund managers tend to keep the NAV of each share equal to a dollar at all times by investing in short-term debt securities they believe to be very safe. So when you invest $250 in a money fund, what you're actually doing is buying 250 shares of the fund. The fund manager then puts your $250 together with the money from other investors and loans it to various governments and/or corporations, receiving IOUs (money market instruments) in return.

In addition to repaying their debts, these governments and corporations must pay the money fund interest on the money they're borrowing. Now here's the good part: The fund then passes these interest payments on to you in the form of **dividends,** typically credited to your account every business day. If you like, most money market funds will deposit these dividends into your bank account.

Many investors, however, choose to have their dividends automatically **reinvested** in the money fund. In this case, their dividends are used to buy them more shares in the fund. This is a painless way to increase the size of your account and keep yourself from spending your dividends.

The **yield** of a money fund is expressed as a percentage and is analogous to the interest rate paid on a savings account. It's calculated by dividing the fund's **dividends per share** by its share price. (With most money funds, the share price is a dollar, making this really easy math.) The yield of each money fund fluctuates day to day. Since money funds all calculate their yields in the same way, you can (and should) compare the yields of several money funds to each other as well as to bank savings accounts to find the best place to put your savings.

To keep a watch on how money fund rates compare to bank savings account rates—and to comparison shop for the best money funds—go to iMoneyNet.com and Cranedata.com.

A WORD ABOUT INFLATION

You may wonder why people don't keep all their money in nice, relatively secure money market funds. After all, even if your money won't grow quite as fast in a money fund as it might in some riskier investment, at least it will be growing, right?

Well, maybe not—at least in the way that matters most. After paying taxes due on your earnings from a money fund, you'll probably have a hard time even keeping up with **inflation**—the tendency of prices to increase steadily over the years. If you earn, say, a 3% yield on a taxable money fund one year but pay 30% in taxes, you'll be left with only 2% at the end of the year. While this doesn't *sound* terrible, if inflation is at 2%, that means everything you buy costs 2% more on average at the end of the year than it did at the beginning (conceptually, anyway). So although you may *look* richer on paper, you're right back where you started.

It's easy to forget about the effects of inflation when you're thinking about long-term investments. To help put things into perspective, take a look at the way inflation has weakened the "purchasing power" of the dollar over the past few decades. Say your parents bought a new car for $5,000 in 1975. If you bought a comparable car today, you'd pay about $22,000. Put another way: $5,000 today buys only about a quarter of what it could buy back in the '70s. Amazing.

Inflation has bounced around a lot over the years: It was occurring at a rate of more than 6% in 1990, less than 2% in 1998, and nearly 5% in 2005; it hit zero during the recession in 2009; and it was hovering around 1% in 2016. While it's hard to predict the future, it seems pretty likely that inflation will erode the value of the dollar over the next few decades. That's why it's so important to earn interest on your money. If you put $20,000 under your mattress and inflation increases at, say, an average of 2% a year, after 30 years, your $20,000 will have reduced in value to the point where it buys only what you can now buy for $11,041. If you'd been earning 3% interest on that money, you'd have the equivalent of about $26,800.

The rate of return you receive on an investment (known as the **nominal rate of return**) minus the rate of inflation is called the **real rate of return**. So if an investment is paying 7% and the inflation rate is 2%, your real rate of return is 5%. Take a look at Figure 5–1 on p. 106. It shows the nominal and real rates of return (without considering taxes) associated with various investments between 1926 and 2015. Don't worry about the exact definitions of these different securities; I'll explain that later. For now, the thing to notice is that stocks and bonds (and although it's not shown in this table, the funds that invest in them) have done a much better job of overcoming the effects of inflation over this period than Treasury bills (which are often found in money funds).

It's clear from the table that if you'd kept your money in a money market fund that invests in Treasury bills, you would barely have kept pace with inflation. Although Treasury bills had a *nominal* return of 3.4%, the real rate of return, after accounting for inflation, was a pitiful 0.5%. And things look even worse when you take taxes into consideration. Although after-tax returns vary depending upon an investor's tax bracket, most investors would actually have *lost* money in Treasury bills over this period. By investing in stocks and bonds, they would have done considerably better.

As I mentioned in the beginning of this chapter, the fact that a particular stock has done better historically than most other stocks tells us little or nothing about how well it's likely to do from now on. Still, it's the best guess of many investment experts that over the long term, stocks and bonds *as a whole* will continue to offer rates of return that are significantly higher than the rate of inflation. Although there's no guarantee that this will actually happen (or even that you won't *lose* money by investing in stocks and bonds over the years), it seems likely that these analysts are guessing right.

So although the safety of money funds makes them a good place to keep your emergency cushion, if you want a fighting chance at keeping up with inflation and can tolerate a bit more risk (meaning: you're okay knowing that you could lose money), your next step should be to consider two more aggressive types of investments: stock funds and bond funds.

STOCK FUNDS

Stock funds invest in—you guessed it—stocks. The appeal of stocks is that your return, over the long term, may be significantly higher than the return you'd get with money market funds. The downside is that with a stock fund, you risk losing money. (See Figure 5–1 on p. 106 for a look at how stocks performed compared to other investments, as well the best and worst years of each over time.)

What Is Stock?

To understand stock funds, you must first understand stock. Stock is sold in units known as shares. A **share of stock** represents a small piece of a company; if you buy stock in a company, you become the owner of a fraction of that company. The more shares you buy, the more of the company you own. The amount of money paid for one share is called the **stock price** or the **price per share**.

Figure 5-1

HOW VARIOUS INVESTMENTS
HAVE FARED OVER TIME

Type of Investment	Average Return (Nominal)*	Average Return (Real)*	Highest Return (Nominal)†	Lowest Return (Nominal)†
U.S. Treasury bills	3.4%	0.5%	14.7%	0.0%
Government bonds (long term)	5.6%	2.6%	40.4%	−14.9%
Government bonds (intermediate term)	5.2%	2.2%	29.1%	−5.1%
Corporate bonds (long term)	6.0%	3.0%	42.6%	−8.1%
Large-company stocks	10.0%	6.9%	54.0%	−43.3%
Small-company stocks	12.0%	8.8%	142.9%	−58.0%

*Compound annual total return, 1926–2015
†Best and worst years, 1926–2015
Data © 2016 Morningstar. All rights reserved. Used with permission.

Stocks are bought and sold each day in a marketplace known as a **stock exchange**. A stock's price rises and falls depending on supply and demand. When a lot of people want to buy a stock, that tends to "bid up" its price, the same way that rival bidders at an art auction might bid up the price of a painting. If, on the other hand, there are more sellers than buyers, the price tends to fall. Anything that might influence investors to buy or sell a company's stock may affect the share price. New information that might lead investors to believe that a company will make more money than previously expected, for example, will generally cause its share price to rise. Unanticipated bad news typically leads to a decrease in price.

In some cases a company's stock price will move up or down for reasons that have nothing to do with changes in the firm's expected profitability. A stock may fall, for example, because a large investor decides to sell lots of shares to raise money for some other purpose and has to settle for a lower price in order to cash out quickly. And in many cases, stock prices go up or down for what appears to be no particular reason at all.

Stocks don't pay interest like a savings account. You make money from stocks by selling your shares for more than you paid for them. The difference between the price you sell for and the price you paid is called a **capital gain** (or a **capital loss**). Certain types of stocks pay **dividends**, which are regular cash payouts companies make to keep shareholders happy. Typically, older, well-established firms—think GE and IBM—pay dividends on their stocks, while newer firms like Facebook and JetBlue do not.

What Is the Stock Market?

You've probably seen headlines reporting that the stock market was up or down. Loosely speaking, the stock market is said to have gone up if the prices of most stocks have risen that day. The barometers most people use to keep track of "the market," though, are not based on *all* the thousands of stocks that people trade, but on a representative sample. The prices of all stocks in the sample are averaged in some way (the details of which may vary) to calculate what's known as an **index**.

The most widely known index is probably the **Dow Jones Industrial Average**, which, despite its fame, is actually based on the stock prices of only thirty large companies, and for that reason doesn't provide an especially accurate reading of the direction of the market as a whole. Another well-known indicator is the **Standard & Poor's index of 500 stocks**. The S&P 500, as it's called, is more representative because it tracks changes in the stock prices of 500 large companies. Someone who tells you that "the market" has gone up is usually referring to one of these two indexes.

Another index, the **CRSP U.S. Total Market Index**, represents nearly 100% of the U.S. stock market, including the stocks of small, medium, and large companies. There are also international indexes, like the **MSCI EAFE Index**, and indexes that track the economies of developing countries, like the **MSCI Emerging Markets Index**. I'll explain each of these shortly.

Different Types of Stock Funds

Stock funds can be divided into two basic categories. The vast majority are **actively managed stock funds,** which means a fund manager uses his or her own judgment to pick and choose among the thousands of stocks available. The other type of stock fund is an **index fund**. An index fund invests in nearly all the stocks that make up a particular index like the S&P 500. Some people refer to index funds as unmanaged or passively managed, since the fund manager exercises little discretion over which stocks go into the fund. Instead, with an index fund, the manager's job is simply to come as close as possible to replicating the performance of the index it tracks.

Which type should you choose?

I recommend that you go with an index fund. Here's why: Although it may seem surprising, a number of academic studies suggest that actively managed stock funds run by "expert" fund managers actually do no better on average than passively managed index funds. (In his extensive research on this topic, Burton Malkiel, a Princeton economics professor and author of the classic finance book *A Random Walk Down Wall Street*, has found that over long periods most active managers have not outperformed the S&P 500 index.)

What is different about an actively managed fund, though, is that you'll be charged much higher fees than you will with an index fund. So why should you invest in an active fund if it charges more but doesn't do any better?

You shouldn't. Instead, stick with index funds, which allow you to participate in the historically attractive returns associated with stocks without charging you too much for the privilege. (I will get into the best ways to buy index funds later in the chapter.)

Of course, don't expect to hear this from the salespeople at most brokerage firms and mutual fund companies. Higher fees may be bad for you, but they're great for the companies that offer actively managed funds, since they allow those companies to pocket more money for themselves.

Stock Funds FAQs

Q: Wouldn't I be best off choosing a top-performing actively managed stock fund?

A: Yes, if you knew which funds were going to perform well in the future. After all, it would be well worth paying a bit extra in expenses if the fund manager could deliver high enough returns to more than pay for them. Researchers have found, though, that funds whose returns have been unusually high in the past don't necessarily perform better than funds that have performed poorly. In fact, the rules require companies to inform people that "past performance does not guarantee future results." (You'll spot this disclaimer on a fund's profile or **prospectus,** a document you can find on the fund company's website that offers all the details about a particular fund.)

Q: But what about those few fund managers who've done well year after year?

A: Maybe they're brilliant, and maybe they're not. But before jumping to conclusions, it's worth remembering that given the number of stock funds that have been formed over the years, it would be really surprising if some of them didn't do better than average for a number of years by sheer chance.

Let's talk odds for a minute. Suppose all fund managers pick their stocks completely at random. The chance that a particular fund will perform better than average (that is, better than half of all the funds out there) during any given year is 50%. There's one

MY FAVORITE INSIDER TRADING SCOOP

Sometimes I meet readers who think I'm holding out on them. "Sure, you recommend index funds in your book," they tell me, "but what investments do you really like?" People believe there's an insider trick to investing, and that if only they knew the truth they'd strike it rich.

I want to be really clear: That's not the case.

Let's put some long-term numbers on this. In 1996, in the first edition of *Get a Financial Life*, I strongly recommended index funds. Over the next twenty years, the average S&P 500 index fund had an annual return after expenses of 8.63%. Meanwhile, the average actively managed stock fund returned 7.29% after expenses. Readers who followed my advice back then and invested $10,000 in index funds earned $52,360, versus the average active fund route, which paid out $40,849—a difference of about $11,500.

In fact, according to the experts at Morningstar, index funds have beaten their actively managed counterparts the majority of the time over the last 35 years. So, for example, if two people had put $10,000 into the stock market 35 years ago—one in an actively managed fund and one in an S&P 500 index fund—the index fund investor would have earned an extra $100,000 today, after factoring in expenses.

That's not to say that an index fund will beat the average active fund every year. But it does mean that over long periods of time, it has been the best bet. The bottom line: Go with index funds.

chance in four (two times two) that this fund will do better than average for two successive years, and one chance in eight that it will be in the top half of its class for three years in a row. Do this ten times, and you'll discover that there's one chance in 1,024 that a given fund will beat the average for ten years running through sheer luck. These may sound like pretty slim odds, but with thousands of fund managers out there picking stocks, we should expect a handful of them to do better than average ten years in a row—enough to convince most anyone that they're financial geniuses even if they're in fact choosing their stocks at random.

To be fair, this doesn't prove that there aren't any mutual funds whose managers are genuine stock-picking geniuses. But even if there are, how are you going to tell them apart from the ones who've just been lucky? My advice: Don't try.

Q: What are the different stock indexes I can invest in?

A: As we discussed, an index fund invests in nearly all the stocks that make up a particular index, such as the S&P 500. But what exactly is the S&P 500? And which index might you want to invest in? Here are five major stock indexes to know:

- **S&P 500.** This index is based on 500 of the largest U.S. companies whose stock is traded on the New York Stock Exchange—the world's largest forum for buying and selling securities. Some companies in the S&P 500 are Apple, Microsoft, and Coca-Cola. A possible drawback of investing in a fund that tracks the S&P 500 is that it includes only the stock of large firms. For more diversification, you may ideally want to invest in an index that includes stocks of small and medium firms, too.

- **CRSP U.S. Total Market Index.** This index, created by the University of Chicago Booth School of Business's Center for Research in Security Prices (that's the CRSP part), tracks nearly 4,000 stocks and covers almost all of the U.S. equity market—from tiny companies to megacorporations like Amazon. If you invest in only one index fund, this index is a good one to consider.

- **Wilshire 5000 Total Market Index.** Similar to the CRSP U.S. Total Market Index, this index comes close to reflecting the performance of the entire U.S. stock market. Despite its name, the Wilshire 5000 currently tracks fewer than 4,000 stocks, with a range of small, medium, and large companies.

- **MSCI EAFE Index.** You may want to consider investing a small portion of your money in the stock markets of other countries. The MSCI EAFE Index tracks the performance of about 1,000 companies based in developed markets in Europe, "Australasia" (a mash-up name for Australia and neighboring islands), and the Far East (hence the acronym EAFE). Though this index may offer a good way to get some exposure to international stocks, it's worth noting that some foreign stock markets can be very volatile, and the fees charged by international fund managers are slightly higher on average than those of U.S. funds.

- **MSCI Emerging Markets Index.** Another level of diversification can come from adding stocks based in "emerging" economies. This index tracks more than 800 companies from 23 developing countries, including China, Brazil, and India. However, since some of these economies have been particularly volatile, you would want to keep this to a very small portion of your investments.

Q: What are exchange-traded funds (ETFs), and how do they differ from stock index mutual funds?

A: **Exchange-traded funds (ETFs)** are a lot like mutual funds: They offer the same type of diversification among dozens, hundreds, or thousands of stocks and bonds, and their fees are often even *lower* than those of index mutual funds.

But there is a technical difference: An ETF is traded like a stock on a stock exchange, with its **market price** going up and down throughout the day. This differs from an index fund's net asset value, which changes only once at the end of the day.

Like a stock, an ETF is easy to buy and sell. But that can be a problem. Research shows that trading in and out of investments often yields lower returns than holding for the long term. So if you are the type of person who may want to jump online to buy or sell whenever prices rise or fall, an ETF may be too tempting.

Assuming you are not an aspiring day trader, ETFs do make sense as part of your investment strategy. You can start with as little as $100 or so per share. (Index mutual funds often require an initial investment of $1,000 or more.) But beware: Although ETFs' annual expenses are low, some firms charge a commission to purchase them. Get your ETFs from one that doesn't.

On p. 124, you will find my recommendations for companies that offer the best index funds and commission-free ETFs.

Q: What percentage of my stock investments should be international?

A: What used to be viewed as risky business is seen today as a smart way to diversify your portfolio. Just don't go overboard. Investing, say, 20% in international funds should be enough to help balance out your losses if U.S. stocks dip.

BOND FUNDS

Bond funds invest in—that's right—bonds. To get a sense of the potential risk involved in a particular bond fund, you need to know the types of bonds in the fund. Generally, bond funds are riskier than money market funds, but less risky than stock funds.

What Is a Bond?

A bond is an IOU issued by a company, a government, or some other institution. When you buy a bond, you're basically lending a sum of money (the **principal**) to the issuer for a fixed period of time (the **term**), which can range from one day to one hundred years. In return for the loan, the issuer pays you interest, computed at a fixed rate called the **coupon rate**. Interest is generally paid monthly or quarterly, but in the case of a **zero coupon bond** you won't receive any interest at all until the end of the bond's term. When a bond reaches **maturity**, you're entitled (at least in theory) to get back your full initial investment.

So What's Risky About a Bond?

The risks associated with buying a bond can be divided into two categories. The first, which is often referred to as **default risk** or **credit risk**, is the possibility that the issuer may fall on hard times and be unable to pay you interest or repay your principal.

The second, which is somewhat more complicated, is known as **interest rate risk**. Here's one way to think about this kind of risk: If interest rates rise unexpectedly during the period in which you own the bond, you won't be able to take advantage of those higher rates. You'll be left with the same fixed coupon rate, which will start to look worse and worse compared to prevailing market rates. And since inflation tends to rise along with interest rates, the dollars you receive when the issuer finally pays you back probably won't buy as much as you'd originally thought they would.

So why not simply sell your bond if interest rates rise unexpectedly and buy another one with a higher coupon rate? Unfortunately, you're not the only one who's thought of this. Nobody is going to buy your low-coupon bond if a new, high-coupon bond can be had for the same price. Since the bond market, like the stock market, obeys the laws of supply and demand, the price you'll be able to get for your bond will drop as soon as interest rates rise. The higher interest rates climb, the less your bond will be worth.

A bond that doesn't have much time left until its final payback date, though, won't drop in value all that much when interest rates rise. This is because its holder won't have to put up with a lower-than-market coupon rate for very long and because inflation won't have much time to erode the value of the principal. A bond with many years left until its final payback, on the other hand, will fall much further when interest rates go up by the same amount.

So far, I've talked only about how interest rate risk can hurt you when interest rates increase. The other side of the coin is that when interest rates *fall* more than the market expects, bonds tend to *rise* in value. Before you quit your job to become a bond trader, though, you should review the exact wording of the previous sentence. It's not enough to know that interest rates are likely to fall if everyone else knows that, too, since those expectations will almost certainly already be reflected in the price you'll have to pay to buy bonds. To "beat the market," you'd have to outguess thousands of experts who spend their time thinking of little else.

My recommendation: Don't even try. The point of this discussion is not to teach you how to make extraordinary profits by predicting the future direction of interest rates but simply to help you understand the two major factors—default risk and interest rate risk—that contribute to the uncertainty surrounding a bond's future performance.

Different Types of Bond Funds

Bond funds differ according to the type of bonds they invest in. There are two key variables to look at. The first is who is issuing the bonds. There are bond funds that invest in bonds issued by the U.S. Treasury; by various federal agencies; by cities, states, and counties; and by corporations.

Why is this important? Depending on the stability of the issuer, each bond falls on a spectrum from dependable to risky. The more stable the issuer, the more dependable the bond. At the dependable end are bonds issued by creditworthy entities, such as the federal government or very solid corporations, that are considered to have a relatively low risk of default. At the risky end of the spectrum are **high-yield** bonds (commonly known as "junk bonds"). These bonds are often issued by financially troubled firms. Because such bonds are issued by relatively unstable companies, they have to pay higher rates to attract investors. A junk bond fund typically invests in the bonds of a *number* of "junky" companies, so the failure of any one company may not constitute a disaster for the fund's investors. Still, if many of these companies were to fail and therefore default on their bonds, investors could earn a much lower return and might even lose a substantial part of the money they originally invested. (See Figure 5–2 on p. 117 for more details about bond ratings.)

The second key variable is the number of years before the bonds in the fund mature. **Short-term bond funds** typically invest in bonds that will mature in fewer than four years, **intermediate-term bond funds** in bonds with maturities of between four and ten years, and **long-term bond funds** in bonds that won't mature for at least ten years.

The length of investment also plays a part in determining how risky it is. All things being equal, long-term bonds are generally riskier than short-term funds. But the relative safety of short-term bond funds comes at a price: Historically, short-term funds haven't performed as well as intermediate- and long-term funds.

The type of bond fund you select will depend in part on how much risk you're willing to take. Funds that invest in the bonds of less stable companies are riskier than those that invest in solid companies; funds that invest in long-term bonds are riskier than funds that invest in the short-term bonds of similar companies. Only you can decide how much risk you're willing to accept for the possibility of a higher return.

I recommend a middle-of-the-road approach that may represent a reasonable compromise if you want to choose a single bond fund and have a more or less average tolerance for risk: a fund that invests entirely or primarily in intermediate-term bonds issued by "highly rated" corporations. While there's no guarantee, there's a good chance that such a fund will provide you with a bit more income than, say, a short-term U.S. Treasury or government bond fund, without subjecting you to a huge amount of default or interest rate risk.

If you have the energy and enthusiasm to evaluate and keep track of more than one bond fund, consider spreading your money among several types of funds that fall at different points on the risk/return spectrum. If not, don't worry; the guidelines in the next section will allow you to hedge your bets even if you choose a single-bond-fund approach.

Bond Funds FAQs

Q: *Where can I get information about the types of bonds in a bond fund?*

A: Head to the fund company's website or Morningstar.com. There you can find the latest stats on the fund and look at the fund's prospectus. You may also want to review the "Portfolio" tab or look up the fund's most recent **shareholder report,** which will give a breakdown of the different **credit ratings** of the bonds that the fund recently held. These ratings are assigned by one of several rating agencies, like Standard & Poor's and Moody's. (Figure 5–2 explains the meaning of various ratings.)

Q: *Within a given category of bond fund, how should I pick a particular fund?*

A: Concentrate on one thing: fees. Studies have shown that bond fund managers have little effect on the performance of bond

Figure 5–2
BOND RATINGS

	S&P	Moody's	Description
Investment grade	AAA	Aaa	Highest quality
	AA	Aa	High quality
	A	A	Good quality
	BBB	Baa	Medium quality
High-yield (junk) bonds	BB	Ba	Risky elements
	B	B	Risky
	CCC	Caa	Riskier
	CC	Ca	Highly risky
	C	C	Extremely poor prospects
	D	—	In default

Sources: Standard & Poor's, Moody's, and Investment Company Institute

INFLATION-PROTECTED BONDS

If you want to own bonds as an investment but can't meet the minimum purchase requirements for a bond fund that interests you, there are still alternatives. You should consider **Series I** savings bonds, or **I Bonds**, a type of savings bond issued and sold by the U.S. Treasury. They're different from the old-fashioned savings bonds that your parents knew about because they have built-in protection against the negative effects of inflation. Now here's the catch: In recent years, I Bonds have often paid really low rates— even lower than bank accounts. But historically they've beaten bank savings accounts, with a median overall interest rate of 3.7% over the past 18 years.

There's another advantage to I Bonds: Because they're government-issued, there's no state or local tax on the interest you earn. You do have to pay federal tax, but not until the bonds are cashed in. This means your money grows tax-free for as long as you hold the bonds. (See p. 132 for an explanation of the magic of tax-free compounding.) And depending upon your income, you may be able to avoid paying any tax on the interest I Bonds earn if

funds, so there's no point in researching managers and paying extra for someone who claims to be better than average.

Q: Are there bond index funds?
A: Yes, there are many low-cost bond index funds and bond index ETFs. The most commonly used bond index is the **Barclays Capital U.S. Aggregate Bond Index**, which tracks the performance of high-grade U.S. government and corporate bonds.

you use the money only for educational expenses under the Education Savings Bond Program. (For more info, go to treasurydirect .gov/indiv/planning/plan_education.htm.)

Another plus is that you don't need a lot of money to get started. I Bonds can be purchased in electronic form with as little as $25 directly from the Treasury website, treasurydirect.gov. The Treasury will also let you set up an automatic investment program that allows your employer to deduct a certain amount from your paycheck and deposit it into your Treasury account. I Bonds can be cashed in any time after 12 months, up to thirty years. (But there's a three-month interest penalty if you cash them in before five years, with some exceptions.)

For investors who have a bit more money to start with, there's another type of inflation-protected government bond: **Treasury Inflation-Protected Securities (TIPS)**. These come in minimum denominations of $100, and twice a year the principal amount (what you invested) is adjusted to keep up with inflation. You can get TIPS directly from the Treasury or through banks, dealers, and brokers, without paying a commission. For more details, visit treasurydirect.gov/indiv/products/prod_tips_glance.htm.

THE RIGHT MIX OF INVESTMENTS

As I've said, your first investing move should be to save three to six months' worth of living expenses in a bank savings account or money market fund. But what happens after that? If you're ready to start investing more proactively, how much money should go into stock and bond funds, and how much should be added to a money market fund?

DON'T TRUST YOUR BRAIN'S
INVESTMENT ADVICE

Now that you understand investing basics, we need to talk about one more vitally important component: your brain. More specifically, how your brain is often doing its very best to get you to make costly investing mistakes.

This phenomenon has received much attention thanks to the field of behavioral economics, which explores how our emotions impact our financial decision-making process.

Here are some concrete steps you can take to ensure your brain doesn't block your best financial interests:

- **Don't get swept up in the moment.** Human nature is such that we tend to assume what's happening now will continue into the future. This seems to be the case with investment decisions, too. When stocks are falling, we tend to think they will keep on falling. And when the market is doing very well, we think the good times will just keep on rolling. This phenomenon is known as **recency bias**. Being swayed by what's happening right now makes it hard to stick to a long-term investment plan. For example, during the financial crisis of 2008, recency bias compelled many investors to sell their stocks. And many of those investors never reinvested in stocks, losing out on the gains from 2009 through 2015, during which time stocks nearly tripled in value.

Unfortunately, there's little agreement even among financial advisors on how much you should risk in the stock market. Historically, a fairly typical recommendation has been to allocate roughly 50% of your assets to stock funds and 30% to bond funds, while keeping 20% in "cash"—meaning money market funds or bank

- **Keep overconfidence in check.** When it comes to investing, research shows that men get into more trouble with overconfidence than women. One study by Brad Barber and Terrance Odean, both University of California, Davis, economists at the time, found that men were much more active traders, thinking they could beat the market. Meanwhile, women traded less often and earned an annualized return that was 1.4 percentage points better than the guys'.

- **Automate your investments.** Just as there are benefits to automating your savings (as I discussed in Chapter 2), there are benefits to investing on autopilot. You can have a set amount regularly withdrawn from your checking account and transferred into an investment account.

- **See yourself old.** You're going to be young forever, right? Wrong. But it's sure hard to appreciate that fact unless you can envision your older self. Literally. In one study at Stanford, college students who were shown a computer-generated rendering of themselves decades older committed to saving more than twice as much for retirement as other study participants who were shown just a current photo of themselves. You can conduct this experiment on yourself using apps, such as Oldify, that can give you a somewhat realistic (and irreverent) glimpse into your future.

savings accounts. This type of breakdown would put a lot of your money into those investments that have had the highest returns, while keeping some of it in safer places, just in case. Most important, you avoid putting all your eggs in one basket, taking advantage once again of the benefits of diversification.

Some say that young people should put even more of their assets—say, 70% to 80%—in stock funds, since these investors have much more time to ride out the downturns of the market. There is also an old rule of thumb to subtract your age from 100 to get the percentage of your money you should put in stocks, while the rest goes into bonds and money funds. For example, a 25-year-old would invest 75% in stocks and 25% in bonds, and then gradually reduce her risk over time as she approaches retirement. Like any cut-and-dried rule, this one has drawbacks as well as advantages, but it can be a useful starting point.

Once again, you'll have to decide for yourself how much risk you're willing to take in pursuit of bigger rewards. To help determine the right mix for you, consider these questions:

- **What's your risk tolerance?** Are you a risk taker by nature? Do you like to gamble? Are you willing to lose $10 for the chance of earning $30? If so, you might be okay with putting a lot of your money in stocks. But if you're afraid of risk and sickened by the thought of losing money—and you would consider it acceptable just to keep pace with inflation—a large percentage of your investment portfolio should probably be in a money market fund or bank savings account.

- **Are you diversified?** As mentioned above, to reduce the overall risk in your portfolio, you'll want to have a mix of investments. Before you make any decisions, examine the types of investments in your company retirement plan. If you invested your company 401(k) plan mainly in stock funds, for example, you'll probably want your other investments to include some bond and money market funds. (For details on 401(k)s, see Chapter 6.)

- **What are your goals?** If you have $30,000 that you'll need to use in the next year or two for a down payment on a home, don't invest it in a stock or bond fund where you could lose a lot of it if the market crashes or interest rates soar. But if you're just trying to build up your savings over the next ten or twenty years (or longer!) without a fixed goal in sight, you might want to take some risk in the hope of bigger returns.

One final note: Don't be discouraged if you can't create the perfect investment mix immediately. If you don't yet have enough money to meet the minimums required for separate investments in both a stock fund and a bond fund, it's important not to use that as an excuse to postpone investing. Start with a stock index ETF, for instance, then begin investing in a bond fund after you've accumulated some more savings.

INVESTMENT FEES
REALLY MATTER

Because there's little evidence that one fund manager is any more likely to beat the market than another, it makes sense to focus on the one thing that will definitely affect your investment results: the fee you are charged to invest in the fund.

This fee is called the **annual expense ratio**. It is computed by dividing the fund's **total annual operating expenses** by the value of all securities held by the fund. The fund's operating expenses are passed on to its investors, so the higher the expense ratio, the less you'll earn on your investment. If, for example, you invest in a fund that earns a 7% annual return on the securities it holds but has a 2% expense ratio, your investment will grow at a rate of only 5% per year.

As of this writing, expense ratios average a little under 1% a year for actively managed stock funds and 0.60% for actively managed bond funds. Compare that to just 0.11% on average for index stock funds and 0.10% for index bond funds. For money market funds, the average expense ratio is 0.13%. As we've discussed, there's no reason to believe that low-expense funds will perform any worse than high-expense ones. The lesson is simple: Invest in funds with the lowest expense ratios you can find, and ignore anything a broker, financial advisor, or bank employee might try to tell you about the great track record or bright prospects of the high-expense fund he or she is trying to push.

Other fee traps you should look out for are **loads** and **commissions**. Loads are typically one-time fees paid to advisors or brokers when you buy certain mutual funds. They aren't included in the fund's expense ratio, so you'll have to look for them separately; they typically range from 1% to 5.4%. Similarly, commissions are fees that some brokerage firms charge you when you buy or sell investments from them. Studies show that investments with loads or commissions perform no better on average than those that are no-load or commission-free.

So why does anyone pay these fees? Because they've been talked into an investment with a load or commission by an advisor who pockets some, if not all, of the fee. Loads and commissions are commonly used to provide generous compensation to the people who sell them, so they're highly motivated to convince you that the fund's superior performance will justify the extra cost. Just say no.

MY FAVORITE LOW-COST FUNDS

Today there are more than 800 financial firms operating in the United States alone, many of which offer dozens or even hundreds of funds. Don't be alarmed, though. I'm going to make this easy. What you're looking for is a company that offers no-load mutual funds or ETFs with low expenses and initial minimum investments that you're able to afford. (For the record, I don't get kickbacks, discounts, or free T-shirts from any of the firms I mention in this book.)

Let's start with ETFs. Two companies that offer a large selection of low-cost, commission-free ETFs are Charles Schwab (Schwab .com) and Vanguard (Vanguard.com). Vanguard's Total Stock Market ETF (0.05% expense ratio) tracks the CRSP U.S. Total Market Index. As of this writing, you could purchase one share of VTI (that's its abbreviated name) for about $100. As you have more money to invest, you can buy as little as one share at a time. The Schwab

U.S. Broad Market ETF (abbreviated as SCHB) has a slightly lower expense ratio (0.03%), but you need to commit to investing $100 a month into your Schwab account until it reaches $1,000. At that point, you can purchase one share at a time for about $50.

You can also buy stock index mutual funds. Although you can find them at a number of places—full-service brokerage firms, discount brokerage firms, mutual fund companies, and banks—I recommend getting your mutual funds directly from one fund company. The main advantage of keeping your investments at one firm is convenience: You'll get one statement covering all your holdings (as well as the ability to check your account online anytime you like), and you'll be able to move your money from one fund to another without much hassle.

As of this writing, the Schwab Total Stock Market Index Fund (SWTSX), which tracks nearly 2,500 stocks, has an expense ratio of only 0.09% and requires an initial investment of $1,000.

Vanguard also has many stock (and bond) index funds. As of this writing, the Vanguard Total Stock Market Index Fund (VTSMX), which tracks the CRSP U.S. Total Market Index, charges 0.16%. Vanguard's 500 Index Fund (VFINX), which tracks the S&P 500, also has an expense ratio of 0.16%. Vanguard requires a minimum initial investment of $3,000 per mutual fund.

SOCIALLY RESPONSIBLE INVESTING

People often ask me for **socially responsible investing (SRI)** recommendations. There are more than four hundred mutual funds and ETFs that fall into this category, but each has a somewhat different idea of what it means to be socially responsible. Some of these funds don't invest in certain industries, such as tobacco, fossil fuels, or firearms. Others use a model known as **impact investing**, zeroing in on, say, firms that treat employees well by providing child care services and promoting women and minorities, or green companies that deal with energy conservation and environmental issues.

BUYING INDIVIDUAL STOCKS

By now you know that my advice to anyone wanting to invest in the stock market is to stick with index funds. Both index mutual funds and index ETFs offer low-cost ways to invest in a broad range of stocks rather than betting on just one stock and hoping it takes off. That said, I feel compelled to offer some advice to readers who want to ignore me and buy individual stocks.

- **Stick with a discount broker.** A typical transaction that would cost you less than $10 at a discount broker could cost $50 at a full-service firm. Also, full-service firms often charge annual maintenance fees that skim a percentage (say, 1% or 2%) off the amount you're investing. But there's no evidence that these would-be experts' advice justifies the steep commissions they charge. And keep in mind that all these brokers, including discount brokers—who are salespeople, not stock analysts—generally make money by getting you to buy or sell stocks. So even if you're comfortable stock picking on your own, you're clearly better off paying lower commissions and going with a discount

Are do-good firms also good investments? That depends. Some people argue that the outlook for these types of companies is stronger in the long run because they pay attention to good business practices. Others disagree but say that investors who want to make an impact must accept that doing good for the world might mean doing worse for your wallet. Of course, even if a company does good for the world, you still want it to be a well-run business. Bottom line: If you want to support socially responsible companies, your best bet may be a mutual fund or ETF with this focus. As always, steer clear of any fund that charges a load or that has an unusually high expense ratio.

broker. Sites like Kiplinger.com and NerdWallet.com periodically publish rankings of the best discount brokers, based on a variety of factors, including price and service. Read them.

- **Avoid the temptation to invest in the latest [insert hot tech company] IPO.** Initial public offerings, or IPOs, mark the first time consumers can buy stock in a company. For example, young investors flocked to Facebook's IPO, expecting the usual "pop"—a dramatic rise in stock price on the first day. Pandemonium ensued when the opposite happened: Instead of the stock price soaring, it dropped unexpectedly and continued to tank in the months that followed. IPOs also sometimes favor friends and family, offering them the chance to buy stock at a lower price than regular investors, which means your earnings won't be as big (and your losses will be even steeper). If you simply can't resist the latest IPO, my advice is to stay the course. Those who stuck with Facebook despite its initial dip bought at around $38 per share, while the price as of this writing is more than $100 per share.

Vanguard has its own socially conscious fund, the Vanguard FTSE Social Index Fund (abbreviated as VFTSX). The expense ratio is just 0.25%, making this one of the cheapest funds in the category, but you'll still need $3,000 to get into it. The Pax World Balanced Fund (PAXWX, a mix of stocks and bonds) requires $1,000 to start, but it's a lot more expensive, charging 0.93% in fees. Many other social funds charge at least 1%. There is a less expensive ETF option: The iShares MSCI KLD 400 Social ETF (DSI) has a 0.5% expense ratio. For more information, consult SocialFunds.com, which analyzes socially aware funds.

DO I NEED A
FINANCIAL ADVISOR?

If you follow my advice outlined in this chapter, you won't need a financial advisor or a planner. If you do want the hand-holding, make sure to choose wisely. Never work with someone who is paid by commission (or loads). You want to work with a fee-only professional who charges you a flat fee (hourly or a percentage of assets). The fee-only system removes a potential conflict of interest: Someone on commission needs to get you to buy and sell to make any money. That's in his or her best financial interest, but not necessarily in yours. To find a fee-only advisor, seek out recommendations from friends, family, and colleagues, or try NAPFA.org.

Another option for investment advice is the new wave of robo-advisors like Wealthfront, SigFig, and Betterment. I like these sites because they each have smart academic researchers involved in them, they recommend low-cost funds, and the additional fees they charge for helping you buy their investment recommendations are very low. The way it works: Each site asks you a list of basic questions like your age, income, and risk tolerance, and then suggests—free of charge—specific ETF investments for you. If you then have them purchase these investments for you, you pay a small fee on top of the expense of the funds themselves. If you'd prefer to invest on your own, you can use these robo-advisors' recommendations as a guide to help you divvy up your money. For instance, if they're recommending 60% in various stock ETFs and 40% in bond ETFs, you can use that breakdown as a road map for investing on your own. These robo-advisors stick to stock and bond ETFs and don't suggest what percentage of your money should be in cash. So just make sure you're putting money you absolutely don't want to lose in places like money funds and bank savings accounts.

And one more note: If you're dealing with a live person, try this test. Ask if the financial advisor likes index funds. If he says no, that almost certainly means he is more interested in lining his own pockets rather than yours.

- Build an emergency savings cushion equal to three to six months' worth of living expenses. Keep that in a bank savings account or a money market fund—depending on which is paying better interest rates—so it's available if you need it.

- Begin investing in stock and bond mutual funds or ETFs. Invest in index funds, since actively managed funds tend to charge higher fees and have not performed any better historically.

- Invest only in no-load, commission-free funds. There's no point in buying funds with hefty fees since there's no evidence that they're better investments.

- Choose a fund with low expenses. As of this writing, expense ratios average a little under 1% for actively managed stock funds and 0.60% for actively managed bond funds. Instead, go with index stock or bond funds, which charge about 0.10% on average.

- When choosing between mutual funds and ETFs, consider two things: your own propensity toward trading (prices of ETFs change throughout the day, like stocks, making it hard for some investors to stay the course), and the minimum initial investment requirements. Some mutual funds require as much as $3,000, while ETFs allow you to start with as little as $100.

6

LIVING THE GOOD LIFE IN 2070

Think It's Crazy to Start Saving Now for Retirement? It's Crazy Not To

SUPPOSE YOU SET aside $1,000 a year (about $19 a week) from age 25 to age 65 in a retirement account earning 7% a year—a total of $40,000. By the time you turn 65, you'll have $213,610.

But if you don't start saving until you're 35 and then invest $1,000 a year for the next 30 years—a total investment of $30,000— you'll have only $101,073 when you turn 65.

You might want to read that example again slowly. By waiting until age 35, you end up with half as much as you'd have if you'd started at age 25.

The moral of this story (a potentially depressing one if you're over 35) and the focus of this chapter: If you don't start saving in a tax-favored retirement account while you're young, you'll miss out on perhaps the best investment opportunity of your life. That's because retirement savings plans offer terrific tax advantages that allow your savings to grow rapidly. In order to maximize the benefit, though, you need to get started right away. The government limits the amount you can set aside each year, so if you don't do it now, you won't be able to make it all up when you're older (and, in theory, anyway, wiser).

But wait. There's another reason to start saving in these accounts: Medical advancements promise to keep people in their twenties and thirties alive years longer than previous generations. Most Americans who reach the retirement age of 67 today can expect to live beyond the age of 85. By the time you retire, the figure could be closer to 90.

One more important big-picture point you should know: The Social Security Administration currently predicts that unless Congress agrees to an overhaul by 2034, there won't be enough money in the fund to pay out full benefits. While Social Security will likely be around in some form when you retire, it was never meant to be your only source of income in retirement. And because the employer-paid pensions enjoyed by our parents and grandparents are largely a thing of the past, now, more than ever, you'll need to have retirement savings of your own to live well.

This chapter will teach you everything you need to know. It will demystify the ins and outs of your options and answer the questions that may have been getting in your way. You'll be happy to learn that you don't have to be rich or financially savvy to put money into a 401(k) or IRA (individual retirement account). You just need to learn the basics spelled out here.

WHAT ARE RETIREMENT SAVINGS PLANS, ANYWAY?

Back in the early 1970s, when Microsoft was just a glimmer in Bill Gates's eye, Congress decided to give savers a break by creating tax-subsidized retirement savings programs. Today, whether you have a traditional job, work freelance, or run your own business, you probably have access to some sort of tax-favored plan. In a traditional setup, you likely have a 401(k) plan. If you work independently (or if your company doesn't offer a 401(k) plan), you can go for an IRA. Of course, Bill Gates doesn't need to worry about running out of retirement savings, but you do.

Here's a quick rundown of your options:

- **401(k)s** are retirement savings plans available to employees of most major companies and many small ones. **403(b)** plans (also called tax-sheltered annuities) are offered to employees of public schools and certain religious or charitable organizations. (Since 403(b)s are similar to 401(k)s, I'll refer only to 401(k)s throughout this chapter.)

- **IRAs** (individual retirement accounts) are available to working people (and their nonworking spouses) and are especially attractive for people who are self-employed or those who work for companies that don't offer retirement savings plans.

The main tax-saving principle behind all these retirement savings plans is simple: Uncle Sam agrees not to tax the money in your retirement account while it is accumulating interest and other earnings. That may not sound like such a big deal. But allowing untaxed interest to pile up year after year can result in thousands of dollars more for you over your lifetime. Why? Because your interest, as it's added to the pot, earns interest on itself, an effect known as **compounding**. I've heard some financial types call this "The Eighth Wonder of the World." (Okay, maybe they need to get out more.) But the point is, when money compounds without being taxed for, say, forty years rather than thirty, it not only grows for a longer period of time, but it also grows more quickly, as the example at the beginning of this chapter shows.

HOW YOUR RETIREMENT SAVINGS GROW

Whichever type of retirement plan you have, the money doesn't just sit there; it's channeled into investments so it can grow. When you sign up for a plan, you're given a choice of investment options.

You pick the ones you want and decide how to divide your money among your selections.

Your choices will depend on the kind of plan you are in. With a 401(k), your employer typically narrows down the investment options for you. Many plans offer you a menu of about twenty choices, which might include shares of your company's own stock (more on this later), some actively managed stock mutual funds, some index funds, a few bond mutual funds, balanced mutual funds (which have a mix of stocks and bonds), money market funds, and international funds. Every time you contribute to your plan, the money is automatically divided up according to your specifications.

IRAs are slightly more complicated because they involve more choices, starting with where to open one. Your best bet is probably a low-cost mutual fund company. One side note: Since retirement accounts allow your money to grow in a tax-favored way, you may want to consider the advantages (and disadvantages) of putting certain investments in them. For instance, it doesn't make sense to put tax-free bond funds into an IRA or 401(k); stick with taxable investments only. (For a discussion of different investment options and the pros and cons of each, see Chapter 5.)

Naturally, there are drawbacks to tax-favored retirement accounts. Your IRA and 401(k) contributions are locked away—if you choose to withdraw any of the funds before you turn 59½, you'll be subject to a stiff penalty. But the tradeoff for limited access is serious tax-free growth in savings for your golden years. You may also wonder if inflation will sap any gains you make in your IRA or 401(k). It's a fair question, but I'm here to tell you that saving for retirement is worthwhile. Give your money decades to grow tax-free, and you'll outpace inflation—and then some. I'll go deeper on all these pluses and minuses later in the chapter.

CONTRIBUTING TO YOUR 401(K)

Many companies offer you a choice between two types of 401(k)s: a **traditional 401(k)** and a **Roth 401(k)**. In this section I'll run through the differences. But don't get too bogged down in the details—later on in this section I'll help you figure out which one is right for you. For now, your big takeaway: You must sign up.

Probably the number one comment I get from people who read previous editions of this book is that they are so glad they forced themselves to sign up for a 401(k) in their twenties. And here's why: Since employers siphon the contributions to your 401(k) from each paycheck, most people don't even notice the money that's being skimmed off. And before long, thanks to tax-favored compounding growth, you have more savings than you ever thought possible.

For 2017, the maximum amount of annual income an employee under age 50 can contribute to a 401(k) is $18,000. (Actually, the maximum you're permitted to contribute may be less, depending on factors such as your salary and your employer's contributions, if any, to your plan.) If you've just started your first job, this may seem like an insane sum, but remember, it's the *maximum*. You can start with much less.

Traditional 401(k)s

Most large employers offer workers the opportunity to start saving in a traditional 401(k). These accounts benefit from two tax breaks—one up front, and one over the long term. First, the government allows you to delay paying taxes on the money you contribute to a traditional 401(k) each year. This is known as a **pretax contribution**. So if you earn $50,000 in a year and you put $1,000 into a traditional 401(k), you're taxed as if you had earned only $49,000. That's appealing because it puts more money in your pocket immediately. Assuming you're in the 25% tax bracket, you'll save $250 that year—the 25% of that $1,000 you would otherwise have had to pay taxes on.

The other tax benefit of a traditional 401(k) is that you get to delay paying taxes on the *interest* (or other earnings) your retirement account generates over the years. This is known as **tax-deferred** growth, since you're putting off, or deferring, paying tax.

It's true that when you withdraw the money from a traditional 401(k) at the time of your retirement, you will have to pay taxes on the whole sum—the amount you contributed plus your earnings. But because the money is able to grow untaxed for many years, paying taxes later rather than sooner could result in thousands of dollars more for you when you retire versus keeping the money in an account that doesn't grow tax-deferred.

Roth 401(k)s

These work a bit differently. Unlike traditional 401(k)s, Roth 401(k)s don't offer an up-front tax break on your contributions. Instead, you pay tax on your income as you normally would and then make an **after-tax contribution**. Once your money is in a Roth 401(k), you never have to pay tax on it again, even many years from now when you retire and start making withdrawals.

What's So Great About 401(k)s, Anyway?

One of the biggest benefits of a 401(k) is that many employers match a portion of the amount you contribute with a contribution of their own. Many companies contribute 50 cents or a dollar for every dollar you put in, up to a fixed maximum (often 2% to 6% of your salary). That's the equivalent of an immediate 50% or even 100% return on your investment. For example, let's say your company matches 50 cents for every dollar you contribute to your 401(k) up to 5% of your salary—and you wisely take advantage. If you make $30,000 a year, you'll contribute $1,500, and your employer will chip in another $750. To take full advantage of this

LETTING THE BOSS PLAN YOUR RETIREMENT

If your company automatically enrolls employees into 401(k)s, make sure to pay attention to *how* that money is then invested. Federal rules require companies to invest money that's auto-enrolled into 401(k)s in certain types of investments, the most popular being **balanced mutual funds** and **target date funds (TDFs)**.

Balanced mutual funds (often called **hybrid funds**) are a blend of stocks and bonds. These funds tend to be somewhere between stock and bond funds in terms of both performance and cost.

Target date funds, also called **lifecycle funds**, are a bit more complicated. They also tend to offer a mix of stocks and bonds, but the mix changes depending on how close you are to your prospective retirement date. The way it works is that you pick the year closest to when you expect to retire, and you're matched up with investments that the TDF company believes will be right for you. In theory, a TDF designed for people who are several decades from retirement will be more heavily weighted with stocks, since

amazing deal, contribute at least the maximum amount for which you are eligible to receive matching funds. If you don't, it's like walking away from free money.

To encourage participation, a growing number of companies automatically enroll employees in the 401(k) by funneling a portion of their salary into the plan. If your company does this, make sure that you contribute at least as much as your company will match; many employers that enroll you automatically start your contribution at a very low level, often 3% or less. Some employers automatically increase your contribution to your 401(k) by a set percentage each year, or with each raise you receive. If your company *doesn't* do this, do it yourself.

the money won't be needed for a long time and they can afford to take a bit more risk. As investors get closer to retirement, TDFs become more heavily weighted toward bonds and cash, since investors need to be sure that the money will be there when they need it.

A TDF company does all the decision making for you since the fund manager is constantly **rebalancing** the mix of stocks, bonds, and other investments to make sure it reflects your target date.

Both balanced funds and TDFs are reasonable, convenient options, but that convenience comes at a cost: They tend to charge higher investment fees than stock and bond index funds. The average TDF currently charges 0.55% a year in total expenses, and the average balanced fund charges 0.77%. That's more than you'd pay for a stock index fund or bond index fund at Vanguard or Schwab. If you're willing to rejigger your investments on your own as you get older, it could result in thousands of dollars more for you come retirement.

The Choice: Traditional 401(k) Versus Roth 401(k)

Generally speaking, the Roth 401(k) makes sense if you're young. But the decision comes down to one basic question: Do you want to pay taxes now, or later? With a Roth 401(k), you pay tax on your contribution before you put it in, when you're still working. With a traditional 401(k), you pay tax on your withdrawals during retirement.

The good news is that there are online calculators to help you make this decision. (More on that coming up.) But first, some backstory: When traditional 401(k)s were first introduced, the assumption was that people would stop working come retirement time, and would therefore be in a lower tax bracket than they were in during their working years. Today, it's common to work well into "retirement," and it is reasonable to assume that you could very well be earning more in the future than you are earning now, when you're just starting out. For that reason, the Roth 401(k) may be the better choice, because any contributions you make today will get taxed at your current (low) rate. With a traditional 401(k), you would pay taxes on withdrawals at your future (presumably higher) rate.

You can crunch the numbers, using your best estimates for your own situation, with a 401(k) comparison calculator such as the one at bankrate.com/calculators/retirement/401-k-retirement-calculator .aspx. No matter which type of 401(k) you choose, contribute at least as much as you need to get the full employer match—more if possible—and then let it grow untouched.

CONTRIBUTING TO AN IRA

Unlike 401(k)s, IRAs are not offered by employers. They're private accounts set up through mutual fund companies, banks, and brokers. (My first choice for an IRA is a low-cost mutual fund company, but more on that later.) Even people who already have a 401(k) can open an IRA.

The maximum you can contribute to an IRA as of 2017 is $5,500 a year, plus an additional $5,500 to your spouse's IRA if he or she doesn't earn any income. If both you and your spouse work, you can each contribute up to $5,500 to your own accounts. These limits apply to your total IRA contribution—whether you have a traditional IRA, a Roth IRA, or a combination of IRAs.

Here's a look at the different IRA types.

Traditional IRAs

These work much like traditional 401(k)s. You get to subtract, or "deduct," your contribution from your income—that's the up-front tax break. So if you earn $50,000 and contribute the maximum $5,500 to an IRA, you pay tax as though you had earned only $44,500.

The money in your traditional IRA also grows without being taxed for many years. Come retirement time, you'll pay income tax on all the money in your account as you withdraw it. Again, this is called tax-deferred growth because you defer paying tax on that money for many years, which helps it grow more quickly.

Traditional IRAs that offer up-front tax breaks are known as **deductible IRAs.** Unfortunately, deductible IRAs are not available to everyone. Whether or not you're eligible depends on your "adjusted gross income" and whether you participate in an employer-sponsored retirement plan. (For details on calculating your adjusted gross income, see Chapter 9.)

Here are the rules. If your employer does *not* offer a 401(k), you're almost always allowed to deduct your full $5,500 contribution to a traditional IRA. (You don't *have* to contribute $5,500, but you're permitted to.) There is one tricky exception: if you're not eligible for a company retirement plan but are married to someone who *is*. In that case, you can make the full contribution to a deductible IRA only if your combined adjusted gross income is $186,000 or less (as of 2017) and you and your spouse file a joint return. So if you drop out of the workplace for a few years to stay home to take care of the kids, for instance, and your spouse has a retirement plan at work, you can still make a full contribution to a deductible IRA as long as your spouse earns $186,000 or less.

But what if your employer *does* offer a retirement plan? In that case, your IRA contribution may not be fully deductible. If you're eligible for an employer-sponsored retirement plan, you can deduct your *full* $5,500 contribution to a traditional IRA if:

- You're single and your adjusted gross income is $62,000 or less

- You're married, you file a joint tax return, and together your adjusted gross income is $99,000 or less

Married people who file separate tax returns, no matter what their incomes, can't claim the full deduction if they participate in retirement plans at work.

If you don't qualify for a fully deductible IRA, you can still put up to $5,500 a year into a **partially deductible IRA** or a **nondeductible IRA**. To find out what part of your contribution may be deductible, check out IRS Publication 590-A, *Contributions to Individual Retirement Arrangements (IRAs)*, at irs.gov/pub/irs-pdf/p590a.pdf. Trust me. It's a great read.

For years, partially deductible IRAs and nondeductible IRAs were considered too much trouble to be worthwhile. Even though they still allowed your money to grow tax-deferred, they didn't offer the full $5,500 up-front tax break that makes deductible IRAs so appealing. They also require extra paperwork. (You'll have to fill out Form 8606 every year when you file your taxes.) But now there's a loophole that can make them more attractive. For details on why nondeductible IRAs are now worth your time, see p. 153.

Roth IRAs

With Roth IRAs, you don't get an up-front tax break on your contributions. (That is, you can't deduct your contribution on your taxes.) But once your money is in a Roth IRA, it will grow tax-free for life. When you retire and start taking your money out of a Roth IRA, you won't have to pay federal, state, or local taxes on it as you would with a traditional IRA or 401(k). For many people—especially young people saving over many years—the Roth IRA is the better deal. (I'll get into the details in a moment.)

One big advantage of Roth IRAs is that you may be able to open one even if you already have a retirement plan at work (which you may not be able to do with a deductible IRA). That's because the eligibility rules for Roth IRAs are simpler than they are for deductible IRAs. It doesn't matter if you and your spouse are eligible for a retirement plan at work—all that matters is your income.

As of 2017, you can make the *full* $5,500 annual contribution to a Roth IRA if:

- You're single and your adjusted gross income is not more than $118,000

- You're married, file jointly, and your adjusted gross income is not more than $186,000

You can still get a Roth IRA even if you have a higher income, but the amount you're allowed to contribute is less than $5,500. As long as you earn under $133,000 as a single person or $196,000 as a couple filing jointly, you can make a partial contribution. It's a sliding scale, so if you want to know where you fall, fill out Worksheet 2-2 in IRS Publication 590-A. One quirky rule: Married people filing separately can never make the full Roth contribution. There are rare cases—if either has a very low income—where they can make partial contributions. Again, see Worksheet 2-2 in Publication 590-A.

The Choice: Traditional IRA Versus Roth IRA

If you want to put money in an IRA, you'll need to decide which kind. Although Roth IRAs are generally considered the better option for younger people, there are a few questions you should ask yourself.

- **Do I qualify for a deductible traditional IRA?** No mystery here: If you don't qualify for the full $5,500 deductible IRA, go with the Roth.

- **Can I afford to make the full $5,500 contribution if I go with a Roth?** With a traditional IRA, a $5,500 contribution would result in a $1,375 tax deduction if you're in the 25% tax bracket. In real terms, this means that the full $5,500 contribution would end up costing you just $4,125 out of pocket. But Roth IRAs are not deductible, which means your $5,500 contribution to a Roth would cost you . . . $5,500. If you can afford to put the full $5,500 in a Roth IRA, you'll be doing your future self a big favor. If you can't, go with a traditional IRA.

A WORD ABOUT 529 INVESTMENT PLANS

If you plan to have kids—or have one or two now—you may have heard about these programs that help you save long term for their college education. You may wonder if they're something to consider. (You may also wonder why I'm bringing them up here in the retirement chapter.) The reason is that these plans offer tax advantages that are somewhat similar to the benefits you get from 401(k)s and IRAs. My advice, even if you have children, is to max out your 401(k) plan (up to the amount your company matches) and a Roth IRA before you consider a 529. That's because 529 plans have strict limits on how you can use the money. If you're one of the rare few who have already maxed out your retirement plans, then, and *only* then, should you start investigating 529s at Savingforcollege.com.

- **Will I be in a substantially lower or higher tax bracket when I retire?** As I said earlier, it's very hard to predict today what your tax situation will look like thirty or forty years from now. When you're in your twenties, you assume you will be richer when you're old, but the fact is many people do fall into a lower tax bracket when they retire because they stop receiving regular income from their jobs. This matters because Roth IRA contributions are taxed today, while traditional IRA contributions are taxed when you take them out. So if you strongly suspect that you will be in a lower tax bracket when you retire than the one you're in today, a traditional IRA may make more sense.

- **Will I need to withdraw my IRA money in the next few years?** This is a big one. You can withdraw the money you've put into a Roth IRA at any time without penalty (though you will have to pay a penalty if you withdraw any of the interest on that money). Although this is not advisable, it does provide more emergency protection than a traditional IRA, which you can't tap at all under most circumstances without paying tax and penalties. (For details on withdrawing money from IRAs, see p. 145).

My advice generally is to put as much money as you can in a Roth IRA and leave it there. But if you think a traditional IRA would be better for you, look into the details before you make any decisions. Check out the IRA comparison calculator at bankrate .com/calculators/retirement/roth-traditional-ira-calculator.aspx.

GETTING AT THE MONEY IN YOUR 401(K) OR IRA IF YOU REALLY NEED IT

On the surface, IRAs and 401(k)s have a major downside for young people. Once you put your money into these accounts, you may have to wait until you reach the age of 59½ to withdraw it without paying a penalty. If you try to take money out of a traditional IRA before then, for instance, you'll get hit with a 10% penalty, plus income tax on the amount you withdraw. The rules can be even tougher with 401(k)s.

These strict rules are meant to prevent savers from raiding their retirement plans. But if you don't have any other options, you should know that the rules aren't actually as rigid as they seem. Here are the details.

Borrowing from a 401(k)

Withdrawing money early from a 401(k) is difficult, for reasons I'll explain in a moment. But most 401(k)s offer an escape hatch: They allow you to *borrow* the money at rates that are sometimes more favorable than a bank's. When you borrow from your 401(k), you are essentially borrowing money from yourself, and the payments you make—including interest—go right back into your own account.

A LESSON IN HOW A LITTLE ADDS UP TO A LOT

Although he has never earned more than $40,000 a year, Peter, 40, has more than $182,000 in retirement savings. How did he do it? Peter socks away 15% of his salary each year through his longtime employer's 401(k) plan. (With his modest salary, he doesn't have to worry about bumping up against the government's yearly limit—which is now up to $18,000.) His starting salary at age 22 was just $25,000 a year, but he immediately began contributing the maximum he could to his company plan (even though his company offered no matching program), and has continued to do so ever since. For each of the three years he lived with his parents after college (he moved out at age 25), Peter also deposited an additional $2,000 into an IRA. Although it's true that Peter profited from the fact that stock and bond funds did well overall since he began placing his retirement savings in them—he has averaged a 7% annual return—his real achievement has been his determination to contribute to his 401(k) every year. If he continues to save the maximum in his 401(k), gets a 3% cost-of-living salary increase each year, and continues to earn 7% a year on his investments, he will have more than $460,000 by the time he turns 50. Amazing.

But there's a big danger to doing this: If you lose your job after taking out a 401(k) loan, you may have to pay back the entire amount—often within 60 days—to avoid a 10% penalty and income taxes. In general, loans must be paid back within five years (although if you use the money to buy your primary home you may be able to pay it back over a longer period). Bottom line: While you really don't want to plan to borrow, it's good to know the option is there for emergencies.

Withdrawing from a 401(k)

To withdraw money from either a Roth 401(k) or a traditional 401(k) early, you must prove to your employer that you need it for something urgent, such as paying medical bills, and that you have nowhere else to turn. If you do meet these conditions, here are the tax details you'll need to know.

- If you withdraw from a Roth 401(k) early, your *contributions* may be withdrawn tax-free. But Roth 401(k) *earnings* that you withdraw early are subject to income taxes and a 10% penalty.

- If you withdraw from a traditional 401(k) early, *all* the money is subject to income taxes and a 10% penalty.

Regardless of which type of 401(k) you have, don't let the withdrawal rules persuade you not to contribute. The advantage of tax-favored compounding is so great, in fact, that after about ten years, the money you would have earned could outweigh the 10% penalty you'd have to pay for making an early withdrawal.

Withdrawing from an IRA

The rules for IRA withdrawals differ depending on what kind of IRA you have. With Roth IRAs, you can withdraw the money you've *contributed* to them at any time without paying the 10% penalty. You also won't pay tax on the money since you've already paid that up front. The *earnings* from your Roth IRA are a different story. You'll generally have to pay both the penalty and the tax if you withdraw the *interest* on your contributions before you're 59½ and before you've held the account for at least five years. With traditional IRAs, you'll generally have to pay both income tax and a 10% penalty on IRA money you withdraw before the age of 59½. For details, see IRS Publication 590-B, *Distributions from Individual Retirement Arrangements (IRAs)*, at irs.gov/pub/irs-pdf/p590b.pdf.

The government also lets you withdraw money from *any* IRA, without paying the 10% penalty, for any of the following reasons, as long as you've had the IRA open for five years. (You will, however, have to pay taxes.)

- Higher education expenses for yourself, your spouse, or your children (including tuition, fees, books, and possibly room and board)

- Unreimbursed medical expenses if they exceed 10% of your adjusted gross income (see Chapter 9 to figure out what that means), or health insurance premiums you pay while you're unemployed

- Home-buying costs (up to $10,000) such as a down payment or closing fees (*lifetime* cap per person, reserved for people who have not owned a home in at least two years)

One last tip: If you need your money from either kind of IRA for a short period of time, you can't take out a loan like you can with many 401(k) plans. Instead, you can temporarily withdraw it once a year, without tax or penalty, as long as you pay it all back within 60 days. Of course, this is easier said than done and should be reserved for a true emergency only. If you fail to pay it back within 60 days, it's treated just like a normal withdrawal: Taxes and the 10% penalty are charged.

INFLATION AND TAXATION

Personal finance articles and books often offer dramatic examples of the rewards of saving without ever mentioning inflation. So far in this chapter, I haven't done much better. It's time for me to come clean.

Although saving over a long period of time really is a good idea, the fact is that it won't make you as rich as it might seem from the examples given so far. As you may remember from Chapter 5, infla-

DIVIDING YOUR RETIREMENT SAVINGS PIE

Most experts urge young people to put a large part of their retirement money into stocks—and I agree—but there's no magic formula for coming up with a guaranteed successful mix.

Many employers offer advice. Some provide access to online calculators that can be helpful. Others offer face-to-face meetings with a financial advisor, but the expert may have a vested interest in selling you the investment that pays him the highest commission (even though there are rules against this). Still others offer their employees access to free advice and tools from Financial Engines (FinancialEngines.com). One of my favorite sites, it uses sophisticated mathematical models created by Nobel Prize–winning economist Bill Sharpe to help you determine the best mix.

Even if you're left on your own, don't sweat it too much. What's really important is that you start investing, and make sure to put a big chunk of your money in stock funds. (For more info on these, see p. 105.)

tion can drastically reduce the purchasing power of the dollar over time. Consider, for example, the scenario I outlined at the beginning of this chapter—the $213,610 you'd have forty years from now would not buy nearly as much as $213,610 can buy today.*

This doesn't mean you shouldn't save. As the numbers show, you still come out way ahead if you start saving in a retirement account while you're young—even after inflation. When money is

* There's a less obvious way inflation comes into play in this example. If you started saving at age 25 rather than 35, each of the $1,000 annual deposits you made during the first ten years would have more "purchasing power" during the year you made it than the $1,000 you deposited each year after that. Although your ten-year head start would leave you with a much larger retirement nest egg, your initial deposits would thus be "more expensive" for you than the ones you made after your 35th birthday. As a result, the benefits of saving early would be offset somewhat by the effects of inflation.

allowed to grow for decades without being taxed, the results are extraordinary.

Consider the following example. Suppose you put $5,500 into each of two accounts—a Roth IRA and a taxable account—in 2017. Let's also assume that each account earns 7% a year, the annual inflation rate is 1%, and you're in a 25% federal tax bracket. After 30 years, the $5,500 in the Roth IRA will have grown to approximately $31,000 (in 2017 dollars). The $5,500 in the taxable account, on the other hand, will have increased to only about $23,000 (again in 2017 dollars) once taxes are deducted. The bottom line: You will have earned about 45% more ($25,500 versus $17,500) by putting your money in a tax-favored account than you would have with a taxable one.

RETIREMENT PLAN FAQS

Okay. Now you've got the point: You don't want to miss out on the benefits of saving in a retirement plan when you're young. This section will answer a few questions to help you get started.

The Facts on 401(k)s

Q: Am I eligible for a 401(k)?

A: Ask your employer. You may be required to work for your employer for up to a year before you can contribute.

Q: One of my 401(k) investment options is stock in my company. Should I bite?

A: Probably not. When you work for a company, you already have a huge "investment" in it. If the business runs into difficult times, you're at risk twice: Not only could you lose your job, but you could also see your retirement portfolio plummet. Some employers match employee contributions with shares of company stock, so you may already be heavily invested in your firm. Even if your company puts its match in its own stock, most employers will let you immediately convert those shares into other investment alternatives offered in your 401(k); make sure to take advantage of this option. In any event, by law you have the right to do that once you have three years on the job.

Q: The funds available in my 401(k) charge high fees. Should I ask my employer to add lower-cost options?

A: Yes. Your employer is obligated by federal law to try to keep expenses low. The higher the fees charged by the funds in your 401(k), the less you'll earn. So if you don't have a low-cost index fund available in your plan, politely ask your plan administrator to add one. (See p. 124 for my favorite low-cost funds.)

Q: What's the safest thing I can put my 401(k) money into?

A: Money market funds are likely to be your lowest-risk option. They're nearly as safe as bank accounts. The problem—and it's a *big* problem—is that they don't keep up with inflation, so the *value* of your money will decline. Historically, other choices in your 401(k) (like stock and bond mutual funds) have done much better than money market funds. But if the market should tumble for a long period, money market funds are an understandable choice for people who are terrified of losing the money they invested. They're a way to enjoy the benefits of a 401(k)—tax breaks and matching contributions from your employer—without taking on the risk of the market. But this is not a strategy that's likely to provide the long-term growth you'll want in these accounts.

Q: What happens to my 401(k) if I get laid off or change jobs?

A: No matter what you do, resist the temptation to cash in your 401(k). Many people do this when they change jobs, but that's a terrible idea. With a traditional 401(k), you will probably have to pay tax on the entire sum, plus the 10% penalty. With a Roth 401(k), you'll probably pay tax and a 10% penalty on the earnings.

Instead, if you move to another company, you should try to transfer your 401(k) money into your new company's 401(k) or into an IRA. It's important that you tell your old employer that you want a **direct rollover** into your new company's 401(k) or an IRA.

Although the rules allow your former employer to pay out, or "distribute," the money from a 401(k) directly to you, there are several reasons to avoid this method. If you are paid the money directly, the plan must withhold 20% of the amount you are due and send it to the IRS (which will hold on to it until you file your taxes for that year). You are then responsible for replacing that 20% from your other savings when you make the transfer into your new plan. If you can't come up with the money in 60 days, you'll have to pay tax on that 20%, plus a penalty. If it's a Roth 401(k), you'll pay tax on the earnings portion of that 20%, plus a penalty.

If your account is over $5,000, another option is to leave your 401(k) money with your old company. Once you leave a company, you're no longer eligible to contribute to its 401(k), but your account will continue to grow if your investments do well. If you like the investment options at your old company's 401(k) better than the ones in your new company's plan, this may be a good option for you.

Q: What happens if I have an outstanding loan against my 401(k) and I quit or I'm fired?

A: This is a situation you should try to avoid. Most companies will ask you to pay back the entire loan in one lump sum when you leave the firm, often within 60 days. If you can't, the amount you owe may be treated as money withdrawn (instead of borrowed) from the plan. For a traditional 401(k), you may therefore owe taxes plus the 10% penalty. If you can't pay back the money you borrowed from a Roth 401(k), you may wind up owing taxes and a 10% penalty on the earnings portion of your loan. This is yet another reason to avoid borrowing from your 401(k) if at all possible.

Q: They tell me I'm vested. What does that mean?

A: To be **vested** is to have a nonforfeitable right to the money your employer contributed to your retirement plan on your behalf. Many company retirement plans require you to work for the firm for a certain number of years before you become fully vested (meaning you're entitled to 100% of the money your employer contributed for you). At some companies you are immediately vested, but at others it can take several years. If your company has a gradual vesting policy, you might be 20% vested after two years at a company, 40% after three years, and so on. Once you become vested, however, it doesn't mean you may withdraw your money without paying the 10% penalty and taxes on your earnings. If you're not vested and you need to get your money when you leave the firm, you can withdraw the money you contributed (plus earnings on those contributions), but you can't keep any of the money your employer contributed for you (or the earnings on those employer contributions). If you're partially vested, you'll get to keep a portion of the money your employer contributed for you, plus earnings. Knowing your company's vesting schedule can help you time a career move. Keep in mind that for vesting purposes, some companies consider a "year" of service to be less than a full calendar year (for instance, five months and a day). That's why you should consult your company's employee benefits or human resources department to find out the exact date you'll be vested.

Q: Can my employer raid my 401(k) to help himself?

A: If the company you work for is facing rough financial times, you may wonder whether your boss can dip into the 401(k) to pay his bills. The answer is no. Your employer is not legally allowed to use the 401(k) money for business purposes. It's completely off-limits. What's more, if your employer files for bankruptcy, the 401(k) money is protected and none of the employer's creditors can touch your account. The person (or company) who is legally responsible for ensuring that no one tampers with your 401(k) is called the trustee. The trustee might be, for example, a bank or the president of your company. And what if your employer decides to end the plan? You'll still be okay, because you'll receive all the money you put in plus earnings, as well as any contributions your employer made on your behalf plus earnings. You also become fully vested if your employer decides to drop the plan, if you aren't already.

The Scoop on IRAs

Q: Where should I invest my IRA money?
A: Find a low-cost fund company that offers you the option of investing your IRA in stock index funds or stock index ETFs with low expense ratios. Some companies require a high initial contribution to open an IRA, so look for one you can afford. One of the best choices is Vanguard, which allows you to open an IRA for the price of one of its ETF shares (about $100), with no fees—plus you can continue to invest one share at a time. If you prefer stock index funds, Schwab requires $1,000 to open an account with its index fund, although you can start with $100 if you commit to investing another $100 each month until you reach $1,000. No matter where you invest, pick a firm that allows you to build up your IRA automatically via direct deposit, or through recurring transfers from your savings or checking account. For specific investments and how to buy them, see p. 124.

Q: What's the timing for getting an IRA?
A: The deadline is April 15 of the *following* year. If, for example, you suddenly realize on January 1, 2018, that you forgot to make your 2017 IRA contribution, you can still contribute and get the tax benefit for 2017. In fact, you have until April 17, 2018 (which happens to be Tax Day that year), to contribute to a traditional IRA or Roth IRA for tax year 2017 (and, in the case of a deductible traditional IRA, to deduct it on your 2017 return). Note: You can also put in your contribution for 2018 as early as January 1, 2018. If you can afford to, definitely do so. Your money will have that much longer to grow tax-free.

Q: Can my parents give me the money to open an IRA?
A: Yes. As long as you (or your spouse) have *earned* at least that same amount during the year it is contributed to the IRA, it doesn't have to be your money that's deposited. (See Chapter 9 for more details on how the IRS defines "earned" money.)

Q: Are there any IRA fees I should watch out for?
A: Yes. A few companies tack on an IRA maintenance fee that could be as high as $50 a year. There may also be fees for opening

or closing the account. Sometimes the fund company will waive the fee if you maintain a specified minimum amount in your account, or if you have other accounts at the same institution.

Q: I want a Roth IRA but earn too much. Should I bother getting a nondeductible traditional IRA?

A: Yes. Due to a quirky tax rule, as of this writing, you can open a nondeductible IRA, contribute to it, and convert it to a Roth IRA within 60 days. You can do this no matter how much money you earn. After that, you've got a Roth and the money will grow tax-free forever.

You can also convert any traditional IRA to a Roth IRA at any time, but you'll need to pay the taxes on the deductible contributions you made. If you need help deciding, try the Roth IRA conversion calculator at dinkytown.net/java/RothTransfer.html.

Q: What's a myRA?

A: The **myRA** (that's pronounced "my-R-A") is a retirement savings plan for people who don't have a lot of money and don't have access to 401(k)s. You can start a myRA with any amount—even $10—from your paycheck, and keep going, building your savings up to a limit of $5,500 a year. (By contrast, you'll need about $100 to open a Roth IRA and buy an index exchange-traded fund [ETF], or as much as $3,000 to open a Roth IRA and buy an index fund.) What's more, there are no myRA account fees, and the expense ratios on the investment options within the account are lower than you'd find almost anywhere else.

To open a myRA, go to myRA.gov. To contribute, your income must be lower than $133,000 for individuals or $196,000 for married couples filing a joint tax return. When your myRA balance reaches $15,000, or after thirty years (whichever comes first), your money must be moved out of the myRA and into a Roth IRA.

The downside of myRAs: The money you put in them will be held in safe, low-interest savings bonds backed by the U.S. Treasury, meaning your money may have trouble even keeping up with inflation. You may be better off opening a Roth IRA at Vanguard and buying a low-cost stock index ETF. (See p. 124.)

THE RETIREMENT PRIORITY BOX

Overwhelmed with all the retirement savings options? Here's a prioritized rundown of the ways you can save. Many people starting out will be unable to manage more than the first step. That's a good start. But if you have additional money to sock away for retirement, keep going down the list. Note: If you're self-employed, some of these don't apply, so see below for your options.

1. **Contribute to a 401(k) with employer matching.** The best deal around, the match alone can generate an immediate 50% to 100% return on your money (once you're vested). Either flavor of 401(k)—traditional or Roth—provides years of tax-advantaged growth. Don't put money in any other retirement account until you have reached the limit of what your employer is willing to match.

2. **Open an IRA (fully deductible traditional or Roth).** After you've reached the match level on your 401(k), the Roth IRA offers completely tax-free growth forever. The deductible traditional

IF YOU'RE SELF-EMPLOYED

Whether you're a full-time freelance writer, an entrepreneur with a start-up, or an artisan selling your goods on Etsy, consider opening a retirement savings plan designed for self-employed people. If you're lucky enough to be doing so well that you have already maxed out your traditional or Roth IRA ($5,500 limit in 2017), these plans allow you to contribute much more. Even better, they don't have income caps.

I know it is tempting to put every last dime into your business.

IRA offers an up-front tax break and then years of tax-deferred growth. Either kind of IRA generally allows you to withdraw your money penalty-free to buy a home or pay for educational expenses.

3. **Open a partially deductible or nondeductible traditional IRA.** If you have contributed the maximum to your 401(k) that your employer will match and you're not eligible for a deductible or Roth IRA, this is your next best choice. The reason: A loophole in the tax code allows you to convert your nondeductible IRA into a Roth. (For details, see p. 153.)

4. **Contribute to a 401(k) without employer matching.** If you've already contributed the maximum to options 1 through 3 above, try to max out your 401(k)—even if it's a stretch on your budget. There are still tax savings to be had there.

5. **Save beyond a 401(k) or IRA.** Once you've exhausted your tax-favored retirement savings options—IRAs and 401(k)s—it might be time to consider a tax-deferred 529 savings plan for your future college student, too. (See the box on p. 142.)

Don't. As a self-employed person, you need to take some of your income and channel it into a tax-favored retirement savings plan. Trust me, this is important.

The first type of self-employment retirement plan is called a **SIMPLE IRA.** As the name suggests, it's the least complicated kind of self-employment retirement plan. It works pretty much like a traditional IRA, except it allows you to set aside (and deduct) more money—up to $12,500 a year—even if that accounts for all your self-employment income. You may be able to contribute even more than that, but the rules are fairly complex, so talk to an accountant before making any decisions. If you don't have employees, a

SIMPLE IRA is easy to set up; if you do have people working for you, you may have to contribute for them as well. One catch you should be aware of: If you want to set up a SIMPLE plan, you have to do it before October 1 of the current tax year.

If you want to contribute more than the limit on a SIMPLE IRA, consider a **simplified employee pension** or **SEP**, sometimes referred to as a **SEP-IRA**. The main difference is the amount of money you can contribute. You can contribute and deduct 20% of your first $270,000 in net earnings from self-employment to a SEP, which means that, in theory, you could save up to $54,000 a year toward your retirement and take the tax deduction. (Naturally, you can always save less.) To figure out your net earnings, visit IRS.gov or consult an accountant. As with a SIMPLE IRA, a SEP may require you to make contributions for any employees you might have. And just like a traditional IRA, you can open a SEP right up to the April 15 tax filing deadline (or October 15 if you file for an extension).

A third option, the **individual 401(k)**, commonly known as a **solo 401(k)**, works like a 401(k) added to a SEP-IRA. In theory, you can put away as much as $54,000 a year in one of these accounts. The rules are complex, so definitely consult an accountant.

For more details on all of these options, contact a low-cost fund company. Fidelity.com is a good site for information. Also, IRS Publication 560 (*Retirement Plans for Small Business*) provides comparison charts, examples, and worksheets for all of these types of plans. You can find it at irs.gov/pub/irs-pdf/p560.pdf.

BUT I JUST CAN'T AFFORD IT!

There's a little-known but terrific way to get some retirement savings, even if you don't earn much. It's called the saver's credit, and it's a way for the government to reward you for contributing to a retirement plan.

Here's how it works. For every $1 you put into a 401(k) or IRA (up to $2,000 a year if you're single, $4,000 a year if you're a married couple), the government credits you 50 cents at tax time. So if, for example, you put in $500, you may qualify for a credit of up to $250. The details vary, but you can typically qualify for at least some of this saver's credit if you earn less than $31,000 as a single person or $62,000 as a married couple filing jointly.

To take advantage of this, you'll have to file either Form 1040 or 1040A (not the 1040EZ form) when you do your taxes and fill out IRS Form 8880, which you can find at irs.gov/pub /irs-pdf/f8880.pdf.

- Enroll in your company's 401(k) plan or open an IRA (individual retirement account) at a low-cost mutual fund company—right now.

- Looking for easy money? If your company offers a 401(k), contribute at least as much as your employer will match. A 50-cent match on a dollar you contribute is the same as earning a 50% return on your investment.

- Figure out whether a traditional or Roth 401(k), or a traditional or Roth IRA, makes more sense for you. Many younger people have more to gain from Roths. See pp. 137 and 141 for details, and look at the comparison calculator at Bankrate.com.

- Don't cash in your 401(k) when you lose your job or move to another one. Roll it over instead.

- If you're self-employed—e.g., a freelancer or an entrepreneur—check out SIMPLE IRAs, SEP-IRAs, and solo 401(k)s. These plans may permit you to sock away far more for your retirement than you could with just a traditional or Roth IRA.

- Take advantage of the saver's credit (see p. 157) if you're eligible. If your income is relatively low, you can get a rebate of up to $1,000 a year from the government by contributing to an IRA or 401(k).

7

OH, GIVE ME A HOME

Advice on Affording
a Place of Your Own

TODAY, PEOPLE UNDER 35 are much less likely to own a home of their own than at any time since the early 1980s. And for the first time on record, more young people are living at home with their parents than in any other living arrangement.

Depressed yet?

It's actually not all bad news. Let me explain why.

Just a few short years ago, banks got much too lax. They began giving mortgages to just about anyone who could fill out some paperwork and come up with a minuscule down payment (or even none at all)—regardless of whether or not the borrower had a solid job, steady income, or good credit.

At first, it was an exciting time with so many flush-feeling homeowners. But before long, millions of people (yes, millions) couldn't make their payments and lost their homes. Suddenly, the boom went decidedly bust.

So where does this leave us now?

For starters, lenders are much stricter, and potential home buyers face real scrutiny before being granted a mortgage. While that may sound daunting, it does have an upside: Now when you *qualify* for a mortgage, you can feel more secure knowing that you're likely to be able to *afford* it.

This tougher environment also means that now, more than ever, you need to get all of your financial ducks in a row before buying a place of your own. This chapter shows you how to do just that. It will help you figure out how much home you really can afford, direct you to programs that can make buying easier, and teach you how to find attractive rates. Most important, it will help you qualify for the best mortgage you can for a home that you expect to live in for years to come. Even if you're nowhere near the point where you can consider buying, you can benefit from this chapter. The first two sections offer tips on being a smart renter—and when it's actually smarter to rent than to buy.

WHAT EVERY RENTER NEEDS TO KNOW

If buying a place of your own isn't in the cards for the near future, you're going to be a tenant, so make sure you're a smart one. Here are steps you can take to reduce the cost of renting and eliminate the typical headaches you're likely to encounter. Keep them in mind before and after you sign a lease.

- **Try to negotiate the rent.** A lot of people feel squeamish about doing this, but you should force yourself. When you find a place you like, tell the landlord you're very interested but hadn't planned to spend as much as he is asking. Ask in a superpolite way if there's any chance you can get a break—say, paying $50 or $100 less a month or receiving one month free, depending on what the market is like where you live. If you're a desirable candidate (that is, you have a good credit score and have been working at the same job for at least a year), there's a decent chance that the landlord will consider making a reduction. If not, nothing is lost. Of course, in cities where there are tons of renters competing for every apartment (hello, Brooklyn), your odds of getting a break are slim to none. It's important to know what the market is like in your area. To get a rough idea of what people are paying in your neighborhood, check out rental listings on Zillow.com or Craigslist.org.

- **Negotiate the terms of your lease.** Though it isn't exciting, it's important that you read your lease, which might be several pages long. Look for provisions that seem unfair; they may be illegal. In some states, for example, a landlord can't include a clause demanding excessive penalties for late rent. To find out the rules in your area, visit the website of your state or county housing office or office of consumer affairs for information about tenants' rights.

   If there is a chance you might want to sublet the place in the future, ask the landlord if that is okay with him. If he says yes, then ask him to write that into the lease. But if he doesn't like the idea—a lot of landlords are leery of their tenants listing their apartments on vacation rental sites like Airbnb and HomeAway—be absolutely clear that you won't do it, so that you don't jeopardize the deal. If your landlord is okay with your earning extra cash through those services, make sure that doing so is legal in your area. For legal guidance on making money through home sharing services, visit Nolo.com.

   And if there's a chance you may need to move before the lease is up, ask your landlord about including an early-termination clause, which would allow you to break the lease after you give a specified number of days' notice.

   Also, look for clauses that, although legal, may be a pain. Try to negotiate them out of the lease *before* you sign. Examples are provisions that give your landlord the right to enter your apartment without your permission, or the right to raise your rent if his taxes or operating costs increase. Watch out for sections that say no one but you can live in the apartment. Look out for bans on pets, or clauses that require you to pay extra to cover the wear and tear your animal causes. Although you might not have a pet now, you might want to get one in the future.

   Finally, think twice before agreeing to any unreasonable stipulation the landlord may have added to the standard lease agreement. I know of one couple in San Francisco who had to agree to wash their landlord's plants every week with soap and water! That meant that they couldn't go away for more than a week without getting someone to take over this ridiculous chore.

- **Negotiate with the real estate broker if you're dealing with one.** In most cities, if you use a broker to help you find an apartment to rent, you don't pay her a commission. But in some places, like New York City, renters are often expected to pay brokers as much as 15% of the year's rent to secure a place. You can avoid brokers entirely by searching on sites like Craigslist.org and Zillow.com for apartments listed as no-fee deals offered directly by the landlord. If you must use a broker, you often can negotiate. Explain up front that you're a serious customer but are willing to pay a commission of only, say, 10%. If you hunt around, you may find a broker willing to cut a deal.

- **List all your roommates on the lease, and have them all sign it.** Although not every landlord will allow it, including all your roommates on the lease ensures that you will all share legal responsibility in case of a problem. It also protects you if one of your roommates suddenly decides to move out before the lease is up. Even if your landlord won't allow it, consider drafting a contract (you can find some examples at Nolo.com) to reflect the agreement you made with your roommates, and get it signed and notarized. This way you have it in writing that you are each responsible for a share of the rent.

- **Get everything in writing.** Ask for a written lease instead of a verbal agreement, so you know exactly what you're responsible for (utilities like water, electricity, and gas, for example). Also, get any additional promises the landlord makes (such as guarantees to paint walls or fix leaky faucets) included in the lease before you sign.

- **Understand how a security deposit works.** A security deposit is money you give to a landlord to protect him in case you damage the apartment or house. If you don't, the security deposit will be returned to you when the lease is up. Many states limit the size of it to one or two months' rent, and many also restrict the ways in which it can be used. In general, the landlord can use the money to fix damages you cause, but not for basic maintenance on the apartment or house.

Get a receipt for the security deposit from the landlord. In some cities, the landlord is required to put your money in an interest-bearing account and return the initial deposit plus the interest at the end of your tenancy. Contact your state or local housing office for the rules. (Even in states that don't require the landlord to pay you interest, some landlords will, so ask.)

Before you move in, it's a good idea to take pictures of the condition of the apartment and note any issues (no matter how minor they may seem). In addition, take more photos right before you move out as proof that you left the place in good order. If you don't trust your landlord, have a neighbor sign a statement saying there is no damage.

- **If you plan to renew your lease, contact your landlord at least two months before the lease is up and try to negotiate.** In an area with an abundance of available rentals, your landlord may agree to keep the rent the same. But don't wait too long to bring up the subject. If you wait until the week before your lease ends, the landlord will assume you're bluffing when you say you're thinking of moving out.

- **Know your rights.** The law protects renters in many ways. Here are a few:

  » Federal law prohibits a landlord from refusing to rent to you based on your race, sex, religion, disability, national origin, or familial status (meaning whether you're pregnant or have kids under 18). Many cities and states also prohibit housing discrimination based on age, marital status, or sexual orientation. If you think you've been denied housing for any of these reasons, call the U.S. Department of Housing and Urban Development's Housing Discrimination Hotline at 800-669-9777 or fill out the department's Form 903, "Online Complaint," at portal.hud.gov/FHEO903/Form903/Form903Start .action and submit it.

» With a fixed lease, such as for one or two years, the landlord is not allowed to raise the rent during the term of the rental contract and must tell you about an impending rent increase before your lease is up. The amount of time within which you must be told of the rent hike varies from state to state. For month-to-month rentals, you must be notified in writing 30 days before the rent is increased in most states.

» In some states, if you disobey a provision in your lease and your landlord knows about it but accepts your rent anyway, the landlord is not allowed to kick you out for violating the provision. For example, if your lease forbids certain pets like ferrets, but your landlord knows you have one and accepts your rent check anyway, he may not be able to evict you later on this basis. But don't push your luck.

» In most cities, if you provide written notice of major problems such as glitches with heating, electricity, or plumbing, your landlord is required to fix them. Your landlord is not always responsible, however, for taking care of minor problems like leaky faucets or worn-out floors. Check your lease to see what repairs the landlord is responsible for and check the landlord-tenant rules in your city.

» In some states, you can withhold rent if there's been negligence on the part of the landlord, but the rules are very specific about how to do this. Again, contact your county or state housing office or office of consumer affairs to find out the rules in your area before taking this step.

For additional information on your rights as a tenant, try contacting local branches of the Legal Aid Society or your state attorney general's office. Nolo.com provides links to renters' rights sites all over the country.

SHOULD YOU RENT OR BUY?

Many people believe that given the choice, renting is a bad idea. They think it's the equivalent of "throwing money away." But when you're young, it's often smarter to rent than to buy.

Unfortunately, making the decision involves a lot more than simply comparing your monthly rent with the monthly mortgage you'd pay as an owner. You also need to take into account how long you plan to own the home, how much you think the home will increase (or "appreciate") in value, the tax break you'll get for buying, the fees you'll have to pay when you buy, and the rate of return you think you could earn by investing the cash you would save by *not* buying. (This is your **opportunity cost**.) Of course, plenty of emotional factors go into this decision too, but I'll leave those for you to think about. A great way to start weighing all these factors is with the "buy versus rent" calculators at nytimes.com/buyrent and dinkytown.net/java/MortgageRentvsBuy.html. Also consider these tips:

- **If you can't envision yourself in the same place for the next several years, you should rent.** One very important factor in the decision to buy or rent is the thousands of dollars you'll pay in up-front fees when you purchase a home. These charges are called **closing costs** because they're paid when you close the deal and sign the final paperwork on a new home. When you sell it, you can expect to pay thousands more to a real estate broker. If you stay in your place for a number of years, these costs won't make much difference, at least in theory. The hope is that your home's selling price will increase enough to cover them and then some. But if you move after a couple of years and your home's value has not appreciated significantly, you may not be able to sell your home for enough of a profit to cover these costs.

- **If you have an amazing deal on a rental, it might make more sense to rent and stash your savings elsewhere.** In some cities there are still deals to be had. If you're lucky enough to have a **rent-controlled** or **rent-stabilized apartment** (one where the landlord can't charge more than a fixed rent and fixed increases) that's substantially below the going rental rate, you may be better off holding on to it and saving that money for a future down payment.

- **If you don't have a steady income, keep renting.** It's difficult to get a loan without a regular paycheck. And, of course, it can also be tough to make your mortgage payments. Don't put yourself through the angst of trying to buy if you're not ready.

- **Don't assume you always get a tax break for buying.** Most of us have a relative who prattles on about how buying a home is the best tax break around. It's true that the federal government (and most states) allows homeowners to subtract the interest they pay on their mortgages from their taxable income, and that can make a big difference at tax time.

  Say you paid $10,000 in mortgage interest in a year and had an income of $50,000. You would be able to subtract, or deduct, the $10,000 worth of interest and bring your taxable income down to $40,000. Assuming your tax rate is 25%, that would translate into a tax savings of $2,500. If you're buying a low-priced home, however, the tax break may be worth very little. That's because all taxpayers (whether they own a home or not) get a tax break known as the **standard deduction,** the amount they can automatically subtract from their taxable income. For 2017, the standard deduction was $6,350 for single taxpayers and $12,700 for married taxpayers filing jointly. In general, to reap a tax advantage from buying, the annual interest you pay on your mortgage (plus other deductions you get) must be greater than the standard deduction. If you're buying a low-priced home, this may not be the case. And if you don't qualify for a tax break, there's less incentive to buy. (For details on other tax breaks for homeowners, see Chapter 9.)

WHAT LENDERS LOOK FOR

The first question most prospective home buyers ask is "How much home can I afford?" The answer depends not only on how big a mortgage you can obtain but also on whether you can handle the payments comfortably. Your mortgage is said to be "secured by" the home, meaning that if you don't pay it back, the lender can take your home, an action known as **foreclosure**. Unfortunately, that's exactly what happened to roughly five million Americans about a decade ago when lenders gave out mortgages without digging into people's finances. But lenders are much more careful now. Here is what lenders consider when deciding:

- **Your credit record.** Lenders are concerned about whether you have a history of paying off your debt. To find this out, they'll get a copy of your credit reports and credit scores, which reveal how responsible you are when it comes to paying back your loans. (For details, see p. 63.) Borrowers with high scores can get the best deals, which can save them hundreds of dollars a month and *thousands* of dollars a year compared to someone with a mediocre credit record. (See Figure 3–3 on p. 63 to learn how your credit score affects interest rates and overall costs.) And if you have poor credit, it'll be hard to find anyone who will give you a mortgage, period. In addition to your score, lenders also want to see that you haven't defaulted on any loans (credit cards, student loans, car loans) or gone bankrupt, especially within the past two years.

- **Your ability to come up with the cash.** Few if any lenders will give you a loan for the full purchase price of a home. Instead, they require you to contribute some of your own money, called a **down payment,** up front. Lenders tend to want a down payment of at least 10% and ideally 20% of the price of the home, depending on both your credit record and the cost of the home. (There are some special programs, which I'll discuss later, that may allow you to make a smaller down payment.) Coming up with a down payment is one of the main obstacles for first-time home buyers. Even if you're fortunate enough to receive some or all of it as a gift, that comes with its own set of issues. (See p. 177 for more details.)

  In addition to the down payment, the typical home buyer also has to pay about 2% to 5% of a home's price in closing costs; these include fees for inspections, appraisals, title insurance, credit checks, land surveys, and legal services that can add up to thousands of dollars. (Note that in some cases, sellers will agree to pay at least a portion of the closing costs, so you may want to ask; but this is less common in a hot market.) Also, some lenders require buyers to have at least two or three months' worth of mortgage payments saved up in reserve.

- **Your income.** Lenders want to make sure you earn enough to pay the costs of owning a home. To do this they compare your future monthly housing costs (also known as your **PITI,** which stands for principal, interest, property taxes, and insurance) to your pretax monthly income. The traditional guideline used by lenders is that your PITI should not exceed 28% of your pretax monthly income. So, for example, if your salary is $60,000 a year, your gross monthly income is $5,000, and your PITI shouldn't be more than $1,400.

- **Your debt-to-income ratio.** Lenders also want to make sure you aren't already burdened with lots of loans. That's why they look at your current monthly debt commitments (such as auto loan payments, student loan payments, and minimum credit card payments), plus your future monthly housing costs (your PITI), and calculate what portion of your monthly income before taxes will go to these expenses. The percentage they come up with is called your debt-to-income ratio (or **DTI ratio**). Lenders like to see a debt-to-income ratio that doesn't exceed 36%. If your ratio is higher than that, you're unlikely to qualify for a mortgage, unless you have a stellar credit score or are willing to make a very high down payment.

- **Your job history.** In general, if you've worked in the same industry for at least two years, lenders view you more favorably than if you've switched careers during that time. They'll also verify your income with your current employer before giving you a loan. If you're self-employed, be prepared to prove what you earn to a lender who might be skeptical about your ability to afford the monthly payment. That could mean handing over three years of tax returns and reams of documentation about your business.

THE REAL COSTS OF OWNING A HOME

Owning a home can be great. But the fact is, when you become a homeowner, you'll run up a variety of expenses that you may never even have heard of as a renter. Here's a description of each:

- **Principal and interest.** Your monthly mortgage payment consists of two parts: principal and interest. The amount you borrow from the lender is known as the principal. The fee that the bank charges to lend you money is called interest, and it is expressed as an annual percentage. Suppose you get a mortgage of $100,000 and you're expected to pay it back over 30 years. (That's standard.) If the lender charges you an interest rate of 5%, after 30 years you would have paid the lender back the $100,000 in principal plus a total of $93,256 in interest. (Shocking, isn't it?) In the early years of your loan, you're paying back mostly interest and very little principal. As time goes on, you start to pay back more and more of the principal. To soften the blow somewhat, as I mentioned earlier, you get to deduct your interest payments if you itemize your taxes, which can save you money. (For a discussion of what this means, see Chapter 9.)

To get a feel for what your monthly mortgage payment would be, check out Figure 7–1 on p. 173.

- **Property tax.** This is a fee you pay to your town, city, or county. It's based on where you live and the official appraised value of your home, including the land on which it's built. To get a sense of the property taxes levied for various homes in neighborhoods you're interested in, check out Zillow.com or the website of the town, city, or county tax assessor. Taxes are generally between 1% and 3% of a given home's value per year. One bit of consolation: You may be able to deduct part of your property taxes. (See Chapter 9 for details.)

- **Insurance.** Most lenders require you to get **homeowners insurance** to make sure that the cost of repairing or replacing your home in case of a disaster, such as a fire, is covered. Lenders want this because until you pay off the mortgage, your home serves as collateral. If it's completely ruined and you walk away from it (and from your loan obligation), the lender needs to be reimbursed. Depending on where you live, you might be required to buy flood insurance also. (For tips on buying insurance, including renters coverage, see Chapter 8.)

    If you make a down payment of less than 20%, you'll also be required to buy **private mortgage insurance (PMI)**. PMI protects the lender if you default on your mortgage. Once you've reached 20% of your home's **equity** (the value of your house minus what you owe), you can ask your lender to discontinue PMI coverage. Lenders are legally required to do so once you've paid off 22% of the purchase price, as long as you've made all of your payments on time in the prior two years.

PMI amounts to anywhere from 0.3% to 1.3% of your total annual mortgage cost. (There's a calculator for estimating your PMI at hsh.com/calc-pmi.html.) You can pay it in monthly or annual installments; ask your lender what your payment options are and decide which makes more sense, depending on your budget. The good news is that you may be able to deduct the premiums you pay on PMI from your taxable income. (For more details, see p. 274.)

Many people who take out 30-year mortgages do not actually expect to keep their homes for that long. If you're one of them, you should ask your lender about **lender-paid mortgage insurance (LPMI)**. With LPMI, the lender takes care of the insurance premium, and you pay it back slowly with a somewhat higher interest rate (about 0.25% to 0.5%) over the length of the loan. That means your monthly mortgage insurance payments will be lower, but your total amount paid may be higher—unlike with PMI, you'll keep paying even after you hit the 22% mark. But if you are planning to leave your home in fewer than ten years, that probably won't matter. Ask your lender to run the figures on both scenarios—PMI and LPMI—to see which one is better for you.

- **Condominium and cooperative fees.** Condos and **co-ops** are housing units (usually apartment buildings) that are jointly owned. Each resident owns his or her own unit or apartment, while the common spaces (stairwells, elevators, hallways, lobbies) are owned collectively by all the residents. To pay for the upkeep of these areas, residents pay extra fees, known as **maintenance fees** or **common charges.**

  The primary difference between a co-op and a condo is the way in which the units are owned. In a co-op, residents do not technically own the apartments; instead they own

shares, or units of ownership, in the cooperative. The cooperative owns all the units in the building. In order to buy or sell units in a co-op, residents usually must get approval from the **co-op board,** which is a group of co-op residents. With a condo, residents have more autonomy; because they own the apartment, they can usually buy and sell it without getting permission from any board.

When considering whether to purchase an apartment or condo, it's good to ask questions such as whether you're allowed to rent out your apartment, install air-conditioning, or join two smaller apartments into one. These issues may not seem relevant to you now, but in the future they could matter. Co-ops often have more stringent rules than condos. You should consider asking for a copy of your potential condo or co-op association's bylaws, which regulate everything from the use of outdoor gas grills to when you can put out your garbage for collection.

SPECIAL PROGRAMS FOR HOME BUYERS

There are several home loan programs geared to first-time buyers or people with relatively low incomes. Lenders might not tell you about all of them, so it's up to you to find out what you qualify for. Here are some of the choices:

- **A Federal Housing Administration (FHA) loan.** As a first-time home buyer, you may want to consider an FHA mortgage. The main appeal: The program allows you to make a low down payment of as little as 3.5%. In some cases, borrowers can qualify with slightly lower-than-average credit scores, although they may have to pay higher interest rates.

  One drawback to FHA loans is that sometimes they can be a bit costlier than others because you also have to buy federal mortgage insurance from the FHA (about 1.75% of the loan amount paid up front, plus annual fees of about

Figure 7-1

GETTING A HANDLE ON YOUR MONTHLY MORTGAGE PAYMENTS

In the left-hand column, locate the price of the home you're thinking about buying, as well as options for how much you might contribute for a down payment. On the right is a range of interest rates that a lender might charge you for a 30-year fixed-rate mortgage. As you can see, regardless of the interest rate, you'd have a lower monthly payment with 20% down than with 5% down. (Obvious, yes, but worth pointing out.)

Keep in mind that this table includes only principal and interest payments. It leaves out closing costs, property taxes, homeowners insurance, and private mortgage insurance (PMI). Use the following rules of thumb to come up with very rough estimates of these costs: Annual property taxes are typically between 1% and 3% of the cost of a home; PMI amounts to between 0.3% and 1.3% of your total annual mortgage costs; and homeowners insurance will likely cost you somewhere between $500 and $2,000 a year. These extra costs can vary dramatically, depending on where you live and the amount of your mortgage. For more precise estimates, ask a lender or a local real estate agent.

Cost of Home	Down Payment %	$	4%	6%	8%	10%
$150,000	5%	$ 7,500	$ 680	$ 854	$ 1,046	$ 1,251
	10%	15,000	645	809	991	1,185
	20%	30,000	573	719	881	1,053
$200,000	5%	10,000	907	1,139	1,394	1,667
	10%	20,000	859	1,079	1,321	1,580
	20%	40,000	764	959	1,174	1,404
$300,000	5%	15,000	1,361	1,709	2,091	2,501
	10%	30,000	1,289	1,619	1,981	2,369
	20%	60,000	1,146	1,439	1,761	2,106
$400,000	5%	20,000	1,814	2,278	2,788	3,335
	10%	40,000	1,719	2,158	2,642	3,159
	20%	80,000	1,528	1,919	2,348	2,808
$500,000	5%	25,000	2,268	2,848	3,485	4,168
	10%	50,000	2,148	2,268	3,302	3,949
	20%	100,000	1,910	2,398	2,935	3,510
$600,000	5%	30,000	2,721	3,417	4,182	5,002
	10%	60,000	2,578	3,238	3,962	4,739
	20%	120,000	2,292	2,878	3,522	4,212

Monthly Mortgage Payment with Interest Rate of:

Source: HSH.com

0.80% to 0.85%). But if an FHA loan is the only kind of mortgage you can get, the additional cost may be worth it to you.

There are no income limits on FHA borrowers, and you can get a loan for up to $625,500 or so if you live in a high-cost area. For more information, visit FHA.gov.

- **A "Fannie Mae" or "Freddie Mac" loan.** Fannie Mae and Freddie Mac are the nicknames of two companies, the Federal National Mortgage Association and the Federal Home Loan Mortgage Corporation. The federal government created them to help banks and mortgage companies make home loans to people who might not have qualified otherwise. Fannie and Freddie don't make the loans directly; instead, they make it possible for lenders to do so.

  How can these loans benefit you? If you're a first-time buyer or your income is relatively low, you may be able to make a down payment of as little as 3%. Also, you can sometimes use gifts from friends and relatives to help come up with part of the down payment, which other lenders may not permit. You'll need good credit to get one of these loans.

  Some Fannie and Freddie programs have income limits, so if you earn an above-average salary by the standards of the area where you want to buy, you may not qualify. Loan amounts are generally capped at $625,500 in high-cost areas. For the latest about these programs and what they currently offer, ask a lender, or go to KnowYourOptions .com and myhome.freddiemac.com.

- **State or local housing agency assistance.** Many state and local housing agencies offer special mortgage deals to first-time home buyers, but you've probably never heard of these programs because they're not advertised much. The interest rates on these mortgages tend to be lower than bank rates, potentially saving you hundreds of dollars a month. You may also be able to get help with your down payment through these agencies.

Requirements vary from state to state—some housing agencies have income limits, credit score minimums, caps on home price, or geographic restrictions, for example. Typically, you can participate in the program if your income is no more than your county or state's median household income and the home you want to purchase costs slightly less than the area's average price. But some states will accommodate you with a different program if your income (or home price) is too high to qualify. And certain states have special programs to assist people in particular professions. California, for example, has a program called Extra Credit to help eligible teachers buy homes.

To find the website of your own state housing agency, check out the National Council of State Housing Agencies at ncsha.org/housing-help. (Not every state website provides a list of lenders that participate in state programs, so you may have to call for that information.) You can also explore local options and check your eligibility for them at Downpayment resource.com, which is recommended by the Consumer Financial Protection Bureau.

- **A loan under the Community Reinvestment Act (CRA).** It pays to check with banks in the area in which you want to live and ask if they offer mortgages under the Community Reinvestment Act. The CRA was created by Congress to help people with relatively low incomes buy homes. Depending upon how much you make or whether the home you want to buy is in a low-income area, the bank may have a good deal for you. Be sure to ask, since banks usually don't advertise this program.

- **Assistance from the U.S. Department of Veterans Affairs.** If you've ever been in active duty in the U.S. military for at least 90 continuous days or have served at least six years in the Selected Reserve or the National Guard, you may be eligible for a Veterans Affairs (VA) mortgage from a VA-approved bank or mortgage company. Requirements vary depending on when you served and whether it was during wartime.

VA loans generally do not require any down payment at all if your loan doesn't exceed $417,000 (although this figure varies in different parts of the country), but in some cases the individual lender that supplies the VA loan may require one. You will pay a one-time charge called a **funding fee**, which is basically an up-front payment of your mortgage insurance. The funding fee ranges from 1.25% to 3.3% of the mortgage, depending on the terms of your loan and your military status. If you *are* able to come up with a down payment, the funding fee will be lower. The VA itself imposes no income limits or credit score requirements on applicants, but your lender may. For more information go to benefits.va.gov/homeloans.

- **A U.S. Department of Agriculture (USDA) loan.** If you live in a rural area—which in some cases can be just a 30-minute drive from a large city—you may be eligible for a loan through the USDA's Rural Housing Service. USDA loans typically require no down payment and some offer low interest rates, but there are other up-front costs, and mortgage insurance is required. There is no minimum credit score to qualify, but there are income limits for eligibility. Visit rd.usda .gov/about-rd/agencies/rural-housing-service for more information and a list of approved lenders to contact, and see eligibility.sc.egov.usda.gov for a map of the areas that are considered rural and the income limits for USDA borrowers in each of them.

IF YOU DON'T QUALIFY FOR A MORTGAGE

Lenders want to give mortgages to people who have good jobs, cash for down payments, and long histories of paying their bills on time. So it makes sense that when it comes to people with spotty employment histories, or slim bank accounts, or late payments in the recent past, they're much fussier. They're also quite sophisticated in their ability to weed out riskier customers by using credit scores and other financial formulas. This is yet one more argument in favor of getting your financial life in order before you apply for a mortgage.

One helpful tip: If you *are* turned down for a mortgage, federal law requires that a lender must tell you why. So make sure to ask.

Here are some tips to help you boost your chances of getting a mortgage:

- **Improve your credit score.** Perhaps the most important factor a lender will consider is your credit score. The higher your score, the lower the interest rate you'll get on your home loan. For example, a rate of just one percentage point less on a typical 30-year loan of $200,000 could save you more than $40,000. If you have been late in paying any kind of bill or loan in the past, focus on making sure that you begin paying on time consistently from now on. Realistically, it will take a couple of years of on-time payments before lenders will begin to see your credit record as top-notch. (See Chapter 3 for more credit-building tips.) One warning: Steer clear of mortgage brokers who promise to get you a loan despite your credit history. If they can do it at all, the interest will be astronomically high.

- **Save for a down payment.** No-money-down mortgages have mostly gone the way of the landline, and rightfully so. (For an explanation of why a low down payment is risky, see the box on p. 180.) Nowadays, you'll be expected to come up with cash—often at least 10% to 20% of the home's price. The best way to do this is to make regular, automated deposits into a bank savings account. (For details, see p. 26.)

- **Get part of the down payment as a gift.** About one in four first-time home buyers receives money from friends or relatives to cover the down payment. Some lenders require that your down payment consist at least partially of your own money. Others permit the entire down payment to come from a gift. Some lenders require that the gift come from a relative; others allow it to come from a friend. In most cases,

lenders require a letter from the generous friend or relative
stating that the down payment money is a gift, not a loan,
since a loan would mean that you'd have to pay that money
back, in addition to making mortgage payments. (To aid in
this effort, I've heard of newlyweds who ask for cash to save
up for a down payment rather than register for china.)

Lenders will review your bank records before granting
your loan. If they see that a large sum of money was deposited in your account in the two months or so before you
tried to get a mortgage, they'll ask you to prove that the
money is not a loan. So keep careful records of cash gifts
and make copies of any large checks you receive (like wedding gifts, for instance). Also, if you sell something valuable
(like a car), keep a receipt of the transaction.

SHOPPING FOR
A MORTGAGE

If you were shopping for a car or even a flat-screen TV, you probably wouldn't dream of buying the first one you saw. This should
be true when you shop for a mortgage as well. If you're able to find
an interest rate just half a percentage point lower than the first one
you're offered, you'll save thousands of dollars over the life of the
loan.

You can get a mortgage from a bank, a credit union, or a mortgage company. It doesn't really matter which type of lending institution you go to. What does matter is that you shop around.

You can compare rates offered by different lenders at sites like
HSH.com, Zillow.com, and Bankrate.com. Also, see if your own
bank or credit union can top the best rate you find online. Even if
the advertised offer isn't lower, you may still be able to secure a better deal if you're a loyal customer or you have a stellar credit score,
for instance, by asking the mortgage lender at your local bank.
There are no guarantees, but it doesn't hurt to ask.

To get a rough idea of the interest rate someone with your credit
score and down payment could qualify for, check out the Consumer

Financial Protection Bureau's tool at cfpb.gov/owning-a-home /explore-rates. The rest of this section highlights what you need to look for—and look out for—when you shop for a mortgage.

Fixed Rates Versus Adjustable Rates

All lenders offer two basic types of mortgages. The most common type is a **fixed-rate** mortgage, which is usually paid back over 30 years. A 30-year fixed-rate mortgage has an interest rate that stays the same the whole time you repay it, and one of the key benefits is the peace of mind that comes with knowing that your total monthly principal and interest payment will also stay the same. What's more, if during that period interest rates in the economy decline, people with fixed-rate mortgages are not locked in to their rate. Lenders allow borrowers to **refinance**—the process of switching your old high-rate loan to a new low-rate one.

The other general type of mortgage is the **adjustable-rate mortgage (ARM)**, sometimes known as a variable-rate mortgage. In theory, the interest rate on an ARM changes based on what happens to interest rates in the economy. If rates go down, your ARM interest rate should drop, and so should your monthly payment. If rates go up, your interest rate and monthly payments will rise. With most ARMs, the lender raises or lowers the interest rate only once a year, during the **adjustment period**.

ARMs tempt first-time home buyers because their *initial* interest rate (sometimes called a teaser) is lower than the rates on fixed-rate mortgages. This lower initial rate means lower monthly payments for the first couple of years. But you are taking a gamble; the ARM ultimately could cost you much more than a fixed-rate loan. (See the box on p. 182.)

ARMs have been disastrous for millions of homeowners, but they can make sense for certain borrowers. If, for example, you're absolutely sure that you'll move in a set number of years and find an ARM with a low rate that won't change for at least that long, you could save money. This is tricky and your situation could change, so be careful. Read all the provisions and know the worst-case scenario. Also note that with fixed mortgage rates near historic lows,

---

THE SINKHOLE OF LOW DOWN PAYMENTS

If you don't have a lot of cash, you might think a low down payment would be a lifesaver. But as too many homeowners have learned the hard way, it can be a disaster because it allows you to buy a more expensive home than you can really afford.

Take the case of a buyer with $20,000 to put down on a home. If she put 20% down, she could buy a $100,000 home. But if she used the same $20,000 to put down only 5%, she could theoretically get a $400,000 home.

Of course, that more costly home would also come with much higher monthly payments. With a 30-year mortgage and a 4% interest rate, the $100,000 home would cost her about $380 a month, whereas payments on the $400,000 home would be $1,800 a month. And if she ran into any sort of financial trouble, she would most likely have a problem making those hefty monthly payments.

What's more, if home prices started to plummet, borrowers like her would have an added complication. Take the case of that $100,000 home. If real estate prices dropped by 6%, the

---

the difference between an ARM teaser rate and a fixed rate isn't as great as it has traditionally been—but this could change if overall interest rates rise.

Interest Rates and Mortgage "Points"

As you've figured out by now, the most important factor contributing to the cost of a mortgage is the interest rate; that's what the bank charges you to borrow money, and it's expressed as a percentage of your loan. But this rate can be reduced if you choose (and have the cash) to pay **points**, up-front fees that you pay when you buy the home.

home would be worth $94,000. Since the buyer made a 20% down payment of $20,000, she would have an $80,000 mortgage. If she couldn't make the mortgage payments and was forced to sell the house for $94,000, she could pay off the $80,000 mortgage and walk away with $14,000 of the original down payment—a $6,000 loss. Bad news, but not devastating.

But what if she owned the $400,000 home? If she made a $20,000 down payment, she would have a $380,000 mortgage. After a 6% drop in real estate prices, that home would be worth $376,000. In other words, she would actually *owe* the bank $4,000 more than the actual value of her home. And if she was forced to sell the house at that value to pay off her debts, she would suffer a loss of $24,000—the entire down payment plus an additional $4,000.

If you owe more than your home is worth, you have what is known as an "upside-down" or "underwater" mortgage—a situation that ensnared millions of homeowners about a decade ago. You do not want to be one of them.

Here's how it works: One point equals 1% of the loan. So one point on a $100,000 loan costs $1,000. If you pay more points to the bank, you'll get a lower interest rate, which is why they're sometimes called discount points.

What combination should you look for? That is determined by how long you plan to live in your home. If you're going to be there for many years, it makes sense to pay more points and get a lower interest rate. The lower payments you'll have with a lower rate will more than make up for the few thousand dollars you paid in points. Also, points are sometimes tax-deductible; check Publication 936, *Home Mortgage Interest Deduction*, at irs.gov/pub /irs-pdf/p936.pdf for more information. If you don't plan to stay in your new home for very long, it's better to pay fewer points, or

THE PROBLEM WITH ADJUSTABLE-RATE MORTGAGES

When Nicole and Jimmy fell in love with their dream house, they were thrilled to find a lender offering an adjustable-rate mortgage (ARM) with an introductory rate of 3%. They assumed that if interest rates in the economy held steady, their rate would remain the same. Unfortunately, that's not the way it always works. Even if the interest rates in the economy fell slightly, their ARM rate could increase to 5% the next year. On a $200,000 mortgage, that would raise their monthly payment from around $850 a month to nearly $1,100.

That's not to say that ARMs are all bad. In some cases, they can make sense if you need to keep mortgage payments down for a few years, for example. But you absolutely need to be aware of the worst-case scenario and see if you could handle it. Here is what all prospective ARM customers need to know:

- **The benchmark the ARM rate is pegged to.** Your ARM's rate fluctuates based on a financial benchmark like the London Interbank Offered Rate (LIBOR), Cost of Funds Index (COFI), or the One-Year Treasury Constant Maturity (CMT). It's not as if one is better than the others, but you should know which benchmark applies to your loan. If you stay in your home long enough, your ARM will adjust, and you'll want to have an idea of what the new rate could be.

- **The introductory or "teaser" rate.** Sometimes a lender will offer you a low interest rate for the first year or two. Don't let this rate fool you. In the case of Nicole and Jimmy, 3% was the initial rate. Their ARM was pegged to the COFI, which was 1% when they got their loan. So when their ARM adjusts for the first time, the new rate they pay will be based on the current rate of the COFI *plus* a fixed number of percentage points (typically two to four) called a **margin**. Nicole and Jimmy's margin is three percentage points.

- **The cap.** With an ARM you need to be sure you can afford the worst-case scenario. Most ARMs have an annual cap, which is the maximum amount the rate can increase in any one year. Nicole and Jimmy's ARM has an annual cap of two percentage points. Here's why the cap protects them somewhat. If the COFI rises to 3% at adjustment time, the lender would ordinarily add three percentage points (the margin) to it, resulting in a new rate of 6%. But since Nicole and Jimmy's ARM has an annual cap of two percentage points, the lender will increase their rate to just 5% (their current 3% teaser rate plus the two percentage point cap). It's also smart to look for an ARM with a lifetime cap of five or six percentage points. That way you'll know exactly how bad it can get.

- **How often it adjusts.** In addition to knowing when the ARM's interest rate adjusts for the first time, you should be clear on how often it can adjust after that. Some ARMs can change their interest rate every year, or even every month. There are also **hybrid ARMs**, which start as a fixed-rate mortgage for a few years and then switch to an ARM thereafter. For example, with a 5/1 hybrid ARM, the first number ("5") tells you your interest rate is fixed for the first five years. The second number ("1") tells you it will adjust every year thereafter. (There are also 3/1, 7/1, and 10/1 ARMs.) The longer the fixed-rate period, the higher the interest rate. So, if you intend to move within five years, you might not need to worry about the risk of future rate adjustments with a 5/1 ARM. But be careful: It's difficult to be really sure when you'll move, and if you're wrong, you could face a big spike in your monthly payments.

perhaps none at all. To calculate whether you would save money by paying points, use the mortgage points calculator at bankrate.com /calculators/mortgages/mortgage-loan-points-calculator.aspx.

No matter which rate/point combination you choose, it's important to shop around for the lender that offers you the most attractive deal. To make this process easier, the federal government requires lenders to tell you a mortgage's **annual percentage rate (APR)**. The APR is what you'd get if you took most of the charges you're paying on the mortgage (including the interest, points, private mortgage insurance, and certain fees) and expressed them as one annual rate.

This makes comparison shopping much easier. You just need to make sure you're comparing APRs of the same types of loans (say, a 30-year fixed-rate mortgage). It's not an exact science, though. The APR doesn't take into account certain charges like appraisal and document preparation fees. Plus, the APR can be affected by a lender's specific policies. For example, the application fee may not be taken into account when calculating the APR. So in addition to asking for the APR, ask each lender for a list of fees that are not included in the APR. Also, if you're interested in an adjustable-rate mortgage, don't rely on the APR alone, since other factors come into play. (See the box on p. 182 for further explanation.)

Fifteen-Year Versus Thirty-Year Mortgages

By far the most common type of mortgage is a fixed-rate loan that lasts for 30 years. Another type of mortgage you may consider is a **15-year fixed-rate mortgage**. This type of loan is more difficult to qualify for than a 30-year mortgage, and it often has a lower interest rate than a 30-year fixed-rate loan. Since you pay it off in 15 years rather than 30, you're able to build up **equity**, or ownership, in the home sooner.

Although some people view a 15-year mortgage as a disciplined way to pay off their home loans faster, it's not always the best choice. Even with a lower rate, the monthly payments on a 15-year mortgage are higher than those on a 30-year loan because of the shorter term. Depending on your situation, it may make more sense to go with the lower monthly payments on a 30-year loan and use the cash you're not pouring into your home for other investments. For example, you may be better off putting the money into a 401(k) in which your employer matches your contributions.

Also, instead of locking yourself into the higher monthly payments on a 15-year mortgage, you may want to get a 30-year loan that allows you to pay it off faster when you want to. Be sure you get a mortgage without **prepayment penalties** (which are fees for paying off your loan early) so you have this option. You can see how much interest you'll save through prepayments at hsh.com /calc-prepay.html.

A Mortgage to Avoid

One loan to stay away from is a **balloon mortgage**. The way it works is that you make small monthly payments for a fixed number of years—from five to seven—and then you're required to pay off the remainder of the loan in one lump sum. People sometimes opt for balloon mortgages if they plan to sell their home in a few years or if they anticipate that they'll be getting a chunk of cash—such as an inheritance—before the loan comes due. But if something goes wrong and you can't make the final massive payment (or if you're unable to refinance), you could lose your home.

MAKING THE PROCESS GO SMOOTHLY

If you've gotten this far in the chapter, you have a good basic understanding of what you need to know to get a mortgage. When you're actually ready to begin your search, though, you're likely to encounter some hassles. Here are some tips to make the search as painless as possible:

- **Get a copy of your credit report and credit score from all three bureaus before you do anything.** Even if you've never been late on a payment, you should do this. (See Chapter 3 for details on how.) Credit reporting agencies are notorious for making mistakes. If you have an above-average credit score (the average fluctuates, but it's usually around 700), that's an immediate signal to a lender that you are a particularly good risk.

- **Before you start house hunting, check with your bank or a mortgage company to see if you can get "prequalified" for a mortgage.** Prequalification is a way for lenders to give prospective buyers a sense of whether they can qualify for a mortgage and, if so, how large a loan they can get. It's something you can do very quickly online or by phone. Although prequalification doesn't mean you have a guaranteed mortgage from the lender, it is a way to get a rough idea of what kind of mortgage you *might* be able to get. Once you have a ballpark figure, you can use it when shopping around for a loan, as long as you are comparing similar loan products.

  A word of warning: Even in today's more cautious lending environment, banks have a vested interest in getting you into the largest loan you qualify for because they make more money in interest that way. Just because a bank tells you that you can afford a certain loan doesn't mean you should take it. You need to be realistic about what payments you can handle while keeping your current lifestyle, or whether you're willing to scale back in other areas to make the payments on time.

- **If you find a lender offering a good deal, consider getting a "preapproved" mortgage.** Although "prequalified" and "preapproved" sound similar, their meanings are very different. While prequalification is quick and comes with no guarantee, **preapproval** is serious. It's a process by which the lender does a thorough analysis of your financial situation and commits to offering you a mortgage before you find a home you want to buy. You'll probably be able to fill out the preapproval application online, but you may still have to submit the necessary paperwork in hard copy (including verification of employment, bank statements, and tax documents). The lender will also look at your credit report and credit score. If everything checks out, the lender will give you a letter of commitment that says you're entitled to a loan. (Lenders sometimes charge a couple hundred dollars for this service, but they may waive it if you ask.) For a list of the info you need to have handy when you apply for preapproval, see Figure 7–2 on p. 188.

A preapproved loan can even be used as a bargaining chip with a homeowner who is anxious to sell. The seller may prefer you over other bidders—or even may be willing to knock down the price a bit—if he or she discovers that you have been preapproved, because that means the deal is more likely to get done.

- **Once you've shopped on your own, consider enlisting the help of a mortgage broker.** These are people who may be able to help you find a better deal on a mortgage than you could find on your own because of their relationships with certain lenders. For example, mortgage brokers can be particularly helpful if you're self-employed and facing an uphill battle to prove your creditworthiness to a lender. A mortgage broker may also be able to expedite the process for you. Ask friends and relatives for referrals. Before you sign up, find out exactly what you'll be charged for the service. The broker may charge you (or the lender) a fee—often 1% to 2% of the loan amount. So use a broker only if the mortgage he or she finds you, minus any fee you have to pay, is a better deal than the best one you could get directly from a lender. And don't pay anything up front.

- **Find out if you can lock in a rate.** Some lenders will allow you to lock in a mortgage interest rate at the time that you get approved for your mortgage. This "lock-in" protects you in the event that interest rates rise before the closing, which is when you sign the paperwork and then officially own the home. Many lenders offer a 30-day rate lock at no cost, though they may charge extra for longer lock-in periods. Make sure to understand the details. Also make sure

Figure 7–2

PAPERWORK YOU WILL NEED
TO APPLY FOR MORTGAGE PREAPPROVAL

GENERAL INFORMATION

Name and co-borrowers' names

Age

Marital status

Social Security number

Landlord contact info

Number of children

Address

Telephone number

Residence history (last two years)

INCOME

Employer's name and address

Job title

Date hired

Federal tax returns (last two years)

Salary

Proof of any other income (e.g., child support)

Bonuses

Average overtime or commissions

Employment history (last two years)

Most recent pay stubs and W-2 form (or 1099s if self-employed)

ASSETS
Total sums in:

Bank (including savings, checking, money market accounts, CDs)

Mutual funds and ETFs

Stocks

Bonds

Other investments, including real estate

Retirement accounts

Cash value life insurance

Car (year bought and current value)

Gifts from friends or relatives to help with down payment

DEBTS AND EXPENSES
Current balances and monthly payments on:

Credit cards

Student loans

Rent

Utilities

Car loans

Other loans

that there's a provision that protects you in case interest rates *fall*. Known as a "float-down" option, this enables you to adjust your locked-in rate one time to a lower rate before the closing—though there may be a fee for this option, so ask.

- **Avoid excessive fees.** Some lenders try to boost their profits by tacking on extra fees just a few days before closing. Often, they have ambiguous names like "document preparation," and they can add up to hundreds of dollars. Compare these final costs to the ones on the Loan Estimate form you received when you first submitted the loan application. With few exceptions, the final costs are not allowed to be more than 10% higher than the estimate. If you see increases, changes, or additions you aren't sure about, you should dispute them and try to negotiate a better deal. (You may be surprised at how successful this can be.) For detailed advice on double-checking these final costs, visit cfpb.gov /owning-a-home/closing-disclosure.

- **Cozy up to your loan processor.** The road to actually getting your mortgage can be time-consuming and frustrating. You can't just fill out your application and keep your fingers crossed. You have to stay on top of it. The basic rule: Be assertive but polite. Call once a week for a status update from the **loan processor**, the person overseeing your mortgage application. If you've filled out an application online, the advice is still the same. If you aren't getting answers, ask to speak to a manager.

- **Don't always trust your real estate agent.** First-time buyers tend to put too much faith in real estate agents (also known as real estate brokers). An agent's goal is to get you to buy the house or apartment he or she shows you, not to get you the best deal or to find you the perfect home. He or she typically splits a sales commission of 6% of the home's price with the seller's agent. On a $200,000 home, that's $6,000 for each agent. And the more you pay, the more they get.

BE CAUTIOUS WHEN BORROWING AGAINST YOUR HOME

If you own a home, you may be able to borrow money from your bank in the form of a **home equity loan (HEL)** or a **home equity line of credit (HELOC)**. Here's how it works. You're usually allowed to borrow a percentage of your home's value (traditionally around 80%), minus the balance on your mortgage. For example, say you own a home valued at $200,000 and you have $120,000 remaining on your mortgage. You could borrow $40,000 (that's 80% of $200,000—or $160,000—minus $120,000).

With HELs and HELOCs you get a tax break that you don't get with credit cards or auto loans. But there's also a huge pitfall: If you can't make your payments, you risk losing your home and still ending up owing money to the bank.

With a HEL, you get all the money at once in a lump sum and repay it over 5 to 15 years. The interest rate is typically fixed throughout the life of the loan.

With a HELOC, you get a set credit line on which to draw over time, like a credit card. You can choose when, how often, and how much to draw from that line. Each month you can make the minimum payment or pay more. HELOCs generally have variable interest rates, which means they change when rates rise or fall. One hidden danger of home equity lines: Banks reserve the right to drop your credit limit at any time to what you currently owe and stop you from using any more credit.

Here are some points to consider *before* you take out a HEL or a HELOC:

- **Understand how the tax break works.** The interest you pay on a HEL or HELOC of up to $100,000 is deductible, meaning you can subtract it from your taxable income when you fill out your tax return if you itemize your deductions. (See p. 269.) The interest on amounts over $100,000 is not deductible unless you're using the money for home improvements. (In that case, you can deduct the interest on a loan of up to $1 million.)

Say you owe $1,000 on your HEL or HELOC and your interest rate is 8%. If you pay it off in one year, you will also pay $80 in interest. If you're in the 25% tax bracket, you will save $20 (25% of $80) at tax time if you itemize your deductions.

- **Factor in up-front fees.** Some lenders charge hundreds of dollars in initial fees when they grant HELs and HELOCs. Look for a lender that does not.

- **Shop around.** Credit unions often offer lower rates than banks. You can also compare interest rates on HELs and HELOCs at Bankrate.com and MyBankTracker.com.

- **Know the worst-case scenario with your interest rate.** The adjustable interest rates on HELOCs can start low, but then can increase several percentage points in a year or two. Ask your lender how much the rate can rise.

- **Don't drag out repayment.** With a HELOC, each month you can choose to make the minimum payment or pay more, so it can be tempting to make small payments. Don't. If you transfer your car loan to a HELOC to get the tax break, it's a smart idea to pay off your home equity line over the same number of years it would have taken to pay off your car loan. Remember, if for any reason you can't make your payments—say you lose your job or have a medical emergency—your home is on the line.

If you live in a state that requires an attorney to be present during the closing, use a lawyer you find on your own—not one who's recommended by the agent. Get a referral from friends or family. Or try your regional Better Business Bureau at BBB.org. And when you're looking for a mortgage, be skeptical of the advice of your real estate agent; many mortgage companies offer incentives to real estate brokers who steer business to them.

One final suggestion: Comb your local real estate listings and sites like FSBO.com for places that are being sold directly by the owner. If you don't use a broker, you may be able to get the seller to accept a lower price.

- If you're about to rent an apartment, read the lease carefully. Try to have unwanted provisions taken out before you sign.

- If you're thinking about buying a home, get your financial house in order first. Lenders will look at your credit score, income, savings, debt, and job history. See p. 167 for details.

- Before you go hunting for a home, get "prequalified" for a mortgage. Prequalification will not guarantee you a home loan, but it will give you an idea of how big a mortgage you can afford. It's also a good idea to get "preapproved." This way, if you do find your dream home, you're increasing your odds that you'll get a loan in time to buy it.

- When shopping for a mortgage, be sure to research all the loans available to you. Check online and with several banks, credit unions, and mortgage brokers. Websites like HSH.com, Zillow .com, and Bankrate.com are great places to start. Also check out your state's housing agency (ncsha.org/housing-help). Careful shopping can save you thousands of dollars in the long run.

- Be wary of adjustable-rate mortgages (ARMs). Make sure you know how high your interest rate could rise in the future—and how high your monthly payments could go. Run the numbers for the worst-case scenario. In most cases, it's best to get a fixed-rate mortgage instead. See p. 179 for details.

- Don't give up if you don't qualify for a mortgage. Work on improving your credit score and accumulating money in your savings account for a down payment (often at least 10% to 20% of the home's price). Some lenders allow friends or family to give you money for a down payment, as long as you can prove it's not a loan. See p. 177.

8

INSURANCE: WHAT YOU NEED AND WHAT YOU DON'T

Finding the Right Policies
and Skipping Coverage
You Can Do Without

FOR MOST OF us, there are two classes of insurance: insurance we have too much of and insurance we have too little of. Into the first category goes the life insurance policy you were talked into buying when you graduated from college and the laptop insurance you signed up for "just in case." Into the second group goes the renters insurance you never even thought about purchasing and the health insurance you feel is just too expensive and not really necessary. This chapter will help you decide how much protection you should have, if any, in each of the basic categories: health, auto, disability, home, and life. It will alert you to types of policies to avoid, show you how to maximize insurance-related benefits from your employer, and offer you advice on how to find the cheapest comprehensive policies.

No matter what type of insurance you think you need, read the first three sections—"Getting the Best Deal," "Checking Out Credentials," and "Making the Most of Your Employer's Plans." Then you can skip around to the specific types of insurance you need.

GETTING THE BEST DEAL

The point of insurance is to protect you and your family from financial loss due to illness, accident, or natural disaster. The charge you pay for all types of insurance is called the **premium**. Remember this term. You'll hear it a lot.

Premiums can vary tremendously from one insurance company to the next. Take the case of car insurance. Studies have shown that insurers in the same city often sell the same exact policies for radically different rates. A 20-year-old guy living in Chicago, for example, could pay as little as $2,600 or as much as $7,100 annually for the same amount of auto liability protection! You might be able to save yourself thousands of dollars if you shop around.

Before I get into the details of the various types of coverage, here are some general tips that will help you save money when you buy insurance:

- **Compare quotes online.** Just like with flights or hotels, there are comparison sites (also known as aggregators) that will help you find the best deals on all kinds of insurance. Most play the role of matchmaker, rather than actually selling the policies. Fill in your information and they'll immediately provide you with a list of companies and policies to consider, usually with quotes for how much coverage will cost. In some cases, the sites may send your information to an agent (more about them in the next bullet). Other sites will link you directly to the insurance company you select. Aggregators may work with different companies, so it's in your best interest to try more than one. Note that each site tends to specialize in a different type of insurance: life, homeowners, etc. I'll point you to some of my favorites throughout the chapter.

- **Contact an insurance agent directly.** An agent is someone who is licensed to sell insurance independently or on behalf of an insurance company. He or she will offer guidance about how much coverage you need. There are two kinds of agents: independent agents who sell policies from a number of companies, and "captive" agents who work for just one company. Both independent agents and captive agents work for commissions, so they are understandably eager to sell you a policy. But don't feel obliged to buy from an agent just because he or she did some research for you. That's the agent's job. *Your* job is to go with whomever gives you the best deal.

- **Find insurance companies that sell directly to consumers.** Some companies don't sell through agents at all. These firms often charge less because they don't have to pay the salaries and commissions of a sales force. You might find them on comparison sites, or if you already know their names (GEICO, for instance), go directly to each company's website. You won't receive as much advice on what to buy as you would from an agent, but if you know the type of policy you need (and you should after you read this chapter!), definitely get a quote.

- **Get the highest deductible you can afford.** With certain types of coverage—health insurance, homeowners insurance, and some auto insurance—you must pay some of the costs out of your own pocket before the insurance pays for anything. This fixed amount is known as a **deductible**. For example, a health insurance policy with a $1,000 annual deductible requires you to pay for the first $1,000 worth of medical bills each year with your own money. Expenses beyond $1,000 will be paid, at least in part, by the insurance company.

  One way to get a lower premium (there's that word again) is to get a policy with a higher deductible. Say you're a 32-year-old single Los Angeles resident with a $48,000 income purchasing a health insurance policy from Blue Shield of California. If you opt for a "platinum" policy with no deductible, you'll pay around $560 a month. If instead you choose a basic plan with a deductible of $1,850, you'll pay a premium of around $320 a month—about 43% less. The same principle applies to renters insurance, homeowners insurance, and auto insurance.

This rule isn't right for everyone, of course. It makes sense to choose a lower premium only if you have enough savings to cover the higher deductible. Also, with policies that have higher deductibles, you'll end up covering certain costs yourself—for example, some doctor's visits, or minor car and home repairs. Pay attention to your individual situation. If you tend to go to doctors a lot or you're prone to fender benders, a lower deductible might make more sense. Otherwise, a higher deductible is probably a smart option.

CHECKING OUT CREDENTIALS

You're not going to spend your life (or even several days of your life) investigating every detail of a particular insurance company or

---

CAR INSURANCE: YOU'D BETTER SHOP AROUND

Lainie, 24, was about to move from New York City to Alexandria, Virginia, and had to purchase auto insurance for her 2013 Ford Taurus. She wanted a $500 deductible, had a spotless driving record, wouldn't be using the car to commute to work, and would be driving only about 2,000 miles a year. She put this info into several insurance comparison sites. One company quoted Lainie an annual rate of $5,100. Another said it would charge $2,900 a year. The third quoted her an annual rate of just $2,650. An added bonus: When Lainie called the company with the best rate and mentioned that she was turning 25 in a few months, the agent she spoke with said she'd get a $72 annual discount once she turned 25. The bottom line: In just 20 minutes Lainie saved nearly $2,500 by comparison shopping.

agent, but it does pay to do some legwork. The following tips can help you avoid potential disaster:

- **Check on the insurer's financial health.** It's obviously a good idea to do business with a financially sound company. Even though states have "guaranty funds" that are supposed to protect consumers up to certain limits, if insurance companies go bankrupt, the rules and level of protection vary. You could wait a long time before you collect on a claim—and even then, you may not get all that you hoped for.

   There are four major rating agencies that judge the financial security and soundness of insurance companies: A. M. Best, Fitch Ratings, Moody's, and Standard & Poor's. Stick with an insurer that gets high grades from at least two of these. But even then, you won't be guaranteed that a company is completely sound. For instance, A. M. Best gave one insurer an A+ rating just two weeks before it failed. You can get free information online from the rating agencies once you register at AMBest.com, FitchRatings.com, Moodys.com, and Standardandpoors.com. Just look for what's called the **corporate finance** or **corporate credit rating**; skip any reports that you have to pay to read.

   Each rating agency has a somewhat different scale, so check to make sure you are interpreting the grades correctly. For example, a "B" from A. M. Best is considered "fair," but a "B" from Moody's is actually a weak grade, indicating that a company may be vulnerable to financial troubles.

- **If you use an agent, ask about qualifications.** First, you'll want to make sure that your agent is licensed in your state and has no complaints filed against him or her. Your state insurance department (which you can find by going to the National Association of Insurance Commissioners at map .naic.org and clicking on your state) will have this information. Find an agent who has taken the courses required to obtain professional credentials. For instance, when you're buying life insurance, look for an agent who has "CLU" after his or her name. This stands for Chartered Life Underwriter. If you're looking for car, homeowners, or renters coverage, the designation to look for is "CPCU" (Chartered Property Casualty Underwriter). To find individuals with a CLU, try Designationcheck.com, a site hosted by the American College of Financial Services. You can enter your zip code and get a list of pros in your area with CLU credentials. To verify that an agent is a CPCU, go to theinstitutes.org /designationholders.

MAKING THE MOST OF YOUR EMPLOYER'S PLANS

Many companies pay a portion of your health insurance premiums. Some also give you a small, fixed amount of life and disability insurance. The type and amount of insurance employees get varies from employer to employer. The best way to learn about your plan is to read the information your employer provides. (I know, I know—this is about as much fun as memorizing the periodic table. But the time you spend will be worth it.) Then make an appointment with someone who can answer questions about benefits at your company.

In the health, disability, and life insurance sections below, I've listed specific steps that will help you evaluate your employer's offerings. Meanwhile, here are some general rules to keep in mind:

- If your company has a "flexible benefits plan," make the most of it. About a quarter of U.S. companies offer a flexible benefits plan (also known as a **flex plan** or a **cafeteria plan**). This program gives employees the opportunity to choose among a variety of benefits. Options often include health insurance, life insurance, and disability insurance.

  Here's how it generally works: The employer gives you a fixed number of "credits" to spend on benefits. You decide how to use the credits. For instance, you may opt for a top-of-the-line health insurance plan but forgo life insurance. Or if your spouse has a terrific employer-sponsored health insurance plan that covers you, you could decline your own company's health insurance and opt for extra disability insurance. These plans can be extremely beneficial if you study your choices carefully and spend your credits wisely.

- **If possible, purchase health insurance on a before-tax basis.** If your employer offers this option, it means you won't have to pay taxes on the portion of your salary that goes toward your premium. (Some companies also let you set pretax dollars aside to pay for commuting or day care. Any of these little perks can save you hundreds of dollars a year.)

- **If your company offers a flexible spending account (FSA), use it but don't overfund it!** An FSA is a special tax-favored account offered by most large employers. Don't confuse a flexible spending *account* with a flexible benefits *plan*. (Clearly, employee benefits personnel could use a little help coming up with more creative names.) An FSA is an account in which you can set aside a fixed amount of your own money—up to $2,600, taken from your paycheck during the year—to pay for specific medical expenses that aren't covered by health insurance. (Many companies also offer a separate dependent care FSA in which you can save up to an additional $5,000 for child care expenses.)

  One thing that makes an FSA different from a savings account is that you can put the money into the FSA and use it to pay for medical care on a before-tax basis—saving you money. FSA money is commonly used to pay for eyeglasses, contact lenses, allergy shots, dental care, prescription drugs, chiropractic sessions, and transportation to or from the hospital or doctor's office. You can also use the money to pay the deductibles and other expenses on your medical and dental plans. The IRS is very clear on a few things that are and aren't allowed. Contact lenses? No problem. Dancing lessons? Not so much. Look at Publication 502, *Medical and Dental Expenses*, at irs.gov/pub/irs-pdf/p502.pdf for details. Rules on other expenses may vary from company to company. Educate yourself before you sign up, and always ask the plan administrator before you assume a health-related expense is *not* covered.

One big point: Check with your HR office to find out if you need to use up all of your FSA funds by the end of the plan year. Federal guidelines allow companies to roll over up to $500 of unused money to the next plan year or offer employees a couple of months' extension to use up leftover funds. Know your company's rules.

An added perk: You don't actually have to wait to build up the money in your FSA to have access to it. It's prefunded, which means the entire amount you've agreed to contribute over the next 12 months is available to you as soon as your new plan year starts (even though it's siphoned in equal installments from your paychecks over the course of the year).

HEALTH INSURANCE

Everyone needs health insurance and, as of this writing, you are required to have it by law. If you're lucky, you're offered coverage through your job. Although you'll have to pay for some portion of the annual cost, the amount you pay is much less than what you'd pay if you had to purchase insurance on your own. If you don't have an employer who provides coverage for you, you're responsible for doing the legwork to find the best coverage for yourself. The good news is that as of this writing, federal rules say you can be covered by your parents' plan if you're under 26 years old (more on that later).

No matter how or where you get it, coverage still costs real money. If you have to buy an individual policy, it may be even more expensive, so you might be tempted to go without it. Don't. For the 2017 tax year, you'd pay a penalty of $695 if you're single or 2.5% of your income—whichever is greater (but no more than the total you'd pay for a year's worth of premiums for a basic health plan). Even more important, if you become very sick or have a horrible accident, you could bankrupt yourself and your loved ones in order to pay your medical bills.

This section will help you find the right coverage, whether your employer offers it or you're shopping for health insurance solo.

Cracking the Health Code

The jargon used in the health insurance industry is so baffling at times, it's enough to make anyone feel, well, sick. But to make the right decisions, you need to learn the essential terms.

While plans vary widely, in general you'll be facing several types of costs. Most health insurance policies—whether obtained through your employer or purchased on your own—require you to pay an annual deductible, usually for services beyond routine preventive care like annual physicals or vaccinations. (As of this writing, the average from an employer is around $1,318 for singles.) Once your medical bills exceed the annual deductible, you'll still pay part of the cost, but the insurer will also start chipping in. In addition, you'll probably pay a **co-payment** (or **co-pay**)— a fixed sum of money that's usually less than $25—every time you go to the doctor. (A smaller share of people pay **coinsurance**, which can be roughly 20% of the cost of your doctor's visit.) For hospital visits or outpatient surgery, you may have to pay a higher percentage of the costs via increased coinsurance or a larger co-payment.

With me so far? Whatever the various costs are called, all health insurance policies have a ceiling on the total amount you will have to shell out in any given year. This is called the **out-of-pocket limit**, and it cannot, by law, be more than $7,150 for an individual in 2017.

The Basic Types of Health Insurance Plans

Whether you get health insurance from your employer or need to shop for it on your own, it's important to understand the various kinds of plans.

But before I break them down, you should know that the vast majority of plans will give you a list of affiliated doctors called a **network**. If you stick with doctors in your network, your costs will be much lower than if you use doctors outside of it. A similar principle applies to different types of medications. If you take any medicines regularly, make sure to check out what they'll cost under your plan, or if they're covered at all.

The most common type of health insurance plan is known as a **preferred provider organization (PPO)**. It's called this because you'll get a network of doctors and hospitals deemed, you guessed it, "preferred providers." As long as you stick to the network, you pay lower rates (on average, about a $25 co-payment for doctor's visits). You don't need a referral from your primary care physician to see a specialist (such as a dermatologist or a cardiologist). But you will pay extra to use a doctor out of the network—typically, a pricier co-payment, a higher deductible, and possibly other charges.

Another common type of plan is a **health maintenance organization (HMO)**, which is often cheaper but also offers less flexibility. With an HMO you usually have to get a referral from your primary doctor—your gatekeeper—to see a specialist. Also, your choice of physicians is limited to your network. If you want to see a specialist outside the network, you'll usually have to foot the *entire* bill yourself. These inconveniences, at least in theory, are outweighed by HMOs' low cost: Many plans won't make you pay any deductible, so your total cost per doctor's visit is usually limited to your co-payment.

Now, on to the third option. A **point-of-service (POS)** plan is essentially a hybrid of the two plans above. As with an HMO, you pay less if you stay within your network, and you're required to go through your primary care doctor for a referral when you need to see a specialist. Unlike an HMO, however, a POS plan will pick up some costs for outside-the-network service.

One type of health plan that is being aggressively promoted by employers is called a **high deductible health plan (HDHP)**. These are commonly structured as PPOs, but, as you might have guessed, have a very high deductible (usually $2,000 or more). To make them sound appealing, they're sometimes called "consumer-directed plans." And while these high deductible plans tend to have lower premiums, and they usually cover the cost of preventive care like wellness visits, immunizations, and health screenings *before* your annual deductible is met, there is a downside. If you get sick or have an accident, you could pay thousands of dollars out of your pocket to meet your deductible. So if you don't have a savings cushion, an HDHP is not for you.

If you are considering a high deductible plan through work, see if your employer offers a **health savings account (HSA)**. An HSA lets you put money away to pay for medical expenses via before-tax contributions from your paycheck. You'll need this money if you're hit with any major health bills. If you end up not using the money in your HSA while you're working, all is not lost. It grows tax-free and can be used to pay for medical expenses in retirement.

Finally, if you're young and healthy, something called a **catastrophic plan** can be tempting. That's because these plans, which are generally available only to people under 30 years old, charge extremely low premiums (typically around $175 a month). But here's the catch: You'll have to pay for all of your medical expenses (other than preventive care) out of pocket until you've met the (very high) deductible—up to $7,150 in 2017. Once you reach that high deductible, however, the rest will be covered by insurance. For that reason, catastrophic plans are considered a safety net for medical emergencies. But if you can afford a better plan, it's worth the extra money for both the protection and the peace of mind.

If You Don't Have Health Insurance Through Work

As I've said, you should have health insurance no matter what. So if you don't get it through work—say you freelance, work for a small start-up that doesn't offer insurance, sling coffee as a barista without benefits, or are unemployed—you need to get it elsewhere.

The easiest way, by far, is to see if you can get coverage through a family member. If you're married and your spouse has insurance through work, look into being added to the policy. Almost all employers provide family coverage to spouses (including same-sex married partners), and many cover unmarried domestic partners as well.

As of this writing, if you're under age 26, you are able to stay on your parents' health plan. A handful of states allow you to remain on your parents' policy even longer. (For example, New Jersey extends the age limit to 31, provided you meet certain criteria.) Going on your parents' plan is allowed even if you are married, are no longer claimed as a dependent on your parents' tax return, have a policy available to you through your work, or live in a different state. This is a great option to consider, but it's not perfect. If you live far from your parents' home, there may not be any doctors in your area who are part of your folks' health plan. If you are healthy and can wait until you are visiting your parents to see a doctor, it might not be an issue. But if you get sick and go to a doctor who is not part of your plan's network, you could run up big bills.

If getting coverage through a family member isn't an option, you will need to shop for an individual plan. As of this writing, your first stop should be the federal health insurance exchange website, **Healthcare.gov**. Simply select your state, and you'll be sent either to what's known as the federal exchange, which offers plans to residents of states that don't have their own marketplace, or a state-run exchange. (A few states have created their own.) Either way, after answering some basic questions, you will get a list of policies to compare. One of the benefits of shopping on a federal or state site is that it will tell you if you're eligible for a special health care credit (which lowers the premium you pay to your insurer each month) or subsidy (which reduces the payments you make when you get care). These can save you hundreds or even thousands of dollars a year. Eligibility is largely based on your income. (See p. 262 for more details on what incomes qualify.)

You can also purchase insurance without going through the federal exchange or a state exchange, and instead head straight to the insurance company. The easiest way to do this is to get quotes from a comparison site such as eHealth.com, through an insurance agent, or directly from insurers. When you purchase insurance this way, you cannot take advantage of any available health care credits or subsidies. But if your income is too high to qualify for these breaks, you should definitely explore other policy options, since you may be able to find better deals. As of this writing, all major plans must follow the same rules and offer the same basic benefits (more details below).

IF YOU LEAVE YOUR JOB,
CONSIDER YOUR HEALTH COVERAGE OPTIONS

If you work for an employer with twenty or more employees, in most cases, your company must offer you the option of continuing your health coverage for 18 months after you leave your job—whether you're fired or you quit. This is thanks to the federal law known as COBRA (the Consolidated Omnibus Budget Reconciliation Act). Religious organizations are exempt, while federal employees are guaranteed a continuation of benefits under a separate law.

But before you sign up for this COBRA benefit, know your options. There's a good chance you could find a better deal. (See p. 204.) COBRA rules say that employers can charge you up to 102% of the total cost of coverage. (So, if you and your employer together pay $500 a month to cover you, you'll pay as much as $510 a month for the same coverage under COBRA.)

The drawback to switching plans is that it may be challenging to find a new plan that allows you to stick with all of the same doctors. Follow the advice about provider networks on p. 203.

Whether you opt for COBRA or a new plan, don't permit a lapse in your coverage. For more information on COBRA, go to dol.gov/cobra and search for "COBRA FAQs."

Final point: No matter where you purchase your plan, you must sign up during the **open enrollment period**, which typically starts in November and lasts for a couple of months. However, certain life events—such as turning 26 (when you can no longer be on your parents' plan in most states), getting married, having a baby (or adopting), moving, or leaving a job—qualify you for a special enrollment period, so check with the insurance company to see if this applies to you.

What to Look for When Choosing a Plan

Whether you're shopping for an individual plan or you're getting your coverage through an employer, you'll have to wade through different features and choose a plan that fits both your budget and your needs. Consider the following:

- **Know what's covered.** Choosing a plan is actually easier now than it was years ago. That's because as of this writing, all insurers must cover ten "essential health benefits." These include prescription drugs, emergency room care, and laboratory services. (For a complete list of essential benefits, go to healthcare.gov/coverage/what-marketplace-plans-cover.) What's more, you can't be turned down if you have a pre-existing condition.

  Still, there are some variations. Coverage of less common treatments like bariatric surgery, infertility treatments, or gender reassignment surgery, for instance, isn't required by law. If there are services that are particularly important to you, make sure to check your plan's **Summary of Benefits and Coverage**, a simple explanatory document that comes with your policy.

- **Make sure your doctors are in the provider network.** Want to be certain that your favorite physicians are part of the plan you are considering? Call their offices and ask if they accept the insurance. Or consult the insurance company's online directory of providers. You can also go to sites like

Zocdoc.com, which can show you some of the doctors in your area who accept the insurance you're contemplating. In general, plans with higher premiums tend to offer a larger network of doctors, hospitals, and labs for you to choose from.

• **Estimate what the plan will cost you.** You pay for your plan in two ways: your fixed monthly premium and your out-of-pocket expenses, which include your deductible, co-payments, and coinsurance. In general, the more you pay for your monthly premium, the less you pay for out-of-pocket expenses when you receive medical care.

When shopping for an individual plan, you'll see that coverage is divided into categories: bronze, silver, gold, and platinum. These categories have nothing to do with the quality of the plan. Rather, they are an indication of cost. So **Bronze** plans tend to have the lowest monthly premiums, but charge you more for co-pays and deductibles. That makes them best for healthy people. **Silver** plans, which have somewhat higher premiums than bronze plans, offer lower co-pays and deductibles. The big appeal? This is the only category of plan that you can purchase with the government subsidy I've been talking about. (Go to Healthcare .gov to see if you qualify.) **Gold** and **Platinum** plans are best for individuals with conditions that require frequent doctor visits. In addition to the cost and type of coverage, you need to think about how long you're willing to wait before seeing a doctor. For instance, with an HMO, it may take several days (sometimes weeks) to get a referral from your primary doctor before you can see a specialist.

One last thing to consider: If you're planning to have a baby in the next year, you need to be informed about costs. As of this writing, all plans are required by law to cover basic prenatal care, childbirth, and care for the newborn. But it's important to compare the specifics of different plans. Each plan's Summary of Benefits and Coverage will include an example of how much you might pay out of pocket if you're having a baby.

CAR INSURANCE

Auto insurance covers harm done to you, your car, other people, and other people's property. The total amount of coverage you need depends on the rules in your state, the condition of your car, the amount of health insurance you have, and the value of the assets you must protect in case you're held responsible for an accident.

Many auto insurers have been raising their rates, sometimes by a large amount, in recent years. Coverage is especially expensive for people in their twenties, because statistically they have more accidents.

Three Basic Types of Auto Coverage

Car insurance consists of three separate kinds of protection: auto liability coverage, medical payments coverage, and collision and comprehensive coverage. Here's a rundown of each:

- **Auto liability coverage.** If you cause an accident with your car and injure someone or damage something, auto liability insurance will pay the other party's medical or repair expenses as well as your legal fees. Of the three major components of auto insurance, auto liability—which comprises both **bodily injury liability** and **property damage liability**—can make up more than half of your premiums.

  Some states, known as **no-fault states**, require drivers (and their insurance companies) to pay for their own costs after a car accident, regardless of who was responsible. But even if you live in a no-fault state, you need liability protection. That's because each no-fault state has a threshold above which a person who causes an accident can be sued. For example, in some no-fault states a driver can be sued if he causes severe physical injury to another driver.

  Every state except New Hampshire requires car owners to purchase at least some minimum amount of liability protection, but you should probably buy more than that. Even if you don't have many assets, you need liability protection in case a court decides to garnish your future wages. Insurance analysts are hesitant to say what the "right" amount of liability protection is, but when pressed, they suggest that the following guideline is reasonable: If you don't have much savings and you don't own a home, get coverage of at least $100,000 per person, $300,000 per accident, and $100,000 for property. If you own a home and have some money saved, consider purchasing an umbrella liability policy, which is coverage above and beyond any auto or homeowners liability protection you have. (For details, see the home insurance section on p. 220.)

- **Medical payments coverage.** This insurance covers your medical and hospital bills (up to a certain dollar amount) if you're injured in a car accident. It also covers the medical and hospital bills (again, up to specific limits) of any passengers in your car. If you live in a no-fault state, you'll generally be required to buy a minimum amount of medical payments coverage, typically called **personal injury protection** or **no-fault insurance**. It covers your medical and hospital bills (and, in some states, your loss of income if you're disabled) regardless of who's to blame for an accident.

  If you live in a "fault" state, you're usually not required to purchase medical payments coverage, but you may want to anyway. Injuries sustained in accidents in which no one can be proven negligent won't be covered by liability insurance. Assuming you have health insurance (you do, right?), you may be wondering if medical payments coverage is redundant. It's not. First of all, while I know *you're* insured, your passengers might not be. Even if they are, medical payments coverage can take care of a whole host of costs that a health plan won't—including any health insurance deductibles and co-pays. In the worst circumstances, it will even cover funeral expenses.

- **Collision and comprehensive coverage.** Collision insurance pays for damage to your car if you bang it into something like a tree, your garage door, or another car. Comprehensive insurance covers damage caused by fire, flood, theft, tornado, falling objects, and just about any other physical damage that's not covered by collision. In all states, both these types of coverage are optional. However, if you took out a loan to buy your car or if you're leasing, the lender or leasing company will most likely require that you purchase them.

  The maximum amount an insurance company will pay under a collision or comprehensive policy is, at least in theory, the cost of replacing the car with a comparable used one. (Unfortunately, some insurers aren't this generous.) After you've paid off your loan, you may want to consider dropping your collision and comprehensive coverage. To decide whether it makes sense to do so, figure out the value of your car (at the Kelley Blue Book site, KBB.com) minus the deductible. Compare that number to your annual premium.

An additional type of insurance required in some states is **uninsured motorist coverage.** This protects you if an uninsured driver crashes into your car. You may also want to consider getting *underinsured motorist coverage,* which will protect you if the driver who crashes into your car has some, but not enough, insurance to cover your costs.

If You Rent a Car, Cover Your Assets

One type of coverage you'll want to have when you rent a car is liability protection. If you also own a car, your standard auto liability and collision damage coverage should insure you when you rent a car. Check with your insurer to get the rules on your policy. (Some, for example, don't cover you if you're renting a car for business.)

If you don't own a car, some credit card companies will give you automatic collision coverage as a perk if you use their cards to pay for rental cars. Check your credit card agreement. If you don't own a car but you do rent cars, purchase liability insurance at the rental counter. Frequent renters who don't own a car may find it cheaper to get something called a **nonowner policy** from an insurance company.

How to Reduce Your Auto Insurance Costs

Your premiums are based on factors such as your age, where you live, the type of car you drive, your gender (women tend to pay less than men, though this difference decreases with age), marital status, credit history, driving record, and how much driving you do. The following suggestions can substantially reduce your premiums:

- **Shop around.** Plenty of websites let you compare car insurance quotes. The trick is finding out whether the quotes they give you really are the best available. Try CarInsurance .com, Compare.com, and NetQuote.com; among them they cover many of the bigger (and smaller) names in the industry. As I've said, some insurers don't turn up often, if ever, on comparison sites, especially companies that sell directly to the public, like GEICO and Progressive. These companies will often have quotes worth seeking out, so if you don't see them, just contact them. And if you or a family member has been in the military, USAA (USAA.com) offers competitive rates, but you'll need to reach out to them directly, too.

- **Drive safely.** It sounds obvious, but insurance companies charge less for drivers who have no violations or accidents. If you have a clean record, point it out when you're pricing policies.

- **Cut down on your driving time.** Some insurance companies charge you less if you spend less time on the road—for example, if you drive fewer than 7,500 miles a year. So if

BABY, YOU CAN'T DRIVE MY CAR

It may seem like no big deal, but when someone asks to borrow your car, you should think twice before saying yes. If you allow someone to drive your car and he or she has an accident, *your* insurer is likely to pay for the damage (less any deductible you have to pay). That means your insurance company may raise your premium just as if you had caused the accident.

you join a carpool or start taking public transportation and your mileage drops, let your insurance company know.

- **Choose your car carefully.** Certain makes and models are harder to damage, less expensive to repair, and less likely to be stolen than others. Insurers use this information when setting rates. You can reduce your collision and comprehensive coverage if you buy a new or used car that's considered low risk, such as a Honda CR-V (versus, say, a luxe Porsche Cayenne). Ask your insurer for a list of such cars, or look at the car insurance rates estimates by model on Insure.com.

- **Get good grades.** If you're currently a student with a B average or better, or are on the dean's list at your school, tell your insurer. Good grades could make you eligible for a discount of 15% to 25% off your premium. In some cases, college graduates are eligible for these discounts until they reach age 25.

- **Grow up.** Most insurers will charge young drivers less as they get older. In fact, auto insurance rates drop an average of 41% from age 20 to 25, according to a study by InsuranceQuotes.com, although men still tend to pay higher rates than women of the same age. Your birthday is a good

BEWARE BEFORE YOU SHARE

If you want the convenience of having a car when you need it but don't want the hassle and expense that come with owning one (like parking and insurance), you may be considering joining a car sharing service like Zipcar or Car2Go that, for a small membership fee, allows you to rent at a set hourly or daily rate. Some car sharing companies even let you rent cars by the minute for quick errands around town.

However, car sharing services have different insurance rules than car rental agencies. Instead of charging you separately for different types of insurance, they automatically include liability and collision coverage in your membership and rental fees. Sounds great, right?

The problem is that this coverage might not give you *enough* protection. Before you sign up, look carefully at the car share company's insurance policy and see if the coverage is adequate. (For the coverage I recommend, see p. 209.) If it's not, check if your own car insurance (if you have it) extends to car sharing. If not, see if your credit card company offers any coverage. Frequent users of car sharing services might want to consider buying a nonowner policy.

time to make sure you're getting the best deal out there. Call your insurer with a reminder.

- **Get hitched.** Insurance companies view married couples as safer than singles. (Of course, this includes same-sex couples.) On average, a single, 20-year-old man pays 25% more for car insurance than a married 20-year-old man, and a single, 20-year-old woman pays 28% more than a married one. As you get older, however, your marital status has less effect on your car insurance costs.

- **See if you're entitled to a household, or "multicar," discount.** If you're married and you and your spouse both have cars, see if you can save money by getting auto coverage from the same company. Insurers often offer discounts if both of your cars are insured on the same policy or by the same company. If you and your partner are unmarried but live together, you typically can receive such a discount as well. If you live with your parents (or if you are a student away at college), you might be able to get a similar discount if your car is insured under your folks' policy.

- **Consider getting your home and auto insurance from the same company.** Some auto insurers will give you a better deal if you purchase, say, renters insurance from them, too.

- **Take a class.** Many auto insurers will offer discounts of 10% to 15% if you take a defensive driving class. Some will even let you take the course online.

- **Get insured through an "affinity group."** As with other kinds of insurance, you can sometimes get a break on car insurance by belonging to a certain group, such as an alumni association or a trade union. Some insurers even offer discounts to people who buy hybrid cars. (The reason: Hybrid owners tend to be safer, more conscientious drivers.) Your employer may also offer group auto insurance.

DISABILITY INSURANCE

What would happen if you had a serious car accident and you couldn't work for ten months?

Only five states—California, Hawaii, New Jersey, New York, and Rhode Island—require employers to provide any income to disabled employees who get hurt off the job. And federal disability benefits from Social Security are extremely difficult to get; the majority of people who apply are rejected.

Your only real protection, therefore, is likely to be private disability insurance. Although you may never have heard of disability insurance, it's something you should have even if you live in one of the states mentioned above. Ideally, your coverage pays 60% to 70% of your income following an accident that leaves you unable to work. (The coverage required by the states above generally falls below that level.) For many young people, disability coverage is more important than life insurance. On average, you're twice as likely to become disabled before retirement as you are to die before retirement. Not exactly a cheery thought, but still important to know.

If you work for a large company, you may already have some disability insurance under a group policy—and that may be all you

---

BAD CREDIT BOOSTS YOUR INSURANCE BILLS

Most people know that with insurance, there's a catch: If your car gets sideswiped or your home is damaged in a fire and you make a claim, your premiums rise. What you may not know is that insurers also look at your credit. People who are in poor financial shape are considered more of a risk, so credit scoring companies like FICO have created special insurance scores to help insurance companies assess applicants. These take into account many of the same factors as your credit score.

If you want to know your insurance scores, ask your insurance provider. Or go to personalreports.lexisnexis.com to get a copy of your auto and home insurance reports. (You're entitled to one free report a year.)

need. If you don't work for a company that offers disability protection, consider buying an individual disability policy.

If Your Employer Offers Disability Insurance

Disability protection is different from **workers compensation**. Workers comp protects you if you're injured while performing your job. Disability insurance, sometimes known as **income protection**, covers you for *any* injury or illness, whether it happens at home, on vacation, or on the job. (Pregnancy, oddly, can count as a short-term disability here, which is one reason why purchasing an individual disability policy can be especially expensive—and valuable—for women.) If you're lucky enough to work for an employer who provides you with disability insurance, assess exactly how much protection it gives you. Many employers offer policies that pay out until the worker reaches age 65. Here are some tips to help you understand your coverage and figure out if you need more:

- **Find out what percentage of your income you'll receive if you're disabled.** A typical policy through your employer will pay at least 50% of your income—usually up to a maximum, such as $5,000 a month—if you suffer a long-term disability. If you earn more than $100,000 a year, consider supplementing your employer's coverage with an individual policy. (More on how to buy your own policy later.)

- **Take advantage of your flexible benefits plan.** Sometimes you're given a choice between disability insurance and life insurance. If you're single with no kids, pick disability.

What to Look For in an Individual Disability Policy

Insurance companies offer all kinds of confusing extras with their disability policies. Below are the basics you will need:

- **A policy that's noncancelable.** This means the insurer generally can't cancel your current policy or raise your premium for any reason.

- **A policy that's guaranteed renewable.** With this feature, you can renew each year without taking a medical exam, and the insurer can't single you out for a rate increase just because you've made a lot of claims.

- **A policy that offers residual benefit protection.** If you're partially disabled, some policies will pay you a portion of your disability benefits, known as residual benefits. This is extremely important coverage in case you're in a situation where an injury or illness allows you to work only part-time.

- **A policy that offers inflation protection.** You don't want your benefits to shrink over time, especially if they're the only income you have to live on. Some policies will give you a cost-of-living allowance, which means they adjust with the rate of inflation year to year.

- **A policy that provides "own occupation" coverage.** This will pay you if you can no longer perform your current job. Without this type of coverage, you could be denied benefits as long as you can work at *any* type of job, regardless of whether it is related to your pre-disability career or not. If instead you had an "any occupation" policy, your benefit may be denied if you are able to perform another job—any job—that replaces about 60% of the income you earned in your previous job.

How to Reduce Your Disability Insurance Costs

The problem with individual disability coverage is that it's not cheap. A 27-year-old paralegal who earns an annual salary of $50,000 might pay about $1,000 or more a year for a top-of-the-line policy. Here are ways to keep your costs down:

- **Compare quotes.** Only a handful of insurance companies specialize in disability coverage. Two of the largest are Northwestern Mutual Life Insurance (Northwesternmutual .com) and MetLife (MetLife.com). Check with PolicyGenius .com to get quotes from several disability insurers.

- **Consider a "graded" or "step-rate" premium.** This allows you to start with a lower premium that increases as you age. With such a policy, for example, the paralegal might pay only about $735 a year for the first year, $742 in the next year, and so on. The advantage here is that those early payments (during what you hope will be your leanest years) are a lot lower than what you'd pay on a standard policy. At a certain age, however, a graded premium policy will likely be charging you more per year than you'd pay if you had a level premium that remained the same every year.

- **Think about how long you can wait before disability payments start.** To get benefits, you'll typically have to wait between one month and a year after becoming disabled. This interval is known as the **elimination period.** Most employers who offer disability coverage also offer short-term benefits that cover some of this period. If you have the three-to-six-month emergency cushion that I recommend, then you can afford to wait a few months for the policy to kick in. The longer the elimination period, the less you'll pay for the policy. The downside is that you may dip into more of your savings than you would like. Once you start receiving your disability payouts, you stop paying premiums.

- **Buy through your employer.** Not all employers will pay for disability coverage. But a growing number of employers now have systems in place to let employees *buy* individual coverage on a voluntary basis. These arrangements can cost significantly less than what you might pay for a policy on your own, especially if you're a woman. (As mentioned earlier, women can expect to pay significantly more than men for individual disability insurance because pregnancy is categorized as a disability, among other factors.) But if you buy a policy through your job, you're protected by workplace equality laws. Check with your human resources department to see whether you have this option. (The downside: If you leave your job, you'll probably lose this disability insurance.)

- **Decrease your benefit period.** Relatively few disabilities last more than a few years. If you're willing to accept the risk, you might be able to save up to 30% on your premium by selecting a benefit period of only five years, instead of being insured until you retire. As you make more money, it's a good idea to slowly lengthen your benefit period.

HOME INSURANCE

If you own a home, you probably have some homeowners insurance. (Most mortgage lenders require it.) But if you're like a lot of homeowners, you don't have enough coverage—or you're paying too much. And if you rent, you may never even have thought about buying any coverage.

Three Basic Types of Coverage If You Own a Home

Homeowners insurance covers the cost of rebuilding or repairing your home (and surrounding structures such as a detached garage) if it's destroyed or damaged by a disaster such as fire, lightning, snow, or windstorm. It also covers the *contents* of your home up to a fixed dollar amount in the event of many of these same disasters—as well as theft. And it can protect you if you're held responsible (or "liable") for injuring people or damaging property, even when you're away from home. Here's a more detailed rundown of each type of protection.

- **Your home's structure.** You need to buy enough insurance to cover the full cost of rebuilding your home. Contact a local builders association or insurance agent and find out the building cost per square foot in your area. Multiply that number by the square footage of your home. This will give you an idea of how much it would cost to rebuild. (A real estate appraiser can also give you the same information but may charge a fee.)

- **The contents of your home.** Standard homeowners policies usually cover your personal property for 50% to 70% of the amount for which you insured your home's structure. You can increase the amount of coverage for a fee. Make sure your **personal property insurance** covers you for **replacement cost**, not **actual cash value.** Coverage for replacement cost gives you enough money to buy new comparable items to replace your belongings. Coverage for actual cash value pays you the amount of money you could get to repair or replace the items, *minus* the depreciation on the items. That amounts to a whole lot less.

  To figure out how much personal property insurance you need, take a **home inventory** of everything you own and estimate (roughly) how much it would cost to replace these items. This is a hassle, but it's worth doing. Make sure you include the approximate purchase date and price of your belongings, including furniture, rugs, electronics, computers, dishes, cookware, artwork, and major appliances. Also list your suits, dresses, shoes, and coats. (Don't forget the expensive stuff, like your wedding dress or tuxedo.) Photos are particularly helpful for documenting valuable items, and it's good to scan or snap pics of receipts, or get them emailed to you, for backup. Record the serial numbers or model numbers for appliances, too. This inventory will come in handy if you ever need to file a claim.

  Consider using the free home inventory app from the Insurance Information Institute at Knowyourstuff.org, or a similar tool from your insurance company. Be sure to keep a copy of your inventory in the cloud. (Dropbox and Google Drive work nicely.) That way if the worst happens and your house burns to the ground, you will still be able to access it.

- **Damage you do to other people and other people's property.** Homeowners policies include liability protection that covers you for damage you cause to other people inside or outside your home. If you leave a pair of boots in the middle of your kitchen floor and your neighbor trips on them and breaks her leg, your liability insurance will probably cover your legal costs, as well as her medical bills and other expenses, assuming you're held responsible for the injury. If you run a shopping cart over someone's foot in a supermarket, your liability coverage may pay for his or her medical expenses if you're found liable. If you have a pet, your policy will often cover you for damage the pet does to people or their property as well.

    Many homeowners policies come with a standard amount of liability insurance: typically $100,000 per accident. In these litigious times, this may not be enough. To get a rough idea of how much you need, tally up all your major assets, including your home, your car, your other possessions, and your investments (including retirement savings). The amount of liability coverage you get should exceed this amount. Sometimes the additional cost is only $10 or so per month for coverage up to $500,000.

What's Covered and What's Not

Your two main homeowners insurance plan options sound vaguely reminiscent of high school chemistry—broad (HO-2) and special (HO-3). If you can afford it, buy HO-3 coverage. It's the industry standard, it doesn't cost much more than HO-2, and it covers a much wider range of perils. (If you live in a co-op or condo, you'll need to purchase a special policy known as HO-6 to protect your personal property and the unit you own, but not the common property.) But certain situations, such as earthquakes and floods, aren't covered by standard homeowners policies. (See the box on p. 225 for more on disaster insurance.)

There are other limits on what most homeowners policies cover. For example, many policies provide only $1,000 to $2,000 of theft coverage for valuables like jewelry. If this isn't enough to replace what you own, purchase extra protection by adding an **endorsement,** sometimes referred to as a **floater.** This is simply an amendment to your insurance policy to protect a specific item. With an endorsement, you can, for example, increase the coverage on your valuables—such as Grandma's silver tea set—from $2,000 to $10,000, if they are worth that much. (You will need to have these items professionally appraised.) Depending on the items, the cost for this increase in coverage could range from $20 to $100 a year.

Many homeowners policies include **off-premises** protection, which covers your possessions outside your home—whether you're mugged while on vacation or your bike is stolen off the sidewalk. Check your policy carefully.

Most policies include some **loss of use** protection. If your home is damaged and you're forced to live elsewhere for a while, this coverage will pay the cost of your hotel bills, meals, and other basic living expenses, as long as they are reasonable. Don't expect the policy to pay for lavish hotels or restaurants. Typical coverage is 20% of the total amount of insurance you bought for your home's structure.

If you work at home, your home office equipment is usually not covered by your homeowners policy. If the business is small, you can get additional coverage by purchasing an endorsement. For larger businesses, you'll have to purchase a separate policy. Ask an insurance agent for details.

If You Rent, Get Insurance

If you rent an apartment or house, the idea of buying **renters insurance,** also known as **tenants insurance** (or, in insurance industry lingo, an HO-4 policy), may not have crossed your mind. But it should have. The first and most obvious reason to buy it is to protect your personal property. If all your possessions—including your clothes, jewelry, audio equipment, TV, computer, camera, sofa, and bike—were stolen or ruined in a fire, a renters policy would cover you up to a fixed dollar amount. (Contrary to what you may think, your landlord won't be on the hook for most damage done to your stuff.)

In addition to covering your possessions, a renters policy will offer you some liability protection inside and outside your home. If someone slips and falls in your apartment, your renters policy could cover that person's medical bills if you're held liable. If you accidentally leave the tap running when you go to work and ruin the floor, your renters insurance may pay the cost of repairs. (For more general types of water damage, you'll probably need separate flood insurance. See the box on p. 225.) And if you knock over a sculpture in an art gallery, your renters policy may protect you then, too. Renters policies also pay for basic living expenses within reason if your home becomes unusable for a time, the same way that homeowners policies do.

How to Reduce Your Homeowners or Renters Insurance Costs

The first step, as is the case with most types of insurance, is to get a high deductible so you can keep your annual premiums low. Remember, this makes sense only if you have enough savings to cover the higher deductible. Here are five other suggestions that apply whether you own a home or rent:

- **Compare quotes.** Look at NetQuote.com to find home insurance companies serving your area; you'll need to click through to each company's website to get an actual quote. If you don't see State Farm (one of the country's largest homeowners insurers) on any comparison sites, contact a State Farm agent. You can also go to homeowners insurance companies that sell directly to consumers, such as Amica (Amica.com). Active-duty or retired military personnel and their families can try USAA (USAA.com) as well.

PLANNING FOR THE WORST: DISASTER INSURANCE

In 2012, Hurricane Sandy damaged or destroyed hundreds of thousands of homes on the East Coast, and the topic of flood insurance once again became a matter of concern for homeowners nationwide. (You may also remember the Gulf Coast devastation wrought by Hurricane Katrina in 2005.) Fact is, flooding is the most common natural disaster in the United States, but too many homeowners and renters have no idea that the typical policy won't cover water damage caused by storms or other natural disasters.

The good news is that the federal government offers flood protection through the National Flood Insurance Program (FloodSmart.gov). Look up your home's location and see if you're in a high-risk area, and if so make sure to purchase coverage. There are high-risk spots in surprising places; for example, some hilly regions of New England are susceptible to runoff from melting snow in spring. (Who knew?) Even if you're not in a high-risk area, you may want to consider flood insurance. It could protect you from losing everything.

Though it's true that most homeowners and renters policies typically cover hail, tornado, and wind damage—sometimes with a separate, higher deductible—if you live in the tornado belt in the Midwest, you'll want to make sure you have adequate protection, including a policy that offers *replacement* value. (See p. 221 for a discussion of why replacement value is key.)

If you live on the West Coast, you should purchase a separate earthquake insurance policy since homeowners policies won't cover the damage caused by this type of natural disaster. California residents can buy earthquake insurance through the state's Earthquake Authority (Earthquakeauthority.com).

- **Don't file small claims.** If a bike is stolen from your yard or a window gets broken in your house, it's almost always best to eat that expense rather than file a homeowners insurance claim. Even if that claim exceeds your deductible and you get a little money from the insurance company, you likely won't come out ahead. That's because the company will decide that you're a high-risk customer and jack up your premiums when it's time to renew your policy, or even refuse to cover you altogether. This may feel ludicrous and unfair, but it's the way it is. So get a policy with a high deductible (which will be cheaper) and pay for minor repairs or thefts out of pocket. Rely on homeowners insurance only to cover really big losses—like if a tree falls on your house and crushes your roof.

- **Check if you're eligible for any discounts.** If you have dead bolts on your doors, live in an apartment building with a doorman, or even just have smoke detectors, you may be able to get a small discount on your premium. If you have a security alarm *and* a sophisticated sprinkler system, you can get a discount of as much as 20%.

- **Consider moving your car coverage to the same insurance company as your homeowners or renters coverage.** Some companies will offer you a dual-policy discount of up to 15%.

- **Check with your state's insurance department.** It may publish a list of homeowners insurance companies and the premiums they charge. (Visit map.naic.org to find your state's site.) This can help you shop around.

LIFE INSURANCE

If you've never received a friendly email or Facebook message from a life insurance agent, just wait. In the next few years, you'll probably get at least half a dozen, all trying to sell you life insurance. Ignore them. Odds are, you don't need it.

The purpose of life insurance is simple: If you die, it protects the people who rely on your income. So if you have kids (or anyone else financially dependent on you), you need it. If you're married without kids, and your spouse could handle the basic housing and living expenses without you, you don't need it. If you're single and you aren't financially responsible for anyone but yourself, you don't need it. (Of course, there are always exceptions, but these are good guidelines.)

Two Types of Life Insurance

The most basic form of life insurance is **term life insurance**. It's called that because it protects you for a specific period of time (a term). When the term runs out, you can usually renew the policy and begin another term. If you die during the term, the insurance company will pay out a specified amount of money to your beneficiaries. This payment is called the **death benefit**.

When you're young, the premium you pay for term insurance is very low. For a death benefit of $100,000, a 25-year-old nonsmoker

---

EXPLORE AN UMBRELLA LIABILITY POLICY

If you have a lot of assets—or you have the potential to earn a high salary—you should consider getting an **umbrella liability policy**. This special type of policy expands the liability protection provided by your car and homeowners coverage. It also may protect you in case you're sued for something unrelated to your car or home, such as slander. The price of a $1 million umbrella liability policy is a few hundred dollars a year. Umbrella policies are usually a better deal than buying more auto liability and home liability coverage.

might pay about \$180 a year for a 20-year policy. This premium may stay the same for many years or increase slightly from year to year, depending on which type of term policy you get.

Term life insurance gives you the most coverage for your money when you're young. But don't be surprised if insurance agents discourage you from buying it. The commissions on such policies are low. Often, it's pure self-interest on their part.

Most life insurance agents will instead urge you to buy a "permanent" or **cash value policy**. (For a sampling of some of the

WHEN TO CONSIDER A CASH VALUE POLICY

There's one quite rarified set of circumstances under which it may make sense to buy a cash value life insurance policy. If you (1) need life insurance; (2) are already putting the maximum allowable amount into tax-favored retirement savings plans, such as IRAs and 401(k)s; and (3) are contributing as much as you need to your children's college education in a tax-free 529 college savings plan, you may then want to consider what's called a **low-load** cash value policy, which has relatively low commissions and expenses. Companies that sell low-load cash value life policies include Ameritas (Ameritasdirect.com) and TIAA (TIAA.org); if you or a parent has a military background, explore USAA (USAA.com). Keep in mind that not all of these insurers sell policies in all states.

Because cash value life insurance can be both expensive and confusing, it's an area where expert advice might help. "Fee-only" insurance consultants are considered unbiased because they don't get commissions from the insurance or investments they recommend. Glenn Daily, one of the pioneers in this field, keeps a short list of fee-only consultants on his website, glenndaily.com/links.htm.

most common pitches, see the box on p. 230.) With a cash value policy, the insurance company takes your annual premium and deducts various commissions and expenses (which are usually very high), then puts what's left into a kind of savings account for you, known as your cash value. Because of quirky tax rules, that money grows tax-deferred and is tax-free to your heirs if held until death.

But the reality is, if you do need life insurance, you're almost always better off buying term insurance (which is cheaper) and investing the money you save in a tax-favored retirement savings plan like an IRA or a 401(k).

How to Shop for Term Insurance

By now it's probably clear that you're better off purchasing a term policy. There are two basic types. **Annual renewable term** is coverage that doesn't require you to take a yearly medical exam to renew it, though your premium will usually increase somewhat each year. A **level-premium term** policy lasts for a fixed number of years (twenty years is the most popular) and allows you to lock in a premium for a set period of time. Some level-premium term deals will lock in your premium and your coverage for the entire term. But beware, "level premium" can sometimes be a misnomer: Other deals may only lock in the *coverage* for the entire term, while your *premium* could go up after just a few years. So make sure you know the details of your policy so that you can avoid rising premiums. In either case, once your coverage period ends, you usually have to pass a medical exam to renew at attractive rates; otherwise, your premium will increase dramatically.

Although an annual renewable term policy may cost less at the beginning, a level-premium term policy may be less expensive in the long run. Look for a policy that guarantees the premium for at least ten years. Make sure that your level-premium term policy also includes a free "conversion provision" that gives you the right to switch to a cash value policy at a later date regardless of your health, potentially saving you money.

You have many options when shopping for term insurance, no

matter what type. Try contacting individual, direct-to-consumer firms like TIAA (TIAA.org) and Ameritas (Ameritasdirect.com). You can also check out comparison sites including the highly regarded Term4Sale.com. Other sites worth checking out include SelectQuote.com and LifeInsure.com.

WHY THE PITCHES DON'T MAKE SENSE

Perhaps you've heard the saying that life insurance isn't bought, it's sold. The reason? Life insurance agents can be very aggressive and extremely compelling. Who can blame them? The commission an agent gets from selling a cash value policy is substantial. Here's what's really behind all those persuasive-sounding come-ons.

The pitch: "Maybe you don't need life insurance now, but you should buy today when you're young and healthy to protect your insurability in the future."

The reality: The chances of your developing a health problem that renders you unable to qualify for life insurance before you reach age 35 are very slim. Since you have limited funds now, why spend your money on insurance you don't need?

The pitch: "Even though you're single, you need life insurance to pay your funeral costs and your debts."

The reality: Your parents, other relatives, or friends will probably be willing to pay for your funeral in the extremely unlikely event that you die young with no assets. As for your debts, unless you cosigned a loan with parents, partners, or friends, no one else will be responsible for paying them. If you have any assets, your creditors will sell them to pay your debts. Otherwise, the creditors will simply take the loss.

How Much Coverage Do You Need?

You need enough life insurance to provide for your dependents (spouse and kids) so that they can carry on a decent lifestyle if you die prematurely. If you have young children, you need to figure out how much they would need to live on for at least the next 15 to 20 years.

The pitch: *"If you have a child, you should buy a policy to cover his or her life."*

The reality: A child is the last person who needs a life insurance policy. Parents need life insurance. Buying coverage on your child's life is a waste of money, despite what late-night infomercials may claim.

The pitch: *"Cash value life insurance offers tax-favored growth and is a great forced-savings plan."*

The reality: This is true, but you can get the same tax-favored growth and forced savings by diverting money into a 401(k), IRA, or 529 plan, without paying a commission to an agent. And with retirement plans, you may also qualify for an up-front tax deduction. (For details, see Chapter 6.)

The pitch: *"Buying term insurance is like renting. Buying cash value insurance is like buying. When the term is up, you don't have anything to show for it. But look how much money you'll have in twenty years if you buy a cash value life insurance policy."*

The reality: Life insurance companies are notorious for using extremely attractive, overly optimistic future rates of return when selling cash value policies. There's no guarantee that your returns will be as good as an agent says.

One rough rule of thumb says you should buy a policy that will pay seven to ten times your annual before-tax income if you die, but many people need more than that—especially if they have several young children. If you have certain aspirations for your kids—for example, if you want to send them to expensive private schools—or if your spouse doesn't work, you will likely need more. The calculators at 360financialliteracy.org/calculators /life-insurance-calculator and basic.esplanner.com will help you crunch all the numbers.

If Your Job Offers Life Insurance

Many large employers provide some life insurance for employees. Your company might pay for a term policy with a death benefit of $50,000—more than enough if you're single and have no dependents. If you need more, you might be better off buying this directly from an insurance company rather than through your employer. That's because some employers charge all employees the same rate for life insurance, regardless of age. If that's the case with your employer, as a 25-year-old you would be paying the same premium as a 45-year-old, for example, which would be much higher than what you could be paying. Also, policies you get through work may be hard (or at least expensive) to take with you if you switch jobs. Find out about your employer's offerings and also price several term policies on your own using the comparison sites on p. 230.

INSURANCE YOU PROBABLY DON'T NEED

It's very tempting to buy quickie insurance on impulse. After all, it seems so cheap—just $10 a day to get collision coverage at the rental car counter, or $30 for $300,000 worth of life insurance at the airport. But before you throw money at this kind of coverage, evaluate it carefully. In most cases, you don't need it.

- **Rental car collision protection.** If you've ever rented a car, you were probably asked if you wanted to buy the **loss damage waiver**, which is just a fancy name for collision insurance. Next time, do a little research in advance to see if you really need to buy it at the rental counter. Often, your credit card agreement automatically protects you with collision coverage when you charge a car rental on the card. And if you already have collision coverage on your car, find out if your policy extends to rentals. You should also check whether your auto liability coverage extends to rentals. Although both often do, there are exceptions. Say, if you normally drive a Camry at home but rent a sporty convertible on vacation. If your policy does cover you, skip the extra coverage at the rental counter. (See p. 211 for more on the ins and outs of insuring rental cars.)

- **Flight accident insurance.** If you need to insure your life, the cheapest way to do it when you're young is to buy a term life insurance policy. (See the previous section.) Don't waste money buying life insurance when you buy your ticket online. Sure, it's tempting (this type of insurance plays on our fear of flying), and it also seems cheap, but it doesn't make sense. Your chances of slipping and killing yourself on the ground are much greater than your chances of dying in a plane crash. Plus, many credit card companies give you automatic flight insurance, usually called travel accident insurance, if you charge your tickets on their card, so be sure to check.

- **Travel and trip cancellation insurance.** Policies promising to protect your vacation against flight cancellation, delays, or even lost luggage have proliferated, but as long as it's a short domestic trip you're booking yourself, you're unlikely to need any of it. For one thing, cancellation and baggage insurance is a very common credit card benefit—as long as you charged the tickets on your card, you're probably already covered.

  The exception is if you're going abroad, in which case travel medical protection may be a good idea. (That depends on what your health insurance will cover while you're over-seas, so check your policy.) Some credit cards, especially those with an international or airline focus, come with some travel medical coverage as well. Check with your issuer to make sure you've got what you need.

- **Extended warranties or service contracts.** When you buy a new dishwasher, wireless speaker system, or car, the sales-person will push hard to get you to buy a service plan or extended warranty. That's because these add-ons are hugely profitable for the retailer. But they are almost never a good deal for you. Many major appliances and electronics already include a one-year warranty, so you would be doubling up on insurance. Beyond the initial year, you're better off pay-

WHY YOU MAY NEED A WILL

Since we're on the topic of life insurance, this is as good a time as any to discuss the subject of wills. The truth is, I don't know any-one in his or her twenties who has a will. But that doesn't mean you don't need one.

If you're single, for example, you may want to leave all your possessions (even if that's just a car and a small savings account) to a friend or sibling. Without a will, your property will be dis-tributed to your closest relatives according to state law. If you're married without children, you may assume that your spouse will get everything in the event of your death. But depending on the state you live in, your parents may be entitled to a share of what you leave behind. If you're a parent, you may not want to think about what would happen to your children if you and your part-ner are no longer around. But without a will, a probate court will select a guardian for them. You get the picture.

ing for repairs yourself in the rare case that your new dishwasher stops working within the first five years.

- **Laptop insurance.** Most laptops come with a one-year warranty for parts and labor. But warranties don't cover accidental damage like spilling a cup of coffee on the keyboard or dropping it. For additional insurance against accidental damage, you could spend a few hundred dollars for three years of coverage. (If you have a $1,000 computer, that's a big chunk of the purchase price—hardly worth it if you plan to replace your laptop in three to five years.) If you're prone to dumping lattes on your keyboard, you might consider accidental damage insurance for one year. Before paying for a longer period, however,

The easiest way to tackle this task is to get a lawyer to draw up a will for you. If you don't own real estate or have much in the way of assets and your situation is straightforward, this should cost less than $1,000. (Many lawyers charge a flat fee for wills instead of billing by the hour, so ask.) For a list of local lawyers specializing in wills, go to the American College of Trust and Estate Counsel at actec.org/fellows/public-search or the National Association of Estate Planners & Councils at naepc.org/designations/estate_planners. If you can't afford the lawyer's fee, you have no children, your situation is uncomplicated, and you're willing to spend the time, you can attempt to write your own will. One software kit that can help is Quicken's WillMaker Plus, or you can check out sites like Nolo.com or Rocketlawyer.com. And keep in mind that once you start earning more money and accumulating more assets, you're going to need to update your will. That is the time to have a lawyer review it.

consider how many years you think you'll keep your laptop before upgrading.

- **Pet insurance.** With monthly premiums averaging around $25 for cats and $35 for dogs, you are generally better off paying the vet bills yourself, especially if your plan includes a high deductible. If your dog is getting old or has a preexisting condition, premium prices, deductibles, and coinsurance are even more unaffordable.

- **Smartphone insurance.** In a world of $100 screen repairs, it sounds reasonable to get this. But you could spend close to $200 on a typical insurance policy over the course of a two-year phone contract and have to pay a deductible of $100 or so before your insurance pays for any repairs. You're better off investing in a good phone case. OtterBox and LifeProof are particularly sturdy and highly rated ones.

- **Identity theft insurance.** If your identity is stolen, restoring your good name can be time-consuming and expensive. Identity theft insurance can cover the costs—such as attorney fees and lost wages—by charging you as much as $300 a year. Skip this expense and instead employ sound practices like monitoring your bank and credit card accounts. For more on how to combat identity theft, see p. 69.

- **Wedding insurance.** These policies pay for nonrefundable deposits if a wedding is canceled or interrupted because of a natural disaster, death, illness, vendor bankruptcy, or other problems. You'll probably end up spending a few hundred for a policy, plus $200 or so more for $1 million in liability coverage. Before you even consider buying it, see if the vendors you are using offer you liability protection or if your homeowners insurance offers coverage. What's more, most of these policies exclude the biggest risk of all: cold feet.

- You need to have health insurance. If your employer does not cover you, find affordable coverage by going to the federal health insurance exchange (Healthcare.gov). If your state has its own exchange, you'll be linked directly to it. If you don't qualify for a subsidy on the exchange, shop at a comparison site such as eHealth.com as well to find the best plan for you. (For general shopping tips, see p. 207.)

- For car insurance, check comparison sites (some good ones are CarInsurance.com, Compare.com, and NetQuote.com) and companies that sell directly to consumers. (See p. 209.)

- Get disability insurance to protect yourself—ideally, coverage that would pay you 60% to 70% of your income if you become disabled. Check MetLife.com or PolicyGenius.com. (For advice on reducing the cost of your coverage, see p. 218.)

- If you own your home, purchase enough homeowners insurance to not only rebuild your house but also to replace your possessions. To keep premiums low, choose a high deductible.

- Buy renters insurance if you rent a house or an apartment. It protects your possessions if they're ruined in a fire or stolen, and it also offers you some liability coverage both inside and away from your home.

- If you have kids or anyone else dependent on your income, buy term life insurance (try Term4Sale.com, SelectQuote.com, or LifeInsure.com) and write up a will. If you don't have dependents, you probably don't need any life insurance at all, but you probably still need a will.

- It's generally smart to avoid extended warranties as well as "quickie" insurance for things like flights and rental cars. In most cases, they're not worth it.

9

HOW TO MAKE YOUR LIFE LESS TAXING

Put More Money in Your Pocket
and Less in Uncle Sam's

YOU CAN RUN from many financial subjects, but you can't hide from taxes. Still, if you're like most people, you find the tax code complex, the forms confusing, and the IRS (Internal Revenue Service) intimidating.

This chapter will help you overcome your fears—and help you avoid paying more than necessary. You'll learn exactly what kind of taxes you pay, how to figure out which tax bracket you're in, and, most important, specific strategies that can save you money. I'll also point out the best tax prep software to guide you through filing your return.

Maybe you do your own taxes—something I recommend you try at least once. Maybe you hire someone to do them. No matter what, it's important to get familiar with the nuts and bolts to ensure that you won't miss out on any money-saving breaks for years to come.

Although exploring the intricacies of the tax code isn't anyone's idea of a good time (except for that accountant I once dated), making an effort to understand the basics will pay off. The following will give you a good overview, but keep in mind that tax law is constantly changing. So while I've made every effort to provide the most accurate, up-to-date information, you'll need to check the current rules when you file. I'll point out the relevant free publications from IRS.gov throughout.

WHY IS YOUR PAYCHECK
SO SMALL?

When you received your first paycheck from your first job, it was painfully clear that your before-tax salary, also known as your **gross income,** was an illusion. Your *actual* take-home pay, or **net income,** was much smaller. The reason, you quickly figured out, was that your employer deducted Social Security tax; Medicare tax; and federal, state, and local income taxes from your paycheck.

Your employer subtracts, or "withholds," tax because the U.S. tax system uses a "pay-as-you-go" method, meaning we pay tax on the money we earn as we earn it. If you're a freelancer or self-employed, you're responsible for making sure you pay the correct taxes each quarter (every three months). If you're an employee, your employer withholds income tax from each paycheck based on salary and the information on the **Form W-4** that you filled out when you were hired. On a worksheet attached to the W-4, you answered some basic questions to help you calculate the number of **withholding allowances** you're entitled to. A withholding allowance represents an estimate of the exemptions and deductions you are likely to be entitled to in the coming year. (You'll learn all about exemptions and deductions later on.) The more withholding allowances you take, the less income tax your employer withholds from your paycheck; the fewer allowances you take, the more tax is withheld. The number of allowances you're eligible for depends on a variety of factors, including your marital status, whether you have kids, and whether you own a home.

THE TAXES YOU PAY

Here's a rundown of the major taxes you'll encounter:

- **Income tax.** The federal government, and some state and local governments, require you to pay tax on your **earned income**, which is the money you receive for work you do. The federal government and certain state and local governments also require you to pay tax on income you receive from investments. Such **unearned income** includes the interest you get from your savings account and the dividends or capital gains you receive from mutual funds, stocks, and bonds.

- **Social Security and Medicare payroll tax (FICA).** Everyone who works must contribute a portion of his or her wages to a fund that provides retirement income for older Americans, as well as disability benefits for those who can't work (that's the Social Security part) and health insurance for this same crowd (that's the Medicare part). If you're an employee of a company, the Social Security tax you pay is 6.2% of your income, up to a maximum income of $127,200 in 2017. For most employees, the Medicare tax is 1.45%, with no maximum. So the typical employee contribution to Medicare and Social Security is 7.65% of your income, and your employer matches that amount, meaning altogether the contribution is 15.3%. If you're self-employed, you have to cover the full 15.3% yourself; this is referred to as the **self-employment tax.** Many states also impose state unemployment and disability insurance taxes.

- **Property tax.** Some state and local governments require residents to pay tax on certain types of property. In Virginia, Kentucky, and Connecticut, for example, residents must pay **personal property tax** on the value of their cars each year. And if you own a home, you usually have to pay real estate tax, also known as **real property tax**, to your municipality and/or county. This figure is based on the value of your home and the land on which it is built.

- **Sales tax.** Most states and many cities and counties impose tax on the items you buy (sofas, tortilla chips, sneakers) and the services you use (dry cleaning, haircuts, lawn care).

- **Capital gains tax.** Your profit or gain when you sell an investment is subject to something called capital gains tax. Gains from investments that you've had for a year or less—known as **short-term gains**—are taxed at your regular income tax rate. (That is, if you're in the 25% income tax bracket, you will pay 25% tax on these gains.) But gains from investments that you've held for more than one year are considered **long-term capital gains**, and are generally taxed at a lower rate. And if your tax bracket is 15% or lower, you likely won't have to pay any taxes on long-term capital gains.

FIGURING OUT YOUR TAX RATE

When people talk about their tax bracket or tax rate, they're usually referring to their federal income tax bracket or rate. Federal income tax generally makes up the largest share of your total tax bill. Your federal income tax rate depends on how much income—including wages, bonuses, tips, and earnings from investments—you received over the course of the year. (It also depends on your marital status and the tax breaks you're eligible for, which I'll tell you more about later.)

The federal government has a "graduated" tax system that requires people with higher incomes to pay a higher percentage of their incomes in taxes. A range of income levels is grouped together in what is called a **tax bracket**. A **tax rate** is assigned to each tax bracket. To figure out your tax bracket, you first need to calculate your **taxable income,** which you can do by following the step-by-step instructions on your tax return or by answering the prompts on your tax software. For example, if you were single and your taxable income was between $0 and $9,325 in 2017, you would be in the 10% tax bracket. The dollar amounts that fall within each bracket are adjusted for inflation every year. Every few years, the president, with the help of Congress, changes the number of brackets and adjusts the range of incomes in each bracket in order to win friends and influence people. As of this writing, there are seven brackets and therefore seven rates: 10%, 15%, 25%, 28%, 33%, 35%, and 39.6%. But figuring out the tax you owe involves more than finding out which rate corresponds to your income.

Take a look at the tables in Figure 9–1 on p. 245. If you're single and have a taxable income of $9,000 (maybe you're a student), that would put you in the 10% tax bracket. Simple. But say your income was $50,000. Here's where it gets complicated. Not all your income will fall into the same bracket. The first $9,325 will be taxed at the 10% rate, the next $28,625 will be taxed at the 15% rate, and the remaining $12,050 will be taxed at the 25% rate. In this example, 25% is known as your **marginal tax rate,** the rate at which the "last dollar you earn" gets taxed—and the highest rate at which any of your money is taxed. Knowing your marginal rate will help you evaluate the merits of making certain investments.

Depending on where you live, you may have to pay state and local income taxes, too. These local and state rates fall into a big range—some areas have no income tax while others have rates in the double digits. To calculate your total federal, state, and local marginal income tax rate, look up your state and local income tax rate on the website of your state's tax department, and add that number to your federal rate.

It's interesting to note that your marginal rate does not indicate what percentage of your income will go toward tax. Your overall rate, known as your **effective tax rate,** is a weighted average of the tax rates that apply to your income. In the $50,000 example above, it's a weighted average of 10%, 15%, and 25% that results in an effective tax rate of about 16.5%.

TAXES AND INHERITANCE

When Milo inherited $15,000 in cash from his Uncle Al, he put it in his bank savings account in January. Milo was thrilled by this windfall, but he worried about whether he would owe tax on the money. Here's how it generally works: You do not owe income tax on money you receive as inheritance, but if you put that money in a bank account, you will have to pay tax on the interest. So Milo had to pay tax on the $300 that his money earned in interest that year. (A handful of states require people who receive an inheritance to pay tax on it, but the executor—the person in charge of sorting through a will and distributing the money to beneficiaries—is responsible for making sure the applicable inheritance taxes are paid.) If you have any concerns about whether or not your inheritance taxes were paid, check with the executor.

FILING YOUR TAX RETURN

The term **filing** simply means filling out your tax forms and sending them to the IRS, the government agency responsible for collecting taxes. Although your employer subtracts money for taxes from your paycheck during the year, the amount withheld is generally an estimate, not the exact amount of tax you actually owe. By filling out tax forms, you learn whether you still owe the IRS money or whether the IRS owes you a refund.

April 15 is usually the last day you can file a tax return and pay tax for the previous calendar year without incurring a penalty. (In years when that date falls on a weekend or holiday, the IRS allows you to file up until the following business day.) If you miss the

Figure 9–1

2017 TAX RATES

Filing Status	For taxable income that is:	Marginal rate is:
Single	not over $9,325	10%
	over $9,325 but not over $37,950	15%
	over $37,950 but not over $91,900	25%
	over $91,900 but not over $191,650	28%
	over $191,650 but not over $416,700	33%
	over $416,700 but not over $418,400	35%
	over $418,400	39.6%
Married couple filing jointly	not over $18,650	10%
	over $18,650 but not over $75,900	15%
	over $75,900 but not over $153,100	25%
	over $153,100 but not over $233,350	28%
	over $233,350 but not over $416,700	33%
	over $416,700 but not over $470,700	35%
	over $470,700	39.6%
Married couple filing separately	not over $9,325	10%
	over $9,325 but not over $37,950	15%
	over $37,950 but not over $76,550	25%
	over $76,550 but not over $116,675	28%
	over $116,675 but not over $208,350	33%
	over $208,350 but not over $235,350	35%
	over $235,350	39.6%

April 15 deadline and owe the IRS money, you may have to pay interest on the amount you owe, plus a penalty.

Start collecting your tax info early in the year. By the end of January, your employer should have sent you a **W-2** form that shows your gross wages and the amount of tax that was withheld from your paycheck over the course of the previous year.

Your bank, mutual fund company, and/or brokerage will each send you a **1099** form, which lists the interest, dividends, and capital gains you earned during the year. If you've done freelance work, you'll probably receive a 1099 from each of the companies you did the work for, so long as you were paid more than $600. (If you were paid less than that amount by anyone, you are still required to report that income, however.) Compare your pay stubs or direct deposit records and financial statements to your W-2 and 1099s to make sure the figures are accurate. If you've received these forms in the mail, scan them and save them electronically in a folder marked "Tax Returns," and create a new folder for each tax year. (For more on which documents to keep and for how long, see Chapter 2.) You'll need them when you fill out your tax return.

Who Has to File a Tax Return?

If you're single and are not claimed as a dependent on your parents' tax return, you generally must file if your gross income is at least $10,400 (as of 2017). For married couples who file a joint return, the minimum income for filing is $20,800. One exception: If you have $400 or more in self-employment earnings, you must file a tax return, even if your income is below the threshold. To help you determine if you need to file, take the IRS quiz "Do I Need to File a Tax Return?" at irs.gov/uac/do-i-need-to-file-a-tax-return.

If you're a full-time student and you're under 24, your parents can claim you as a dependent. Even so, you may have to file. If you earn more than $6,350 in 2017, for instance, or your unearned income is over $1,050 (and not included on your parents' return), you will have to file. The rules are tricky, but tax software (more about that later) will prompt you with questions to figure out the details. When in doubt, you're always better off filing, especially because you may be eligible for refunds.

When Should You File?

You need to file electronically by April 15. (If you are filing a paper return—yes, some people still mail in their returns—it needs to be postmarked by that day.) But if you're expecting a refund, send your tax forms to the IRS as soon as you can in January so that you can get your money fast. If you owe money, though, you want to hang on to your cash as long as possible. Just make sure not to miss the deadline. (See the box on p. 250, which runs down the best ways to pay.)

If you simply can't get it together in time, you can file for an automatic six-month extension by filling out IRS Form 4868 at irs.gov/pub/irs-pdf/f4868.pdf. But if you think you owe money, you must estimate how much you owe and make a payment to the IRS on or before April 15. If you haven't sent all that you owe by April 15, the IRS might charge you interest on the unpaid portion, plus a penalty if you've paid less than 90% of the amount due.

How Should You File?

If you've never done your own taxes, you may be surprised to learn how easy it is. When you file online, whichever tax software you use will walk you through filing by asking you questions. It then selects the right forms for you and, offering step-by-step prompts, helps you take advantage of all of the tax breaks available to you. It also incorporates any last-minute tax law changes into the calculations automatically.

In most cases, your biggest challenge is picking the best way to file online for your circumstances:

- **If your income is $64,000 or less, try the IRS's Free File tool** (available at irs.gov/freefile). Like its name says, Free

File allows you to select tax prep software from more than a dozen participating companies (like TurboTax and H&R Block) for free. After selecting the software, you'll be transferred from IRS.gov to the company's website, where you can fill out your return just as you would if you were paying for the service. (Depending on where you live, you may be able to file your state and local taxes this way for free, too.)

- **If your income is greater than $64,000, you have two choices—one free and one with a small fee.** The free choice is the IRS's Free File Fillable Forms (at Freefilefillableforms .com). These online forms are identical to the paper ones you'd get from the IRS, but the benefit is that they do the math for you. The downside is that you won't be prompted to maximize your tax breaks. (It is the tax man's site, after all.)

  Instead, it's worth spending a little money and using tax prep software, available from sites such as HRBlock.com, TurboTax.com, or TaxAct.com. If you are filing a basic federal and state return, with a 1040A or 1040EZ form, you can generally do so for free. (More on those forms later.) But if you are eligible for more complicated tax breaks, you may pay $50 to $80 for your federal return and $40 for your state return.

No matter how you file your taxes online, doing so will decrease the time it takes to get a refund. Online filers typically get refunds within about 10 days, compared to 21 days or more for those who file paper returns. You can check the status of your refund on the IRS's free app, IRS2Go, within 24 hours of e-filing.

What Is Your Filing Status?

If you're not married but have children or dependent relatives living with you, you may be able to file as a **head of household**. This status generally allows you to pay less tax than an ordinary single person. Married taxpayers—including same-sex couples—have the option to file as **married filing jointly** or **married filing separately** on both their state and federal returns. Usually married filing jointly results in a lower tax bill, but filing separately may have advantages, depending on your situation. Tax prep software walks you through a series of questions designed to determine your filing status. You can also take the quick IRS quiz "What Is My Filing Status?" at irs.gov/uac/what-is-my-filing-status.

If You Can't Pay

Even if you don't have enough money to pay the IRS the tax you owe, you should file your return by April 15. If you don't file, you'll be charged interest plus a monthly penalty of 5% of the amount of tax you owe, up to a maximum penalty of 25% of your total IRS debt.

To avoid these nasty charges, you can request a payment plan. Check out the Online Payment Agreement application at

---

A NOTE TO STUDENTS

Scholarships that pay for tuition, course-related fees, books, and supplies are not considered taxable income if you're working toward a degree. But if you received a scholarship to, say, study abroad for a year and the course work is not related to a degree, you must count the money you receive as income. And whether you're working toward a degree or not, the portion of a scholarship used to pay for room and board, travel, and research is usually considered taxable income. Your tax software will prompt you with questions to help sort this out. Or you can find details in the IRS's Tax Topic 421, *Scholarships, Fellowship Grants, and Other Grants*, at irs.gov/taxtopics/tc421.html; or Publication 970, *Tax Benefits for Education*, at irs.gov/pub/irs-pdf/p970.pdf.

irs.gov/individuals/online-payment-agreement-application. If you
file on time and request an installment plan, the IRS will still charge
you a monthly penalty—but at a much lower rate of 0.25% of the
balance due—plus interest and a one-time charge of $52 to set up
an automatic payment plan.

If You Need Help

Once you've filed your return, if you have a problem, go to IRS
.gov, or call the IRS at 800-829-1040. If you can't resolve the issue
on your own, or if you think the IRS is treating you unfairly, go
to irs.gov/advocate to find your local Taxpayer Advocate Service
office.

OWE MONEY TO THE IRS?
THE BEST WAYS TO PAY UNCLE SAM

If you're one of the millions of taxpayers who owes the IRS at
tax time, there are a few ways you can settle your tab. The best
choice is to have the money you owe transferred electronically
to the IRS from your checking or savings account before April
15. The IRS doesn't charge a fee for this, and most banks don't,
either (but check). For details, see irs.gov/payments.

The next best option is to use a debit card, which may result
in a small fee of less than $3. Avoid making your payment with
a credit card, since it may include "convenience fees" ranging
from 2% to 4% of your tax bill.

Of course, you can always mail the IRS an old-fashioned
check. (Tell the postal clerk that you want to send it "certified
mail, return receipt requested, please.") Just be sure you make
it payable to the United States Treasury, not the IRS.

MAXIMIZING YOUR
TAX BREAKS

Although the government wants citizens to pay their fair share, it does offer taxpayers ways to reduce the amount of their income that's subject to tax. This section will discuss the various tax breaks for which you may be eligible.

Exemptions and Deductions

One type of tax break available to taxpayers is an **exemption,** a specific amount ($4,050 in 2017) that can be subtracted from your taxable income. If you're single and have no children, you are allowed one personal exemption (as long as you're not being claimed as a dependent on someone else's tax return). If you're married and you file a joint return, you and your spouse are each entitled to a personal exemption. You also get an additional exemption for each child you have. If you earn a very high income, however, you may not be entitled to any exemptions.

The other type of tax break is a **deduction.** This is a specific expense that the government allows you to subtract from your taxable income, thus reducing the amount of tax you pay. (For an example of how this works, see the box on p. 258.) For instance, to encourage people to buy homes, the government allows taxpayers to deduct the interest they pay on their mortgages.

There are two distinct ways to take advantage of deductions. The simpler way is to take the **standard deduction,** which is a fixed dollar amount that all taxpayers are allowed to subtract from their income. Even if you don't participate in activities eligible for tax deductions, you still get the standard deduction. (You don't need this level of detail now, but technically, you subtract your standard deduction from a figure known as your **adjusted gross income,** or **AGI.** Your AGI is basically your gross income minus special deductions known as adjustments.) In 2017, the standard deduction for a single person was $6,350. For a married couple filing a joint return, the standard deduction was $12,700. These figures are adjusted each year for inflation.

A more complicated but potentially more rewarding method is to **itemize** your deductions. Itemizing means listing the specific "items" that are deductible according to current tax rules and then subtracting their cost from your adjusted gross income. If you choose to itemize, you cannot take the standard deduction. But there are a few deductions that you can take *without* itemizing. (See p. 257.)

Whether you should itemize or take the standard deduction depends on the specifics of your financial life. The following two sections describe some potential itemized deductions. The gist: If the total of your itemized expenses is greater than the standard deduction, you should itemize. Otherwise, take the standard deduction. Your tax software will ask you questions and figure out which method saves you more. If you *do* itemize, make sure you can substantiate with receipts the amounts you claim. If you are audited, this is the part of your return that the IRS is likely to scrutinize.

Some Straightforward Itemized Deductions

The rules concerning deductions, even those that seem straightforward, can be very tricky. They also change frequently. This list is only a starting point. Also, if you earn a high income—in 2017, more than $261,500 if you're single and $313,800 for married couples filing jointly—you'll face limits on some itemized deductions.

- **State and local income tax.** On your federal tax form you can deduct the state and local taxes you paid (including amounts withheld from your paycheck) over the course of the year. Because most people pay these taxes automatically out of their paycheck, you're likely to be eligible for this tax break.

- **Sales tax.** Interestingly, you have the option of deducting either state and local income tax *or* state and local sales tax on your federal return (but not both). For people who aren't subject to state income tax, such as Texans, it's a no-brainer: Deduct the sales tax and save money. There are two ways to go about this. You can deduct a standard amount, which is determined by your income, and add any sales tax you paid on certain big-ticket purchases, such as a car. Or, you could go with the more labor-intensive option: Save all your receipts for the entire year and add up the sales tax. To figure out whether it makes more sense to deduct income tax or sales tax, use the IRS's Sales Tax Deduction Calculator at irs.gov/individuals/sales-tax-deduction-calculator to determine how much sales tax you could deduct. Then, compare that figure to your state and local income taxes. (See p. 243.) Choose the higher amount.

- **Property tax.** If you own a home, you can deduct the property taxes (also known as real estate taxes) you pay. If you live in a co-op, it pays property taxes for you as part of your monthly maintenance fee; find out what your share of these taxes is so that you can deduct it.

- **Donations to charity.** If you make a contribution to a group that's considered a qualified tax-exempt organization by the IRS, you can deduct it. Qualified organizations include most religious institutions and educational organizations, and some alumni organizations. If you're unsure whether a particular organization qualifies, ask before you make a donation. If you donate clothes, furniture, or household items to the Salvation Army, for instance, you get to deduct their current market value. Write down a description of each item you donate and how much each is worth. (The IRS is very specific about this. That awesome sweater that you think is worth $50 would probably only bring a few dollars at Goodwill. Search online for donation value guidelines from thrift stores like Goodwill or the Salvation Army.) Make sure to get a receipt from the charity. For noncash donations worth more than $500, you'll have to fill out Form 8283 when you file your tax return. (If you use tax software, you'll be prompted with questions to determine if you need to file this form. If you don't use tax software, you can find it at Freefilefillableforms.com.) If your noncash donation is worth more than $5,000, you'll need to get a professional appraisal. You can also deduct some of the expenses you incur when you do volunteer work, as long as there's no significant element of recreation or vacation in the travel. If you volunteer at a senior center on weekends, for example, you can deduct some of your transportation costs.

If you get any "benefit" (theater tickets, a meal, the ubiquitous tote bag) in exchange for a contribution, you can deduct only the amount of your donation that exceeds the value of the benefit. Say you pay $200 to attend a fund-raising dinner for the Save the Lizards Foundation and the actual value of the dinner is $50; you can deduct $150 on your tax return. The receipt you get from your charity should specify any such "benefits" you have received.

- **Housing costs.** If you own a home, you can deduct the interest you pay on your mortgage. (You cannot deduct the portion of your mortgage payment that goes toward the principal.) You also may be able to deduct some or all of the premium on your private mortgage insurance if your adjusted gross income is $109,000 a year or less.

  Also, in the year you buy a home, you may be able to deduct the "points," even if these points were actually paid by the seller of the home. (See Chapter 7 for an explanation of points.) If you live in a co-op building, the co-op might pay interest on a mortgage for the building. If so, find out what your share of this interest is; you may be able to deduct it.

Some Trickier Itemized Deductions

Certain expenses are deductible only in specific situations. Below are some of those deductions. Again, remember that some are not available to taxpayers with very high incomes. Others have quirky rules. If you are unsure whether you are eligible for one of these deductions, check IRS Publication 529, *Miscellaneous Deductions*, at irs.gov/pub/irs-pdf/p529.pdf, consult your tax preparer, or, if you use tax prep software, let the software guide you.

- **Job-related expenses and other miscellaneous deductions.** This broad category includes a variety of costs. The basic rule is that they must be related to producing income. It's quite tricky, though. You can deduct the combined total of these expenses that exceeds 2% of your adjusted gross income. Here's how that works. Suppose your adjusted gross income is $60,000. You could not deduct the first $1,200 (2% of $60,000) of your "job-related and miscellaneous expenses," but you *could* deduct expenses beyond that amount. Below are examples of job-related expenses:

  » *Work-related home computers, cell phones, and other equipment.* If your employer requires you to purchase equipment, you may be able to deduct its full cost. You must be able to prove that your employer told you the item was necessary for your job, and that you use it more than 50% of the time for business. (Ask your boss to put it in writing.) Even if you don't meet this "50% rule," you may still be able to deduct the cost of the equipment over several years.

  » *Job-search expenses.* The IRS allows you to deduct costs related to a job search as long as you're looking for a position in your *present* occupation. If you're trying to change careers—say, you're a lifeguard looking to study taxidermy—you don't get the deduction. If you're currently out of work, the kind of job you held most recently is considered your occupation. Those looking for their first job don't get the tax break. The expenses you can deduct if you qualify include the fees of career counseling and employment or placement agencies; the cost of preparing your résumé; phone calls; and transportation costs (plus 50% of the cost of meals while traveling) for a long-distance job search. Items like clothes and shoes for interviews are not deductible. (For details on deducting your moving expenses once you get that job, see p. 263.)

» *Work-related educational expenses.* If you take a course that helps you maintain or improve the skills you use to perform your current job, you may be able to deduct your tuition and expenses. Also, if a course is required either by your employer or by law for you to keep your job, you may deduct any costs not reimbursed by your employer. But if you take a course to train for a new line of work or to meet the minimum educational requirements of your profession, you can't deduct the tuition. So a financial analyst can't deduct the cost of taking a cooking course. But a teacher may be able to deduct the tuition of a course on new classroom technology. Same goes for a digital marketer who takes a course on the hot new social media platform.

» *Mandatory uniforms for work.* Suits and ties aren't deductible, but nurse uniforms, firefighter uniforms, postal uniforms, safety shoes and glasses, hard hats, and work gloves are. (If you're a computer programmer who wears a hard hat to work for kicks, it doesn't count.) If your employer reimburses you for these expenses, however, you can't deduct them.

» *Unreimbursed business travel and entertainment expenses.* If you pay these costs yourself, there are very specific rules about how much you're allowed to deduct. In general, you must keep a detailed log of your trips and be prepared to prove the business purpose of each expense.

» *Union dues and initiation fees, professional and business association dues, and job-related subscriptions to trade publications and professional journals.* Make sure to deduct these expenses if you are not reimbursed for them by your employer.

» *Tax preparation fees.* Even though these aren't directly related to work, you can deduct the cost of tax-related software and tax publications. You can also deduct money you pay to a tax preparer.

• **Medical expenses.** You can deduct out-of-pocket medical and dental expenses, for yourself or any dependent, that are greater than 10% of your adjusted gross income. Include premiums you pay for medical insurance, co-payments for doctor visits, the cost of birth control pills or cigarette-quitting programs, prescription medicines not covered by your health plan, and transportation needed for medical care.

• **Losses due to theft and disasters.** You're allowed to deduct the cost of items you lose in a burglary, fire, or other disaster that exceed 10% of your adjusted gross income and are not covered by insurance. The first $100 of losses above the 10% threshold is not deductible.

Some Exceptions: Deductions You Can Take Without Itemizing

As I've explained, you generally have a choice to itemize or take the standard deduction. Most deductions have to be itemized, and their total must be greater than the standard deduction for them to be of any use. But there are exceptions to that rule. Here are three of the most important deductions you can claim even if you take the standard deduction:

• **Contributions to a traditional IRA.** The money you contribute to a traditional IRA (not a Roth IRA) may be deductible if you aren't eligible for an employer-sponsored retirement

FIGURING OUT THE VALUE OF A DEDUCTION

Your tax bracket plays a major role in determining how much a deduction is worth. Suppose you obtained a mortgage to buy a home. Assume in the first year the interest payments you made on the mortgage totaled $10,000. You would be able to subtract, or deduct, that $10,000 from your taxable income for that year. If you're in the 15% tax bracket, that would mean saving yourself $1,500 (15% of $10,000). But if you're in the 25% tax bracket, the $10,000 tax deduction would be worth $2,500 (25% of $10,000). Compare the cash value of your deduction with the standard deduction to figure out whether it's worth itemizing.

plan or if your income falls below a certain level. (See Chapter 6.) If you're in the 25% tax bracket, a deductible $5,500 IRA contribution will save you $1,375 on your tax bill. (The math: $5,500 times 0.25 equals $1,375.) If you're eligible, it's deductible whether you itemize or you take the standard deduction. When you fill out your taxes, you'll be prompted to include IRA contributions. One nice feature about the IRA deduction is that you technically don't have to make your contribution during the tax year in question: The deadline for contributing to an IRA is the same as the deadline for filing your taxes for that year, usually April 15 of the following year.

An aside about 401(k)s: Although you do not have to pay income tax on the money you contribute to traditional 401(k)s, you don't list 401(k) contributions on your tax return because your employer has already subtracted your contributions from your gross pay throughout the year. The net salary on the W-2 you receive already reflects your contribution.

- **Student loan interest.** You are entitled to deduct the *interest* payments you make on your federal and private student loans, up to a maximum of $2,500 in interest per year. The bad news is that you can't deduct money that goes toward repaying the principal. If your **modified adjusted gross income (MAGI)**—which is your adjusted gross income with some deductions, including student loan interest payments, added back in—is at least $80,000 as a single person or $165,000 as a married couple, you're not eligible for this deduction. Note that there's something of a "marriage penalty" when it comes to deducting student loan interest: As a couple, you're only allowed to write off the same amount as an individual (up to $2,500). If you paid $600 or more in interest, you'll get Form 1098-E from your student loan servicer; if you paid less than $600, get in touch with your servicer and ask for the exact amount you paid. For more information, see IRS Publication 970, *Tax Benefits for Education*, at irs.gov/pub/irs-pdf/p970.pdf.

IF YOU CHANGE YOUR NAME, TELL SOCIAL SECURITY

The IRS checks to make sure that the name and Social Security number you list on your tax return match the records of the Social Security Administration. If you change your name—for any reason—without alerting the folks at Social Security, the IRS may delay sending you the refund check you are due. What's more, you might not get credit for the money your employer deducts from your paycheck and sends to Social Security. Go to ssa.gov/forms/ss-5.pdf and submit Form SS-5 to register your new name.

- **Tuition and fees.** The IRS may let you deduct up to $4,000 a year in higher education tuition and fees (including graduate school), provided your modified adjusted gross income is no more than $80,000 as a single person or $160,000 as a married couple. You have to choose between this deduction and one of the education credits available. (See the next section.) You can switch between them from year to year, but you can't take both at one time. Do the math to see which way saves you more money. Obviously, if your income is too high to be eligible for the credits, the deduction is better than nothing at all. Once again, you can find all the details in Publication 970, *Tax Benefits for Education,* at irs.gov/pub/irs-pdf/p970.pdf.

Making the Most of Your Tax Credits

Tax credits are special breaks that are subtracted directly from the tax you owe to the IRS. That's different from a deduction, which only reduces the amount of your taxable income. To put it another way, tax credits can be worth a lot more than tax deductions. But, like deductions, tax credits can change or expire, so check the IRS publications recommended below. If you use tax software, it will help you determine which of the following credits you should take advantage of:

- **Saver's credit.** If your adjusted gross income is $31,000 or less as a single person or $62,000 or less as a married couple filing jointly in 2017, you can get a credit for contributing to a 401(k), IRA, or other retirement account. This is in addition to any other tax break you get from your 401(k) or IRA. For more details, see p. 157.

- **Earned income credit.** In 2017, if you're single, age 25 or older, and earn less than $15,010 (and no one can claim you as a dependent) you may be eligible for this special tax break of up to $510. The income cutoff for married couples without kids is $20,600. If you have a child, your adjusted gross income must be less than $39,617 (single) or $45,207 (married filing jointly) to qualify for a credit of up to $3,400; if you have two children, you must earn less than $45,007 (single) or $50,597 (married filing jointly) for a credit of up to $5,616. For details on eligibility, go to irs.gov/credits-&-deductions /individuals/earned-income-tax-credit.

- **American Opportunity Tax Credit (AOTC).** If you're paying your way through college, you may be eligible for a tax credit of up to $2,500 a year during the first four years. You have to choose between this credit, the one below, and the tuition and fees deduction described on p. 260. The way it works: You get a tax credit for 100% of the first $2,000 you spend on tuition, books, and supplies, plus 25% of the next $2,000. If the amount you're eligible for is more than the taxes you owe, you can get up to $1,000 as a refund.

- **Lifetime Learning Credit.** This credit is worth up to $2,000, and it helps students who have already claimed four years of the AOTC or who are not pursuing a degree program but are acquiring new skills. Since there's no limit to the number of times this credit can be claimed, it's a real boon if you are a perpetual grad student or you just want to take up basket weaving. You have to choose between this credit, the credit above, and the tuition and fees deduction described on p. 260. Here's how it works: You may claim up to 20% of the first $10,000 of eligible tuition and fees as long as your income is less than $56,000 (single) or $112,000 (married filing jointly). For details, check out IRS Publication 970, *Tax Benefits for Education*, at irs.gov /pub/irs-pdf/p970.pdf.

- **Child tax credit.** You can take a tax credit of up to $1,000 for each dependent child who's under 17 at the end of the tax year, including stepchildren and foster children. The credit begins to phase out for singles with incomes over $75,000 and married couples earning more than $110,000. For more information, go to irs.gov/pub/irs-pdf/p972.pdf and check out Publication 972, *Child Tax Credit*, or take the quiz "Is My Child a Qualifying Child for the Child Tax Credit?" at irs.gov/uac/is-my-child-a-qualifying-child-for-the-child-tax -credit.

- **Child care credit.** If you have a child under the age of 13 and you pay someone for child care while you work, the IRS allows you to subtract as much as 35% of your child care expenses (up to $3,000 for one child, or $6,000 for two or more) from your tax debt. You may be eligible for this credit even if you earn a high income. Expenses that qualify include the cost of day care and preschool, after-school care, and summer day camp. For details, see IRS Publication 503, *Child and Dependent Care Expenses*, at irs.gov/pub/irs-pdf /p503.pdf. You can also receive a credit for a sitter, but you will have to pay your sitter totally by the book. That means paying the required employment taxes, such as Medicare and Social Security, for your child care worker. For details, refer to Publication 926, *Household Employer's Tax Guide*, at irs.gov/pub/irs-pdf/p926.pdf.

- **Adoption credit.** If you adopt a child, you may be allowed a credit for specified adoption expenses up to $13,570 in 2017, even if you earn a high income.

- **Premium tax credit.** As of this writing, if you purchase your own health insurance on either your state or the federal health insurance exchange, you may be eligible for a tax credit to help pay for part of your premiums. Credits are available to people with incomes between 100% and 400% of the poverty level for your state. You can get an idea of the size of your credit by using the Kaiser Family Foundation's calculator at kff.org/interactive/subsidy-calculator. You'll need to file Form 8962 to determine your credit. For more information, see IRS Publication 974, *Premium Tax Credit (PTC)*, at irs.gov/pub/irs-pdf/p974.pdf.

- **Home energy credit.** If you own a home and install solar panels or a small wind turbine on your property, you could earn a credit for 30% of the cost. A typical $18,000 solar energy system could net a credit of $5,400. There are no income limits. For details, check out *Instructions for Form 5695: Residential Energy Credits* at irs.gov/pub/irs-pdf /i5695.pdf.

Nine Tax Moves That Could Save You Money

Here are some additional ideas that might work for you come tax time:

1. **Bunch your deductions into one year.** If you don't have enough deductible expenses to make it worth your while to itemize this year, take the standard deduction now and put off additional deductible expenditures until next year. For example, make your charitable contributions next January rather than this December.

2. **See if you can deduct your moving costs.** If you relocated for a full-time job, you may be able to deduct the cost of your move, including transportation, packing, and shipping costs. You don't have to itemize in order to get this deduction. But eligibility rules are tricky. If it's your first job, your new workplace must be 50 miles or more from your old home to get the deduction. If you're changing jobs, the distance between your *new job* and your *old home* must be at least 50 miles more than the distance between your *old job* and your *old home*. (I know. This is outrageously complicated.) You must also work full-time in your new location for at least 39 weeks during your first 12 months there. Special rules apply if you're self-employed. If you recently graduated and didn't have a job at school, your moving expenses may be deductible if your new job is at least 50 miles from your college residence (on or off campus). For a specific explanation

of eligibility, check out IRS Publication 521, *Moving Expenses*, at irs.gov/pub/irs-pdf/p521.pdf.

3. **Figure out if you'd save money by filing jointly or separately.** If you work and your spouse doesn't, it generally pays to file a joint return. If you and your spouse both work, you should figure your tax on a joint return and on separate married returns to see which way saves money. (Annoying, but doing this could save you a lot.) Filing separate married returns may make sense if you have many deductible expenses that are subject to an "adjusted gross income threshold." Say you and your spouse each earns about the same amount of money but you have exceptionally high medical bills. If you file a joint return, your medical bills would have to exceed 10% of your *combined* adjusted gross income in order to be deductible. If you file separately, you can deduct medical costs that exceed 10% of your *own* adjusted gross income (about half the combined income, so you get to deduct more). Of course, all of this information applies equally to same- or opposite-sex married couples.

4. **Check your withholding.** As I detailed on p. 240, you filled out a W-4 when you started your job. Changes in your personal life, as well as changes in the tax law, may result in your having too little or too much tax withheld from your paycheck. If you get married, buy a home, have a baby, or experience any other major financial life change, you should reevaluate your withholding.

   If you receive a big refund from the IRS, you should probably increase the number of withholding allowances you take. Although receiving a cash windfall from the IRS feels great, it isn't a smart financial move. A refund occurs after you've given the IRS too much money. The problem is that the IRS doesn't pay you interest for the excess money withheld from your paycheck during the year. And although some people say that overwithholding is a good forced savings program, I don't agree. You're better off withholding the right amount and funneling small amounts of cash into your savings account automatically throughout the year. (See Chapter 2 for details.) That way you get forced savings *plus* earnings.

There are other ways that adjusting your withholding can help you. If you just graduated from college, for instance, and you'll be working for less than 12 months this calendar year, request a special withholding method known as a part-year option. Then your employer will calculate your withholding based on the number of months you actually earn money this year, rather than basing the withholding on your annual salary. This will prevent overwithholding.

A warning: Don't claim more allowances than you deserve. This will result in your employer's withholding too little tax during the year, and you will owe money at tax time. At minimum you must pay the lesser of two amounts: either 90% of the tax owed in the current year or the amount you paid the previous year. If you don't, you'll be hit with a penalty. To find out how much you should have withheld, use the IRS Withholding Calculator at irs.gov/individuals/irs-withholding-calculator. If you learn that you're withholding too little or too much, ask your employer to adjust the number of withholding allowances on a new W-4.

5.   **Take advantage of state and local deductions.** Some states, including Alabama and Louisiana, allow you to deduct some of your federal income tax on your state return. Some states allow you to deduct the license fees for your car, contributions you make to 529 college savings plans, or charitable donations. And most states give a tax break to homeowners who paid local property taxes. (This is in addition to the federal tax break you

get on property taxes.) Note that state tax breaks vary widely and change often, so check the website of your state's tax department.

6. **Consider taxes when you invest.** As I've said repeatedly, IRAs and 401(k)s are great tax-favored ways to save. If your tax rate is 25% or higher, you may also want to consider investments that offer some tax advantages, such as tax-free money market funds and I Bonds. While it doesn't make sense to choose an investment solely for the tax break, it's a factor to consider.

7. **Take advantage of tax-favored employee benefits.** If you work for a company that offers you the chance to use a flexible spending account (FSA) to pay for child care or for medical expenses that aren't covered by your insurance, sign up. Same thing with health savings accounts (HSAs), which cover out-of-pocket medical expenses. (For details on both types of accounts, see Chapter 8.) And, of course, contribute the maximum you can to your 401(k).

8. **If you're a self-employed performer, see if you're eligible for a special tax break.** Listen up, musicians, actors, and other performing artists: Whether you itemize deductions or not, you may get your first big break from the IRS. That's because you're allowed to deduct business-related expenses (the cost of acting classes, head shots, costumes, etc.) from your income, if your adjusted gross income is $16,000 or less before this deduction. The rules about who can deduct these expenses are complex, so check the details in *Instructions for Form 2106: Employee Business Expenses* at irs.gov/pub/irs-pdf/i2106.pdf.

9. **You may want to consider taxes before you choose your wedding date.** Okay, call me unromantic, but if you both have fairly high incomes, you might save hundreds of

dollars if you marry in January rather than December. That's because you may owe more in taxes by filing a joint return than by filing two single returns. The general rule is that if you and your betrothed earn about the same income, you will probably save money by marrying after the first of the year. If one of you earns much more than the other, it's generally better to get married before the end of the year and file jointly. The fact that married people sometimes pay more tax than singles is known as the **marriage penalty**. Congress has been promising to abolish it for years without following through, so don't hold off on your wedding plans in hopes of that happening.

DEDUCTIONS FOR THE SELF-EMPLOYED

If you work for yourself—that includes anyone who is launching a start-up or who makes a living as an independent consultant or freelancer—you may be eligible for some special deductions.

If you're self-employed, the companies you do contract or freelance work for probably do not withhold taxes from their payments to you. But you can't simply wait until the end of the year to pay the IRS. Instead, you will have to pay tax quarterly based on your estimated annual income. To calculate these taxes, use the Self Employment Tax Calculator at bankrate.com/calculators/tax-planning/self-employed-business-tax-calculator.aspx. For more information, check out the IRS Self-Employed Individuals Tax Center at irs.gov/businesses/small-businesses-&-self-employed/self-employed-individuals-tax-center. If you still have questions, it's probably a good idea to see a tax preparer.

As a self-employed person, you're eligible for many additional deductions. You can deduct half the Social Security and Medicare taxes you pay, for example, and you're allowed to deduct all of your medical insurance premiums. You can deduct business travel expenses, whether or not they exceed 2% of your adjusted gross income. And you may be able to deduct the cost of office supplies and equipment. For in-depth information, see IRS Publication 334, *Tax Guide for Small Business*, at irs.gov/pub/irs -pdf/p334.pdf.

If you work from home, you might even be able to deduct your *home* office expenses. Keep in mind, though, that the IRS has very strict rules regarding home offices. You must use the space that you designate as your home office exclusively for business and on a regular basis. If your desk is in your living room, for example, you will have trouble proving that you use that portion of your home exclusively for work. You can find more information in IRS Publication 587, *Business Use of Your Home*, at irs.gov /pub/irs-pdf/p587.pdf.

As a self-employed person, one of your smartest tax (and savings) moves is to open an IRA. But as of 2017, the most you can contribute annually to an IRA is $5,500. If you have more money to put aside, consider contributing to one of the special types of retirement plans for self-employed people: a SIMPLE IRA, a SEP-IRA, or an individual 401(k). For more on these, see p. 154, and review the rules in IRS Publication 560, *Retirement Plans for Small Business*, at irs.gov/pub/irs-pdf/p560.pdf.

GETTING YOUR TAX LIFE IN ORDER

Probably the most daunting part of the tax process is organizing your financial and tax documents. This section offers a rundown of the various tax forms you may need. It also includes a guide to help you avoid getting lost in a maze of paper or digital files.

A Rundown of the Main Tax Forms

If you use software to file your taxes online, you don't necessarily need to know the names of the forms you are required to fill out. Instead, you'll answer a series of questions and the software will

Figure 9–2

WHAT, ME ITEMIZE?

A lot of young people don't think it's worth the effort to itemize. Take Jennifer, who recently left her job at an architecture firm in Denver to work for a design company in New York City. (Moving costs: $2,000.) Before moving, she donated three bags of clothing, a couch, a dresser, and a bed to the Salvation Army. (Total value: $2,000.) Her salary is $50,000. She bought a computer ($2,000) and a scanner ($200) so she can do more work at home. (Her boss told her to buy them so that he could email her work off-hours from his summer house.) Jennifer uses the computer and scanner exclusively for work. In addition, she paid $2,000 in interest on her student loans in the past year. To understand why it makes sense for her to itemize her deductions on the IRS tax form 1040 rather than take the standard deduction on the 1040A or 1040EZ, see below:

	1040EZ	1040A	1040
Total Income	$50,000	$50,000	$50,000
(minus) Student loan interest payments	0	2,000	2,000
(minus) Moving expenses	0	0	2,000
ADJUSTED GROSS INCOME (AGI)	50,000	48,000	46,000
Personal exemption	4,050	4,050	4,050
Charitable contributions	0	0	2,000
State and local taxes	0	0	4,196
Miscellaneous and business expenses*	0	0	1,280
Other itemized expenses	0	0	0
Total itemized deductions or standard deduction (whichever is greater)	6,350	6,350	7,476
EXEMPTION PLUS DEDUCTIONS	10,400	10,400	11,526
TAXABLE INCOME (AGI minus personal exemption and deductions)	39,600	37,600	34,474
FEDERAL TAX OWED	5,639	5,174	4,708

* Here's how you get $1,280 in miscellaneous and business expenses in the 1040 column. First, you calculate that 2% of Jennifer's adjusted gross income ($46,000) is $920. Then you subtract that amount from the $2,200 ($2,000 for the computer and $200 for the scanner) in total miscellaneous and business expenses. Original source: Ernst & Young LLP determine which forms you need and if, for example, you will save more money by itemizing or by taking the standard deductions. But if you use the IRS's Free File Fillable Forms (different from the hand-holding available from the IRS's Free File tool) or you just want a better understanding of the taxes you file, check out IRS Tax Topic 352, *Which Form—1040, 1040A, or 1040EZ?*, at irs .gov/taxtopics/tc352.html. Here are the main forms you might need:

- **1040EZ.** So named because it's the easiest to fill out. It's generally for single people, or couples filing jointly, with taxable income less than $100,000. To use this form, you must also earn less than $1,500 in taxable interest (from, say, a savings account or an investment). You can't itemize your deductions on the EZ; it's meant for people who are best off with the standard deduction. Two especially good reasons *not* to use the EZ: You can't deduct your student loan interest payments or your contribution to a traditional IRA.

- **1040A.** Almost as simple as the EZ form. To use it, your total taxable income must be less than $100,000, but your taxable interest and dividends can be more than $1,500. This form does not allow you to itemize, but it does permit you to claim some tax credits and take deductions for student loan interest payments, IRA contributions, and tuition and fees.

- **1040.** More complicated, but use this form if you think the value of your itemized deductions is larger than the standard deduction. Also, if your income is $100,000 or more (or you receive certain types of income like self-employment earnings), you are *required* to fill out the 1040. To itemize on the 1040, you must fill out an additional form called **Schedule A,** which will help you figure out the value of your itemized deductions. (For an example of how filling out the 1040 and itemizing can work to your advantage, see Figure 9–2 on p. 269.)

Tax-Related Records: What to Keep and Why

Good record keeping is important when it comes to filing your taxes even if you use a tax preparer. By keeping careful, accurate records ideally in both electronic and hard copy, you'll save time and money. For general advice on setting up a financial filing system, refer back to Figure 2–3 on p. 24. In this section, I will go into greater detail on the tax-related items you should keep and why it's important to keep them.

- **Tax returns: 2017, 2018, 2019, etc.** This includes a copy of your tax return (after you file it), income statements from your employers (W-2s, which also show your 401(k) contributions), and income statements from your bank, fund company, and other sources (1099s). If you are audited, the IRS can request up to three years' worth of tax records. (Actually, if you've underreported your income by 25% or more, the IRS can ask for returns from six years back. And if you've committed fraud, there's no time limit.) If a decade from now the IRS claims that you didn't file, you'll want to be able to prove that you did. You may also need them to apply for a mortgage or other loan, or, in rare cases, as proof of the Social Security benefits you're due.

- **IRAs.** Keep records that indicate when your IRA contributions were made, the amount you invested, the date you opened the IRA, and the source of any money you rolled over from an employer retirement plan into your IRA. This documentation will be useful when you start withdrawing the money upon retirement. It's especially important to hold on to copies of IRS Form 8606, which you'll need to file each year if you make nondeductible contributions to a traditional IRA. When you withdraw money from a nondeductible traditional IRA, you won't be taxed on the money you contributed, only on the earnings. Also, hold on to a copy of the special form (Form 5329) that you'll need to file if you make a penalty-free withdrawal from your IRA, as described in Chapter 6.

- **Home purchase.** Keep the closing statement and any other documents related to the purchase of your home, including mortgage-related documents. You may need these for tax purposes when you sell your home.

- **Home improvements.** A home improvement, also known as a **capital improvement,** is a renovation that increases your home's value. If you own a home, save all receipts related to home improvements. Although you can't deduct these expenses now, you can add them to the original purchase price of your home when you're ready to sell; this reduces the "reported gain" (selling price minus the amount you paid for the house) and therefore the amount of tax you pay on the sale. Routine repairs like painting don't count, but adding a room, putting on a new roof, installing a new toilet, paneling walls, or retiling a floor do.

- **Home sale.** Let's say you sell your home and make a profit. If you're single, you don't have to pay tax on the profit if it's less than $250,000. If you're married filing jointly, you don't have to pay tax if it's under $500,000. In either case, the home must have been your principal residence for at least two of the previous five years. Though these numbers may sound high, you need to hang on to those home improvement receipts. That's because if you buy low and housing prices soar, these records could help you snag a sweet tax break—just keep the receipts for seven years *after the sale,* in case you're audited. (For more information, consult IRS Publication 530, *Tax Information for Homeowners,* at irs.gov/pub/irs-pdf/p530.pdf; or Publication 523, *Selling Your Home,* at irs.gov/pub/irs-pdf/p523.pdf.)

- **Mutual funds and ETFs.** Most funds provide you with a year-end statement that indicates how many shares you bought and sold during the year, and the prices of those shares. You're taxed on any gain you made from selling shares, and you get a tax break on losses. That's why you need to keep the statements. The good news: For transactions from 2012 on, your fund company must keep track of them for you. For older transactions, there are several methods you can use—and some are more advantageous than others. To figure out which method is the best for you, refer to IRS Publication 550, *Investment Income and Expenses*, at irs.gov/pub/irs-pdf/p550.pdf.

- **Stocks and bonds.** For stocks purchased in 2011 and later, brokerages are required to keep track of your gains and losses for you. But if you own individual stocks and bonds purchased before 2011, you will need to keep track of this information yourself. So make sure you save brokerage statements with information on your older stocks.

- **Business-related expenses (unreimbursed).** Save appropriate credit card receipts, entertainment and meal receipts, and receipts for tolls, taxis, parking, gas, car maintenance, tips, union dues, and subscriptions. If you plan to deduct the cost of a laptop or smartphone, in addition to your receipts keep records that detail when you use the equipment for work and when you use it for leisure activity. If you're self-employed, save all receipts from business-related travel. Also, keep a detailed spending record when you go on business trips.

- **Charitable contributions.** Save receipts from charities you donate to as well as any relevant bank or credit card statements.

- **Child care/dependent care expenses.** Hold on to documents indicating the dates and amounts of various fees you paid to an individual or a center to take care of your child so you could work or look for work. (Sorry, the fifty bucks and unlimited ice cream you give the sitter for a night out doesn't count.) Also, keep a log of the cost of meals and lodging expenses paid to a child care worker who lives in your home. To be able to claim the child care credit, you must make sure to pay the required employment taxes—Social Security, Medicare, and unemployment—for your employee. Keep strict records that prove these taxes were paid.

- **Education.** Save records of tuition and fees paid for school, as well as interest payments on your loans, to back up any deductions or credits you claim.

- **Health insurance.** As of this writing, you're required to report whether you had health insurance for the year on your tax return. While you don't have to send proof to the IRS, you should keep your own records. These include insurance cards or payroll statements that show health insurance contributions, as well as Form 1095, which you'll get each year from the government health insurance exchange, your insurer, or your employer. If you took a premium tax credit, you'll need to save proof of the amount you paid. (See p. 262 for more on the premium tax credit.) If you did not have coverage, you will likely owe a penalty when you file your taxes.

- **Medical expenses (unreimbursed).** If you pay any medical costs that your health insurance doesn't reimburse you for, keep the receipts. (If you pay all or part of the premiums on your health insurance, keep track of those expenses as well.) If at the end of the year these expenses exceed 10% of your adjusted gross income, you can deduct the portion that's over this threshold.

- **Miscellaneous deductions.** This catchall file should include receipts for all possible deductions, including tax preparation, job search activities, and certain education expenses. Go through it at the end of the year to determine what is and is not actually deductible.

- **Mortgage interest payments.** If you own a home, keep your 1098 form. This annual statement from your lender indicates how much interest and principal you paid on your mortgage. It may also tell you how much property tax you paid. Co-op owners generally receive a 1098 indicating the portion of the interest they paid on the building's mortgage. Keep your private mortgage insurance (PMI) documents in this file as well. You may be able to deduct the premiums.

- **Property and real estate tax.** The monthly mortgage payment you make to your lender probably includes your property taxes. Lenders typically forward the tax to your local taxing authority. At the end of the year, you'll receive a statement from your lender about the amount of property tax you paid. These payments are deductible, so hold on to these statements.

- **Police reports and insurance claims.** If you've been burglarized or had identity theft problems (see p. 69), save these documents. If you suffered major losses, you may be able to deduct the value of uninsured items.

DO YOU NEED A TAX PREPARER?

After you've done your own taxes, you will not only get a better sense of your financial life, but you'll also see how straightforward the process is thanks to tax software. But if you prefer to use a tax preparer going forward, find a good one. The most obvious—and inexpensive—choices are either big-name chains such as H&R Block or highly rated independent tax preparers in your neighborhood. (Check Yelp.com and other rating sites.) If your return is relatively simple, these preparers are fine. Keep in mind that the level of knowledge can vary dramatically. Look for a tax preparation business that operates year-round rather than one that's open just a few months during tax season. Ask friends and family members to recommend individual preparers. Most chain preparers allow you to request a specific person.

If you have a somewhat complicated return (for example, you recently launched a business or bought a home), you may want to find a preparer with more chops. One of the top credentials is **CPA**, which stands for **certified public accountant**. CPAs have to meet the toughest requirements to get licensed; they also can be expensive. You can generally find one by contacting your state's society of CPAs. Another, usually cheaper, option is an **enrolled agent**; the title refers to any preparer who has worked for the IRS as an auditor or in some similar job for five years or who has passed a difficult two-day exam. You can search for one at NAEA.org. (You can often find an enrolled agent at a chain preparer like H&R Block.) At the very least, find a preparer with a minimum of three years' experience filing returns. Tax attorneys are typically the most expensive alternative and are necessary only if you're in serious trouble with the IRS. Be sure to ask what your particular preparer charges; there may be different rates for different preparers at the same company.

Finally, no matter who fills out your forms, look over the paperwork carefully yourself. A recent undercover study by the Government Accountability Office found that only 2 out of 19 chain tax preparers calculated the correct refund. *You* are responsible for making sure all the information on your return is true and correct. Take the time to read it before you sign and submit it.

- Figure out your marginal tax rate. See Figure 9–1 on p. 245.

- Using tax software from sites like HRBlock.com, TurboTax .com, or TaxAct.com, fill out your tax forms as soon as you have your W-2 and other tax filing materials. If you're owed a refund, have it deposited directly into your bank account. If you owe money to the IRS, wait until early April to file so you can hang on to your cash as long as possible.

- If your adjusted gross income (AGI) is $64,000 or less, use the IRS's Free File software at irs.gov/freefile to file your federal return and possibly your state return at no cost.

- Take full advantage of the tax credits, deductions, and other breaks available to you. (See p. 251.) They are money in your pocket. With prompts from your tax software, you'll know what you qualify for and what you don't.

- If you're expecting a refund, have it deposited directly into your bank account. Your money should arrive within ten days. (If you owe money, authorize Uncle Sam to withdraw it from your account via irs.gov/payments.)

- If you received a big refund from the IRS, fill out a new W-4 form to adjust your withholding. (Consult the Tax Withholding Calculator at irs.gov/individuals/irs-withholding-calculator.) Since the IRS doesn't pay you interest on the money you overpay during the year, you're better off investing it.

- If you owe the IRS money but you can't afford to pay, file your return along with whatever you *can* afford by April 15 and set up an installment plan with the Online Payment Agreement tool at

irs.gov/individuals/online-payment-agreement-application.
You'll have to pay a penalty, but it won't be as stiff as the one for
late filing.

• If you're self-employed, pay your taxes quarterly. For details, visit
the Self-Employed Individuals Tax Center at irs.gov/businesses
/small-businesses-&-self-employed/self-employed-individuals
-tax-center.

10

MAKING THE MOST OF MILITARY BENEFITS

Know What You Deserve
If You Serve

I F Y O U A R E one of the millions who have served in the military, National Guard, or Reserve in the last few years, you've earned some benefits not available to civilians. And that's for good reason. You have made a huge sacrifice for the rest of us, and, frankly, I wish more was being done to thank you.

This chapter gives you an overview of the offerings. For further details, go to the National Military Family Association (Military family.org), Military OneSource (Militaryonesource.mil), and the Consumer Financial Protection Bureau's Office of Servicemember Affairs (cfpb.gov/servicemembers). These are all great resources for veterans and active service members alike.

To start, consider the following benefits:

EDUCATION PERKS

Whether you're thinking about going back to school or are already paying down college debt, make sure you know about these education benefits from the military:

- **Help paying off student loans.** If you went to college before joining, the military may pay off a third of the amount you borrowed in federal student loans or $1,500 (whichever is greater) for every year of active duty. There's a $65,000 cap for the Army and Navy, and $10,000 for the Air Force. The Marines don't offer this program. The types of loans paid back include Direct Loans (aka Staffords), Perkins Loans, and PLUS Loans. So if you borrowed $10,000 and served for two years, the military will cover $6,667. For more information, go to military.com/education. If you plan to pursue a long-term career in the military, you may also qualify for the Public Service Loan Forgiveness program and have your federal student debt wiped out after ten years of reduced monthly payments. (See p. 49 and visit studentaid.gov/publicservice.)

- **Breaks on tuition.** If you're considering going to college—or returning to it—after you serve, there are some important benefits that may help.

    First of all, you may be eligible for as much as $4,500 per year to pay for academic or technical college classes (including online courses) *while* you are serving. The rules vary by military branch, so visit military.com/education for details.

    If you have served since September 11, 2001, the Post-9/11 G.I. Bill may pay for some or all of your college costs *after* you leave the military. This funding covers four academic years, including tuition and fees, housing, books, and sometimes a moving allowance. After you put in 90 days of active duty in the armed services, National Guard, or Reserve, the government will pick up 40% of the cost of the most expensive public undergraduate school in your state. This percentage increases the longer you serve. After three years of active duty (or if you get a disability discharge), the G.I. Bill will pay 100% of the costs up to the price of your state's most expensive public school or $21,000 of private school costs. Some more expensive institutions (both private and out-of-state public universities) will also give you a discount to bring their tuition closer to what the government will pay—so make sure to ask about the "Yellow Ribbon Program"—but you'll probably still have some out-of-pocket costs.

The G.I. Bill will pay for many types of online courses, on-the-job training programs, flight school, apprenticeships, or other nonacademic programs, but not all of them. Check out inquiry.vba.va.gov to find out what programs are covered. Also go to military.com/education/gi-bill for more details about how to take advantage of your G.I. Bill benefits.

One warning: For-profit colleges have been known to aggressively recruit veterans in order to get their G.I. Bill money. Steer clear. These institutions often have poor graduation rates, meaning there's a high risk that you'll leave school *with* student debt for costs incurred beyond what the G.I. Bill pays—but *without* a diploma. To check if the school you're considering is for-profit, search the College Board website BigFuture.org. If it is, you should look for a not-for-profit alternative.

- **Additional college money.** Before you enlist (or reenlist), ask your military recruiter about the possibility of getting extra funding for your future education. Often known as an additional "college fund," "kicker," or "supplemental benefit" for education, it's money (as much as $950 per month) that the government will add to your other G.I. Bill benefits. Recipients are often people who score particularly well on their military entrance exam. But even if your score isn't particularly great, it doesn't hurt to ask.

FINANCIAL ASSISTANCE WITH YOUR HOME

If you're thinking of buying a place or you're having trouble making payments on an existing mortgage, these options may help:

- **A no-down-payment mortgage.** If you're considering buying a home, you may qualify for a no-money-down home loan under the Veterans Affairs (VA) loan program. Veterans generally must have served 24 consecutive months of active duty to take advantage of this deal. For the National Guard or Selected Reserve, the requirement is either six years of service or 90 days of active duty. And if you're currently on active duty, you must have been on it for at least 90 days in a row. This offer is available through lenders who make VA loans; not all lenders do. (See p. 175 for details, or visit benefits.va.gov/homeloans.) But tread carefully. As discussed in Chapter 7, "no-down-payment" loans can be really risky because you are borrowing the entire cost of the home, which means more debt and more interest in the end. Unless you have a very specific reason to buy a home right away, you should probably wait and try to build up a down payment of at least 10%.

- **Help in preventing foreclosure.** If you are having trouble making your mortgage payments, lenders are not allowed to foreclose on your home for twelve months after you leave the military. In addition, if you've been injured in active duty, you may be able to lower or delay your mortgage payments for up to six months while staying in your home, without incurring negative marks on your credit report. To understand your rights, go to knowyouroptions.com/military.

PROTECTING YOUR HEALTH AND YOUR ASSETS

Take care of yourself and your family with the following insurance benefits:

- **Inexpensive health care.** If you're currently in the military, you and your family are likely getting low-cost medical care under the military's health plan, Tricare. If you've left the military, you may be able to enroll in the VA health care system. Bear in mind that those with combat injuries are given higher priority. For tips on navigating the notoriously bureaucratic VA system, visit military.com/vahealth.

- **Deals on other insurance.** Companies like USAA (USAA .com) or Armed Forces Insurance (AFI.org) sell home and auto insurance to active-duty and former military personnel and their immediate families at what often is a good price. Also, if you're currently in active service or if you're a veteran, you're eligible to buy disability and life coverage at a relatively low cost through the government. Check out benefits.va.gov/insurance.

HELP PAYING OFF YOUR DEBT

In addition to the help you can get to pay off federal student loans, the following may offer some relief for your other debts:

- **Reduced payments on credit cards and loans.** The interest rates on debt you took on before you joined the military or were called up from the National Guard or Reserve may be capped at 6% while you are on active duty. This applies to credit card debt, private and federal student loans, and mortgages. But it won't happen automatically; you have to show your creditors that your service has affected your ability to pay your bills. You also may be able to get out of a rental or auto lease early without penalty. To figure out if you're eligible for these protections, and to make sure they are enforced, get free help from the legal assistance office at your institution by searching legalassistance.law.af.mil.

- **More lenient bankruptcy rules.** Declaring bankruptcy is never a wonderful choice, but you may be considering it if you're in deep financial trouble. Chapter 7 bankruptcy (which allows most of your debts to be forgiven) is generally available only to people who make below a certain income in their home states. But if you're a member of the National Guard or a reservist who has served at least 90 days of active duty, these income rules may not apply. Check out the legal advice site Nolo.com for more info on the bankruptcy rules for military families, and also see p. 74 for general advice on bankruptcy.

SUPPORT FOR YOUR FAMILY

Make sure that you are familiar with the following family benefits:

- **Family leave.** If you get seriously injured on military duty, members of your immediate family may be able to take up to 26 weeks off in a 12-month period to care for you without jeopardizing their jobs. (Unfortunately, they won't be paid for that time.) Women serving in the military can go home for at least 12 weeks of paid maternity leave. A married, active-duty service member whose spouse gives birth can go home for 10 days of parental leave. These maternity and parental leaves do not count against the 30 days of annual leave earned by every active-duty service member.

- **Child care.** You can usually get child care at military facilities for kids up to age 12, with the cost based on your family's income level. If you are stationed too far from these child care services, or you're on a waiting list, you may qualify for the military's fee assistance program to help pay for a private provider. For details on applying, visit usa.childcareaware.org/military.

- **Rights for same-sex couples.** The military grants same-sex married couples the same benefits as heterosexual married couples. Plus, gay and lesbian service members assigned overseas and looking to tie the knot can be granted up to 10 extra days off if they need to travel to a location that allows same-sex marriage. (This time off needs to be approved by a commanding officer.)

GUIDANCE ON LEGAL, TAX, AND PERSONAL FINANCE MATTERS

If you need help with day-to-day money or legal matters, these options may work for you:

- **Free legal assistance.** Service members and their families have free access to lawyers at the legal assistance office wherever they are stationed. Visit legalassistance.law.af.mil to find an office near you. An attorney can review a contract or a lease, notarize a legal document, help you draft a power of attorney document so that your spouse can act on your behalf while you're away, or make sure you are granted some of the other military benefits listed in this chapter. Legal assistance offices aren't able to help with certain issues, such as serious criminal cases. They *can* give you a referral to a civilian attorney, whom you will have to pay. If you can't afford a civilian lawyer's fees, ask your legal assistance office to refer you instead to the American Bar Association's Military Pro Bono Project (Militaryprobono .org), which may connect you to an attorney who will take your case for free.

- **Personal finance help.** See if your facility offers free personal finance classes, as well as counseling to help you fix your credit record or make a plan to pay off debt if you're behind on payments. You can select "Personal Financial Management Services" at militaryinstallations.dod.mil to find the nearest location to visit. Or call 800-342-9647 for free counseling from service members resource hub Military OneSource.

- **Job placement after your service.** The Veterans' Employment and Training Service (VETS) is an independent government agency offering free help to service members seeking civilian jobs. You can get assistance with résumé writing and interviewing skills, as well as job placement counseling. Visit dol .gov/vets to locate the nearest VETS office.

- **Tax support.** Service members and their families can get free in-person tax advice, plus help with preparation and filing, via militaryonesource.mil/financial-and-legal/taxes. And here's a helpful rule for active-duty service members: If you are from a state without an income tax (Florida, for instance), you can continue to file your taxes as a legal resident of that state (and pay no state income tax) no matter where you serve.

SECURING YOUR SAVINGS

Consider these ways to plan for the future:

- **Combat-related benefits.** All active-duty, National Guard, and Reserve service members can earn a guaranteed interest rate of 10% on savings up to $10,000 while deployed. The rate extends for 90 days after you get home. Check out the Department of Defense Savings Deposit Program at www.dfas.mil/militarymembers/payentitlements/sdp.html. In addition, the salary you receive while deployed in a combat zone is not subject to federal tax. Finally, the sad reality of military life is that people die. The immediate family of active-duty personnel killed in the line of duty is entitled to receive $100,000 tax-free. For other programs you and your family should be aware of, visit military.com/benefits /survivor-benefits.

- **Tax-favored retirement savings.** Unfortunately, the government's 401(k)-like account, known as the Thrift Savings

Plan, does not currently offer matching contributions for most service members, though this is set to change in 2018. For that reason, until then, you may be better off with a Roth IRA, so see Chapter 6. If you're a reservist called to active duty for at least 180 days, you can take early distributions from your IRA or 401(k) without paying the usual 10% penalty, although you will have to pay any tax owed. (For more details about retirement savings, see Chapter 6.)

• **A long-term pension.** Although many new entrants to the military aren't sure how long they will stay, it's worth knowing that military personnel who serve at least twenty years can draw **retirement pay.** This translates into a pension that starts at 40% to 50% of your preretirement basic pay and is adjusted for inflation thereafter. (Unfortunately, if you leave before the twenty years is up, you don't get any pension at all.) Serve for forty years and your pension can equal 100% of your preretirement income.

FINANCIAL CRAMMING

- The military offers numerous education benefits, including money to repay federal student loans as well as tuition help for further schooling. See military.com/education.

- For deals on home or auto insurance, check out USAA (USAA.com) or Armed Forces Insurance (AFI.org). Visit benefits.va.gov/insurance to shop for low-cost disability and life insurance from the government.

- Service members and their families have access to free, in-person counseling on legal, tax, and general personal finance issues. Check out legalassistance.law.af.mil and militaryonesource.mil/financial-and-legal/taxes, and visit militaryinstallations.dod.mil and select "Personal Financial Management Services."

- If you're a reservist called up to active duty and you have debt, ask the legal assistance office to help you apply to have the interest rates on credit card debt, student loans, and mortgages capped temporarily at 6%.

- You may be able to get a guaranteed interest rate of 10% on your savings up to $10,000 while you're deployed and for another 90 days after you return. Visit www.dfas.mil/militarymembers/payentitlements/sdp.html.

FURTHER READING

IF YOU'VE READ through this entire tome, congratulations! You have all the basic information you need to enjoy a prosperous financial life. If you just can't get enough, below are some very selective recommendations. These are the books I would tell my friends to read if they wanted to know more about various topics. I have also included a handful of websites that may interest you.

BOOKS

Behavioral Economics

Belsky, Gary, and Thomas Gilovich. *Why Smart People Make Big Money Mistakes and How to Correct Them: Lessons from the Life-Changing Science of Behavioral Economics.* New York: Simon & Schuster, 2010. One of my favorite books on behavioral economics—both fun and informative to read.

Dunn, Elizabeth, and Michael Norton. *Happy Money: The Science of Happier Spending.* New York: Simon & Schuster, 2014. It's like *The Happiness Project* for personal finance.

Thaler, Richard H., and Cass R. Sunstein. *Nudge: Improving Decisions About Health, Wealth, and Happiness.* New York: Penguin, 2009. Two distinguished professors take a fascinating look into how tiny interventions can help you save money and enhance your life.

Investing

Malkiel, Burton G. *A Random Walk Down Wall Street: The Time-Tested Strategy for Successful Investing.* New York: W. W. Norton, 2016. This updated classic is a must-read for anyone who wants to learn more about investing.

Tobias, Andrew. *The Only Investment Guide You'll Ever Need*. New York: Mariner, 2016. An excellent (and witty) overview of key investment concepts.

Student Loans

Chany, Kalman A., with Geoff Martz. *Paying for College Without Going Broke*. New York: The Princeton Review, 2016. A comprehensive primer on college financing issues.

Kantrowitz, Mark, and David Levy. *Filing the FAFSA: The Edvisors Guide to Completing the Free Application for Federal Student Aid*. Las Vegas: Edvisors Network, 2015. A step-by-step guide that demystifies this tricky financial aid form—helpful for undergrad and graduate students and their parents. (Free download available at edvisors .com/fafsa/book/user-info.)

Taxes

The following two books are excellent tax guides. Make sure to get the most current editions!

Cohen, Gary N., et al. *EY Tax Guide*. Hoboken, NJ: Wiley, 2016.

Eiss, Elliott, et al. *J. K. Lasser's Your Income Tax*. Hoboken, NJ: Wiley, 2016.

Miscellaneous

Clifford, Denis. *Quick & Legal Will Book*. Berkeley: Nolo, 2014. A good resource if you're thinking of writing a will—includes all the legal forms you'll need.

Howell, Terry. *The Military Advantage*. Annapolis, MD: Naval Institute Press, 2016. With a new edition out each year, this book surveys all the latest military benefits including health care, scholarships, and post-service job placement, plus some little-known discounts.

Kobliner, Beth. *Make Your Kid a Money Genius (Even If You're Not)*. New York: Simon & Schuster, 2017. My guide shows parents how to teach their kids the financial facts of life at every age, from 3 to 23.

Leonard, Robin, and Margaret Reiter. *Solve Your Money Troubles: Debt, Credit & Bankruptcy*. Berkeley: Nolo, 2013. Packed with vital information, plus sample letters to help you negotiate with creditors and budget worksheets to prioritize and manage your debts.

Tyson, Eric, and Ray Brown. *Home Buying Kit for Dummies*. Hoboken, NJ: Wiley, 2012. Everything you need to know about home prices, mortgages, and negotiating the best deal.

WEBSITES

Bankrate.com. A one-stop source for the latest interest rates for bank accounts, credit cards, loans, and more—plus reliable personal finance reads.

BethKobliner.com. From budget calculators to my latest blog posts, my website offers ways to continue improving your financial life.

CFPB.gov. The Consumer Financial Protection Bureau, which serves as a watchdog on topics like student loans, credit cards, mortgages, and more, is constantly coming up with new tools to help you stay in control of your finances.

GetRichSlowly.org. Created by a self-described "average guy" who took control of his finances and worked his way out of debt, this site provides smart coverage on a variety of money topics.

Iwillteachyoutoberich.com. Entrepreneurial-minded millennials aiming to earn more to afford the lifestyle they want will appreciate this blog run by the charismatic Ramit Sethi.

Kiplinger.com. *Kiplinger's Personal Finance* magazine covers all the basics, including the latest investing advice.

Militaryonesource.mil. Comprehensive answers to questions on benefits, taxes, education, retirement, and other money matters for active members of the military and veterans.

Mint.com. An all-in-one app and site for budgeting and tracking investments, plus a blog covering personal finance topics.

NerdWallet.com. Reviews and rankings for every bank, credit card, insurance provider, and loan servicer you can think of, plus insurance quotes, calculators, and in-depth articles.

Nolo.com. A source for online legal forms and legal info, on subjects ranging from forming an LLC to signing a lease to filing for workers comp.

TheBillfold.com. Personal essays, news analysis, and interviews covering "everything you wanted to know about money but were too polite to ask," with a millennial/Gen X bent.

time.com/money. *Money* magazine, where I began my career, continues to offer solid financial advice.

Wiserwomen.org. The Women's Institute for a Secure Retirement features calculators and tips to help you plan for the future.

For a full list of the most up-to-date personal finance resources, please visit bethkobliner.com/resources.

SPECIAL ACKNOWLEDGMENTS

EVERY VERSION OF *Get a Financial Life* has been an enormous team effort, and this fourth edition is no exception. Beginning on p. 297, I've listed more than 800 sources to whom I turned for expertise in both the original and current editions of the book. This special section, however, acknowledges those people who have made contributions above and beyond the call of duty.

First, the financial experts who have given generously of their time in helping me prepare this and the previous editions of *Get a Financial Life*. Special thanks go to investment advisors Lew and Karen Altfest; student loan advisor and president of Campus Consultants Kalman Chany; fee-only insurance consultant Glenn Daily; Virginia Bankers Association professor emeritus at the University of Virginia Richard DeMong; author and head of Market Education at Nav Gerri Detweiler; former vice president of communications at the Consumer Bankers Association Fritz Elmendorf; vice president at HSH.com Keith Gumbinger; president of the Women's Institute for a Secure Retirement Cindy Hounsell; EvaluateLifeInsurance .org's James Hunt; and senior vice president, public affairs, and chief communications officer at the Insurance Information Institute Jeanne Salvatore. For his contributions to the first three editions, I remain grateful to the late Art Spinella, former president of CNW Marketing Research.

I also owe a debt of gratitude to the following people, whose expertise was invaluable in putting together this new edition of the book: principal at Lighthouse Capital Partners Ann Diamond; chief operating officer at TransUnion David Emery; cofounder and CEO of PolicyGenius Jennifer Fitzgerald; director of public education for Experian Rod Griffin; director of content operations and strategic alliances at Military.com Terry Howell; student financial aid expert Mark Kantrowitz; director, Tax Policy & Professional Standards at the AICPA, Melissa Labant; freelance writer and consultant Catherine Lee; estate planning and tax attorney Larry Lehmann; senior vice president and chief financial analyst at Bankrate.com Greg McBride; Rutgers professor and specialist in financial resource management Barbara O'Neill; attorney for the National Consumer Law Center Andrew Pizor; director, Health Care Value Hub at the Consumers Union, Lynn Quincy; assistant editor at *Bon Appétit* Amiel Stanek; research consultant for the Center for Retirement Research at Boston College Francis Vitagliano; and senior vice president and chief economist at the Insurance Information Institute Steven N. Weisbart.

And I greatly appreciate the assistance given by these experts at various stages of writing *Get a Financial Life*: Kent Allison, Camilla Altamura, Roy Assad, John Battaglia, David Berson, Jack Bonné, Raschelle Burton, Ed Chang, Karen Christie, Annette Clearwaters of Clarity Investments + Planning, Steven Enright, Andrew Eschtruth, Wilson Fadely, Karen Ferguson of the Pension Rights Center, Martin Fleisher, Jerry Gattegno, Linda Lee Goldberg, Sheldon Jacobs, James Johnson, Stuart Kessler, L. Harold Levinson, Gail Liberman, Brian Mattes of Vanguard, Keith Maurer, Randall McCathren, credit card guru Robert McKinley, Michael Moebs, Walter Molony, Bob Murray, Edward L. Neumann, Tom Ochsenschlager, Marty O'Malley, Glenn Pape, Sharon Ridenour, Joseph Ridout, Diane Rivers, Don Roberts, Martin M. Shenkman, Janice Shields, William Speciale, Jack VanDerhei, Craig Watts, Eric A. Wiening of the American Institute for Chartered Casualty Property Underwriters, Rolf Winch, and Scott Witt.

My former coworkers at *Money* were incredibly generous with their time and help when I was writing the first edition of *Get a Financial Life*. They included Caroline Donnelly, Richard Eisenberg, Judy Feldman, Carla Fried, Eric Gelman, Jordan Goodman, Kelly Smith, and Patti Straus. I would especially like to thank Gary

Belsky and Walter Updegrave for their incredibly valuable feedback on the original edition. My gratitude also goes to Tyler Mathisen of CNBC and Frank Lalli, the former managing editor of *Money*, who has been a mentor to me. From *Glamour*, I'd like to thank Cindi Leive, Ellen Seidman, Noelle Howey, and Rebecca Webber.

Many friends and colleagues also offered valuable input at various stages. They include Rick Allen, Robin Alssid, Andrew Bradfield, Richard Burgheim, Larry Burke, Eileen Choi, Nicole Chong, Fran Claro, Joe Claro, Paul Cohen, Jon Cowan, Adam Feldman, Elizabeth Fenner, Anne Fentress, James Gates, Lynn Goldner, Glenn Hodes, Jennifer Jaeck, Michael Kantor, Jonathan Karp, Sam Kerstein, Skye Ketron, John Kildahl, Maki Kitamura, Janet Klosklo, Kenneth Kobliner, Miriam Diamond Kobliner, Perry Kobliner, Michelle Kosch, Steve Kotsen, Kathy Landau, Megan McCrudden, Carmen Morais, Vanessa O'Connell, Max Phillips, Melissa Phipps, Parker Reilly, Ruby Reilly, Jonah Sacks, Mark Safire, Rebecca Scott, Anne Morgan Spalter, Michael Spalter, Lisa Turvey, David Witt, and Dave Zinczenko.

I would also like to single out Jessica Ashbrook, Marisa Bardach, Karen Cheney, Sarah Courteau, Scott DeSimon, Max Dickstein, Valerie Popp, Kaitlin Puccio, Jeffrey Rotter, Leslie Schnur, and Julia Wetherell, who have put in literally hundreds of hours helping me ensure that every data point in the new edition has been meticulously researched, checked, and rechecked. I am also especially indebted to Danielle Claro, whose insight, humor, and remarkable editing skills were, and continue to be, a godsend.

I owe gratitude to Simon & Schuster, notably to Sarah Pinckney Whitmire (my editor on the original version with Bob Asahina), Doris Cooper, the intrepid and talented Michelle Howry (my editor for version three and this current fourth edition) and her assistant Lara Blackman, Christine Lloreda (who guided me through three editions), Kaitlin Olson, Rachel Rader, Trish Todd, and Mark Gompertz. I would like to thank Gordon Kato, who believed in this book from the beginning, and Kate Lee of ICM as well as Suzanne Gluck of the William Morris Agency.

I want to thank Rebecca, Adam, and Jacob for being incredibly patient while I worked during late nights and weekends—and for making me laugh. Special thanks to my dad, Harold Kobliner, who when he pays his bills (yes, he uses stamps and everything!) slips a handmade "flier" describing *Get a Financial Life* in with his check and invoice. ("If you're going to pay 49 cents for the stamp, why not get some free PR?" he wisely asks.) Also, thanks to my mom, Shirley Kobliner, for coming up with this great title (which has still held up!) more than 20 years ago, when I was in my twenties.

And most of all, I would like to thank my husband, David. I started writing *Get a Financial Life* before we were married. I remember I used to procrastinate by organizing, and he'd ask, "Do you want to look back in twenty years and say, 'I sure was organized,' or do you want to look back on writing a book?" Now, more than twenty years (and three kids) later, I can say you were so right, my love. Go, Blue Jays!

ACKNOWLEDGMENTS

THE FOLLOWING IS a list of the hundreds of people who generously gave of their time and expertise over the years to make this book possible. I made my best effort to include everyone who pitched in. If anyone has inadvertently been left out, I apologize.

Introduction

Larry Cohen, SRI International; Carmen Denavas-Walt, U.S. Bureau of the Census; Neal Fogg, Center for Labor Market Studies at Northeastern University; Jeffrey Hackett, National Opinion Research Center at the University of Chicago; Steven Haugen, U.S. Bureau of Labor Statistics; Stephanie Schlandt, Payment Systems; Andrew Sum, Center for Labor Market Studies at Northeastern University; David Tong, SRI International; Stephanie White, U.S. Bureau of Labor Statistics.

Chapter 2: Taking Stock of Your Financial Life

Durant Abernathy, National Foundation for Consumer Credit; Mari Adam, Adam Financial Associates; Kent Allison, PricewaterhouseCoopers; Mark Beal, CPA; David W. Bennett, FMC Financial Group; Debbie Bianucci, Bank Administration Institute; Kent Brunette, American Association of Retired Persons; Anthony Burke, Internal Revenue Service; Gail Cunningham, National Foundation for Credit Counseling; Peg Downey, Money Plans; Ericka Ecker, The Spacialist; Steven Enright, Enright, Mollin, Cascio & Ramusevic; Wilson Fadely, Internal Revenue Service; Linda Hamilton, CPA; Steven Haugen, U.S. Bureau of Labor Statistics; Cindy Hounsell, Women's Institute for a Secure Retirement; Pat Keefe, Credit Union National Association; Ross Levin, Accredited Investors; Greg McBride, Bankrate.com; Ed Mierzwinski, U.S. Public Interest Research Group (PIRG); Ron Montoya, Edmunds.com; Bill Moss, American Express; Tracy Nelson, Paychex; Glenn Pape, Ayco Company; John Pfister, Chicago Title and Trust Company; Jenice Robinson, Institute on Taxation and Economic Policy; John Rogers, Bureau of Labor Statistics; Steve Sanders, Sanders Investment Advisors; Ken Scott, Ken Scott Communications; Kyle Selberg, BankingMyWay.com; William Speciale, David L. Babson & Company; Marilyn Steinmetz, Mutual Service Associates; Kristyn Stout, The Ryland Group; Tracy Van Auker, Paychex; Jeannette Weiland, Bank Administration Institute; Stephanie White, U.S. Bureau of Labor Statistics; Dick Wolfe, ADP; Lisa Zaslow, independent organization consultant.

Chapter 3: Dealing with Debt

John Abadie, NationsBank; Mari Adam, Adam Financial Associates; Fiona Adams, Student Loan Marketing Association (Sallie Mae); Jonathan Adkins, Debt Counselors of America; Deb Adler, New York State Credit Union League; Deborah Ankrom, Student Loan Marketing Association (Sallie Mae); Stephanie Babyak, U.S. Department of Education; Carolyn Balfany, MasterCard Worldwide; Bill Banks, Chemical Bank; Karen Barney, Identity Theft Resource Center; Sandy Baum, The College Board; Gary Beanblossom, U.S. Department of Education; Monica Beaupre, American Express; Ricky Beggs, Black Book; Ed Block, automotive lease consultant; James A. Boyle, College Parents of America; Elaine Cafasso, Oak Brook Bank; Jessica Caldwell, Edmunds.com; Glenn Canner, Federal Reserve Board; Dennis Carroll, National Center for Education Statistics; Nancy Castleman, Good Advice Press; Kalman Chany, Campus Consultants; Tim Christensen, U.S. Department of Education; Karen Christie, Bankrate.com; Sandra Chu, Visa USA; Alex Cobos, Volkswagen of America; Larry Cohen, SRI International; Paul Combe, Knight College Resource Group; James Daly, *Credit Card News*; Linda Del Castillo, Student Loan Marketing Association (Sallie Mae); Jason Delisle, New America Foundation; Richard F. DeMong, McIntire School of Commerce at the University of Virginia; Gerri Detweiler, Credit.com; Claire Diamond, AT&T Universal Card Services; Ken Eaton, Stepp & Rothwell; Robyn Eckard, Kelley Blue Book; Rachel Edelstein, U.S. Department of Education; Liz Eischeid, TransUnion; Marc Eisenson, Good Advice Press; Fritz Elmendorf, Consumer Bankers Association; David Emery, TransUnion; Brad Fay, Roper Organization; Susan Forman, Visa USA; Ian Foss, U.S. Department of Education; Gerhard Fries, Federal Reserve Board; Jean Frohlicher, National Council of Higher Education Loan Programs; Luther Gatling, Budget & Credit Counseling Services; Dave Gelinas, Davidson College; Beth Givens, Privacy Rights Clearinghouse; Jane Glickman, U.S. Department of Education; Linda Goldberg, CarQ; Edward Gonciarz, Goldberg Gonciarz & Scudieri; David Graubard, Kera & Graubard; Jeffrey Green, Faulkner & Grey; Meredith Griffanti, Equifax; Rod Griffin, Experian; Keith Gumbinger, HSH Associates; Robert Hall, Corestates Dealer Services Corporation; Charles Hart, Chart Software; Dayna Hart, General Motors; Ed Harting, Auto Lease Guide; Paul Havemann, HSH Associates; Robert Heady, Bank Rate Monitor; Evan Hendricks, Privacy Times; Stephen Henson, Kelley Blue Book; Stuart Himmelfarb, Roper Organization; Jeanne Hogarth, Federal Reserve Board; Martha Holler, Student Loan Marketing Association (Sallie Mae); Brenda Horner, Consolidated Credit Counseling Services; Wendy Huntington, Student Loan Marketing Association (Sallie Mae); Joseph Hurley, Savingforcollege.com; Edie Irons, Project on Student Debt at the Institute for College Access & Success; Christine Isett, U.S. Department of Education; Robert Johnson, Credit Research Center at Purdue University; Jim Jurinski, University of Portland; Mark Kantrowitz, MK Consulting; Mike Kidwell, Debt Counselors of America; Jacqueline King, The College Board; Dottie Kingsley, Department of Education; Beth Kitchener, MasterCard Worldwide; Tim Klein, Equifax; Ross Kleinman, Student Loan Marketing Association (Sallie Mae); Laura Knapp, The College Board; Paula Knepper, National Center for Education Statistics; Janis Lamar, TRW Information Systems & Services; Ruth Lammert-Reeves, Georgetown University; Tony Langan, Chase Manhattan Bank; Phyllis Laubacher, MasterCard International; Roberta Lazarz, Credit Union National Association; Anne Leider, Octameron Associates; Jean Lesher, American Bankers Association; Aaron Lewis, Edmunds.com; Gail Liberman, Bank Rate Monitor; Lee Anne Linderman, Zions Bancorporation; Ronald S. Loshin, Bank Lease Consultants; Chris Lynn, Oak Brook Bank; John Maciarz, General Motors; Norm Magnuson, Associated Credit Bureaus; Drew Malizio, National Center for Education Statistics; Garry Marquiss, Bank One Corporation; John Marsh, Wachovia Bank of Georgia; Colleen Martin, TransUnion; Nancy Mathis, Congressman Joseph Kennedy's Office; Todd May, U.S. Department of Education; Greg McBride, Bankrate.com; Randall McCathren, Bank Lease Consultants; Bruce McClary, National Foundation for Credit Counseling; Robert B. McKinley, RAM Research; Sean McQuay, NerdWallet; David Melançon, Visa USA; Maria Mendler, Citibank; Ed Mierzwinski, U.S. Public Interest Research Group (PIRG); Scott Miller, Student Loan Marketing Association (Sallie Mae); Bob Murray, USA Group; Fatimah P. Nasra, Experian; Martin Neilson, Seafirst Bank; Jim Newell, Student Loan Marketing Association (Sallie Mae); Michael O'Brien, MasterCard International; Kit O'Kelly, European American Bank; Bussie Parker, Debt Counselors of America; Travis Plunkett, Consumer Federation of America; Christina Ra, Credit Karma; Mike Ramirez, CPA; William Redman, European American Bank; Philip Reed, Edmunds.com; Bruce Reid, AT&T Universal Card Services; Andrea Retzky, Congressman Joseph Kennedy's Office; Joseph Ridout, Consumer Action; Mark Rodgers, Citibank; Marcello Rojtman, U.S. Department of Education; Denise Rossitto, Student Loan Marketing Association (Sallie Mae); Yaron Samid, BillGuard (Prosper Daily); Stephanie Schlandt, Payment Systems; Dick Schliesmann, Wells Fargo; Matt Schulz, CreditCards.com; Hans Schumann, AT&T Universal Card Services; Tom Sclafani, American Express; Jeffrey

Scott, Fair Isaac Corporation; Ken Scott, Ken Scott Communications; Nick Sharkey, Ford Motor Credit Company; Tarry E. Shebesta, National Vehicle Leasing Association; Sheila Shekar, Visa USA; Lewis Siegel, Pirro, Collier, Cohen & Halpern; Jenny Smith, Oak Brook Bank; Henry Sommer, Miller, Frank & Miller; Keely Spillane, NerdWallet; Art Spinella, CNW Marketing Research; Jennifer Spoerri, Nolo Press; Anthony Sprauve, Fair Isaac Corporation; Virginia Stafford, American Bankers Association; Anna Stovall, Davidson College; Amy Sudol, Chase Manhattan Bank; Charlene Sullivan, Credit Research Center at Purdue University; Marcia Sullivan, Consumer Bankers Association; Terry Sullivan, General Motors; Ruth Susswein, Bankcard Holders of America; Laura Szabo-Kubitz, Project on Student Debt at the Institute for College Access & Success; Chintan Talati, Kelley Blue Book; Greg Tarmin, American Express; David Tong, SRI International; John Ulzheimer, Credit Sesame; Francine Van Nevel, Credit Union National Association; Jonathan Wahl, Edmunds.com; Senator Elizabeth Warren of Massachusetts; Gail Wasserman, American Express; Craig Watts, Fair Isaac Corporation; Laura Weiss, Consumers Union; Sharlene Weldon, Bankrate.com; Jay Westbrook, University of Texas at Austin School of Law; Lance Wilcox, J. D. Power and Associates; Catherine Williams, Money Management International; Lisa Williamson, Ward's Information Products; Jeff Wischerth, European American Bank; Labat Yancey, Equifax; Anissa Yates, Experian; Steven Zeisel, Consumer Bankers Association; Steve Zwillinger, U.S. Department of Education.

Chapter 4: Basic Banking

Heatherun Allison, Federal Reserve Bank; Kent Allison, PricewaterhouseCoopers; Karen Altfest, L. J. Altfest & Company; Lew Altfest, L. J. Altfest & Company; Angela Amberg, SunTrust Bank; Caryl Austrian, Federal Deposit Insurance Corporation; Peter Bakstansky, Federal Reserve Bank of New York; Brad Ball, Citibank; Linda A. Barlow, financial planner; David Barr, Federal Deposit Insurance Corporation; Richard Beebe, Bank of America; Debbie Bianucci, Bank Administration Institute; Brian Black, Bank Administration

Institute; Alexander Bove, Law Offices of Alexander Bove, Jr.; Dan
Brennan, Federal Reserve Bank of St. Louis; Jim Bruene, Online
Banking Report; Neal Chambliss, Furash & Company; Diane
Coffey, Dreyfus Corporation; Jeff Comerford, Equitable; Tom
Crosson, Consumer Bankers Association; Troy B. Daum, Wealth
Analytics; Elda Di Re, Ernst & Young; Lorna Doubet, Wells Fargo;
Fritz Elmendorf, Consumer Bankers Association; Steven Enright,
Enright Financial Advisors; Tom Feltner, Consumer Federation of
America; Alan Fisher, California Reinvestment Coalition; Linda
Foley, Identity Theft Resource Center; Linda Gladson, Varner &
Brandt; Elizabeth Greak, Corner & Greak Financial Consultants;
Joe Hagan, TNS Global; John Hall, American Bankers Associa-
tion; Eric Halperin, Center for Responsible Lending; Jennifer Har-
lan, Society Bank; Kathlyn Hoekstra, Federal Deposit Insurance
Corporation; Gunnar Hughes, Twentieth Century Services; Shel-
don Jacobs, *The No-Load Fund Investor*; Caroline Jervey, Bauer
Communications; Doug Johnson, American Bankers Association;
Jerry Karbon, Credit Union National Association; Cathy Keary,
Merrill Lynch; Pat Keefe, Credit Union National Association; Ken
Kehrer, Kenneth Kehrer Associates; David Klavitter, Credit Union
National Association; Tom Klipstine, General Motors; Stephen
Ledford, Global Concepts; Dina Lee, Ernst & Young; Lawrence
Lehmann, National Association of Estate Planners and Councils;
Ross Levin, Accredited Investors; Gail Liberman, Bank Rate Moni-
tor; Scott MacDonald, Southwestern Graduate School of Banking
at Southern Methodist University; Jane Mahoney, Equitable; Joyce
Manchester, Congressional Budget Office; Brian Mattes, Vanguard;
Greg McBride, Bankrate.com; Diana Mehl, BanxQuote; Michael
Moebs, Moebs Services; Anne Moore, Synergistics Research Corpo-
ration; Edward L. Neumann, Furash & Company; Steve Norwitz,
T. Rowe Price Associates; Karen Oetzel, Credit Union National
Association; Obrea Poindexter, Division of Consumer and Com-
munity Affairs, Federal Reserve Board; Barbara Raasch, Ernst &
Young; Christopher Renyi, Forrester Research; Ellen Ringel, Price
Waterhouse; Kevin Roach, Price Waterhouse; Richard Robida,
Speer & Associates; Mark Rodgers, Citibank; Jay Rosenstein,
Federal Deposit Insurance Corporation; Mimi Rossetti, Payment
Systems; James Royal, Informa; Brian Ruby, Green Dot; John

Sabelhaus, Urban Institute; Pam Sabin, Fiserv; Judith Saxe, Kronish Lieb Weiner & Hellman; Joel A. Schoenmeyer, attorney at law; Kyle Selberg, BankingMyWay.com; Janice Shields, Center of Study for Responsive Law; Robert Siciliano, IDTheftSecurity.com; Jonathan Skinner, Frank Batten School of Leadership and Public Policy, University of Virginia; Chrissy Snyder, Janus Capital Corporation; Barton Sotnick, Federal Reserve Bank of New York; William Speciale, David L. Babson & Company; Virginia Stafford, American Bankers Association; Ellen Stuart, Chemical Bank; Michele Stuvin, Executive Enterprises; Jack Tatom, Federal Reserve Bank of St. Louis; Christina Tetreault, Consumer Federation of America; Paul Thompson, Credit Union National Association; Ken Tumin, Deposit Accounts; Joseph Votava, Nixon, Peabody; Chad Watkins, Informa; Sandra Weiksner, Cleary Gottlieb Steen & Hamilton.

Chapter 5: All You Really Need to Know About Investing

Camilla Altamura, Lipper Analytical Services; Lew Altfest, L. J. Altfest & Company; Alexa Auerbach, Morningstar; Marc Beauchamp, North American Securities Administrators Association; Christine Benz, Morningstar; Jennifer Bright, R. L. Polk & Company; Paul Britt, ETF.com; Maria Bruno, Vanguard; Jim Cain, Lehman Brothers; Dan Caplinger, Motley Fool; Anand Chokkavelu, Motley Fool; Lisa Cholnoky, Smith Barney; Peter Cinquegrani, Investment Company Institute; Annette Clearwaters, Clarity Investments + Planning; Mark Coler, Mercer & Associates; John Collins, Investment Company Institute; Bob Connor, Smith Barney; Pete Crane, iMoneyNet; Kim Crawley, Morgan Stanley; Don Criniti, Fidelity Investments; Diane Cullen, Dalbar Financial Services; Ann Diamond, Lighthouse Capital Partners; Jon M. Diat, Standard & Poor's; Courtney Goethals Dobrow, Morningstar; Holly Duncan, Financial Engines; Richard Erickson, USAA; Dominic Falaschetti, Ibbotson Associates; Georgina Fiordalisi, Duff & Phelps; Nick Gendron, Lehman Brothers; Lynne Goldman, Cerulli Associates; Trista Hannan, Morningstar; Michael Herbst, Morningstar; Rowena Itchon, T. Rowe Price Associates; Sheldon Jacobs, The No-Load Fund Investor; Paula Kahanek, Ibbotson Associates; Dawn Kahler, Wiesenberger/Thomson Financial; Charles Kassouf, Mercer & Associates; Teri Kilduff, Fidelity Investments; Russ Kinnel, Morningstar; Patrice Kozlowski, Dreyfus Corporation; Mike Krasner, iMoneyNet; Annette Larson, Morningstar; Keith Lawson, Investment Company Institute; Marilyn Leiker, Lipper Analytical Services; Mark N. Lindblom, Morgan Stanley; Stephanie Linkous, United Services Advisors; Pam Livingston, E*Trade; Jeanine Magill, Morningstar; John Markese, American Association of Individual Investors; Anthony Massaro, Vanguard; Brian Mattes, Vanguard; Rachel McTague, Investment Company Institute; Patrick McVeigh, Franklin Research & Development; Norman Mehl, BanxQuote; Bob Mescal, Institute for Econometric Research; Marilyn Morrison, Fidelity Investments; Maggie Muraca, Motley Fool; Chip Norton, IBC/Donoghue; Steve Norwitz, T. Rowe Price Associates; Roger Nyhus, Frank Russell Company; Glen King Parker, Institute of Econometric Research; Chris Phillips, Frank Russell Company; Teri Redinger, IBC/Donoghue; Matthew Scott, Domini Social Investments; Ramy Shaalan, Wiesenberger/Thomson Financial; Mo Shafroth, Charles Schwab; Carling Spelhaug, Morningstar; Kimberly Stamel, Morningstar; Michelle Swartzentruber, Morningstar; Tom Taggart, Charles Schwab; Thomas Tays, United Services Advisors; Jon Teall, Lipper Analytical Services; Lukasz Thieme, Lipper Analytical Services; Robyn Tice, Fidelity Investments; Maurice Turner, Working Assets Capital Management; Julie Ann Urban, Ibbotson Associates; Michael Van Dam, Morningstar; Andrea Vassallo, Financial Engines; Ken Volpert, Vanguard; Bob Waid, Wilshire Associates; Alison Wertheim, Charles Schwab; John Woerth, Vanguard; Mark Wright, Morningstar.

Chapter 6: Living the Good Life in 2070

Kent Allison, PricewaterhouseCoopers; Ted Barna, PricewaterhouseCoopers; Harvey Berger, Grant Thornton; Andrea Bierstein, Western New England College School of Law; Joanna Bolden, American Association of Retired Persons; Jack Bonné, Gateway Asset Management; Kent Brunette, American Association of Retired Persons; Anthony Burke, Internal Revenue Service; Heather Chappel, PricewaterhouseCoopers; Steve Ciolino, Ernst & Young; Joe

Conway, Towers Perrin; Gloria Della, U.S. Department of Labor; Karl Ebert, Dinkytown.net; Asma Emneina, Financial Engines; Steven Enright, Enright Financial Advisors; Andrew Eschtruth, Center for Retirement Research at Boston College; Wilson Fadely, Internal Revenue Service; Karen Ferguson, Pension Rights Center; Edward Ferrigno, Profit Sharing/401k Council of America; Martin Fleisher, pension consultant; Phil Gambino, Social Security Administration; Jerry Gattegno, Deloitte & Touche; Hal Glassman, Department of Labor; Mary Ann Green, MBL Life Assurance; Hattie Greenan, Plan Sponsor Council of America; Amy Grzybowski, Center for Retirement Research at Boston College; Tom Hakala, KPMG Peat Marwick; Ed Hansen, Mercer & Associates; Cindy Hounsell, Women's Institute for a Secure Retirement; Christopher L. Jones, Financial Engines; Richard Koski, Buck Consultants; Ross Levin, Accredited Investors; Jules Lichtenstein, U.S. Small Business Administration; Tom Margenau, Social Security Administration; John Markese, American Association of Individual Investors; Doug Mollin, Enright, Mollin, Cascio & Ramusevic; Mike Packard, Pension Benefit Guaranty Corporation; Glenn Pape, Ernst & Young; R. Michael Parry, American Planning Group; Carolyn Pemberton, Employee Benefit Research Institute; Stephanie Poe, Mercer & Associates; Mark Puccia, Standard & Poor's; Tangela Richardson, Social Security Administration; Robert Runde, American Planning Group; Rania Sedhom, Buck Consultants; Christine Seltz, Hewitt Associates; Greg Spencer, U.S. Bureau of the Census; Susan Stawick, Internal Revenue Service; David Strauss, Pension Benefit Guaranty Corporation; Jack VanDerhei, Employee Benefit Research Institute; James Velten, Coopers & Lybrand; Pamela Villarreal, National Center for Policy Analysis; Francis Vitagliano, Center for Retirement Research at Boston College; Paul Westbrook, Westbrook Financial Advisors; David Wray, Profit Sharing/401k Council of America; Caryn Zappone, Hewitt Associates.

Chapter 7: Oh, Give Me a Home

Gopal Ahluwalia, National Association of Home Builders; Ali Ahmad, Mortgage Bankers Association; Mark Beal, CPA; Rick

Beebe, Bank of America; David W. Bennett, FMC Financial Group; Mark Berman, Townsend Consulting Group; David Berson, Federal National Mortgage Association (Fannie Mae); Katherine Billings, Federal Home Loan Mortgage Corporation (Freddie Mac); Amy Bonitatibus, Federal Home Mortgage Corporation (Fannie Mae); Mary Burt, National Association of Mortgage Brokers; Raschelle Burton, Federal National Mortgage Corporation (Fannie Mae); Kevin Bussell, Rent.net; Mark Calabria, National Association of Realtors; Michael Carliner, National Association of Home Builders; Pam Carmichael, HOME Inc.; Andrew Carswell, National Association of Home Builders; Ed Chang, Interet; Brian Chappelle, Mortgage Bankers Association; Larry Clark, International Association of Assessing Officers; Laura Clavier, Merrill Lynch; Wayne Collett, Countrywide Funding Corporation; Nancy Condon, Federal Home Loan Mortgage Corporation (Freddie Mac); William A. Connelly, U.S. Department of Housing and Urban Development; John L. Councilman, National Association of Mortgage Brokers; Gail Cunningham, National Foundation for Credit Counseling; Josh Dare, Federal National Mortgage Association (Fannie Mae); Callie Dosberg, Fannie Mae; Douglas Duncan, Mortgage Bankers Association; Brad Dwin, Hope Now; Michelle Elliott, National Association of Home Builders; Robert Engelstad, Federal National Mortgage Association (Fannie Mae); John Ferchen, Norwest; Mark Ferrulo, Florida Public Interest Research Group (PIRG); Lauren Francis, JPMorgan Chase; Weldon Freeman, Department of Agriculture; Lisa Gagnon, Freddie Mac; Monica Gallagher, Hewitt Associates; Brad German, Freddie Mac; Joe Gilvary, U.S. Bureau of the Census; Vince Gisonti, Deloitte & Touche; Elizabeth Greak, Corner & Greak Financial Consultants; Ginna Green, Center for Responsible Lending; Keith Gumbinger, HSH Associates; Steven Haugen, U.S. Bureau of Labor Statistics; Kevin Hawkins, Federal National Mortgage Association (Fannie Mae); Eric Hersey, National Community Reinvestment Coalition; Mollie Hightower, National Association of Mortgage Brokers; Liz Johnson, National Association of Realtors; Stefanie Johnson, Federal Housing Finance Agency; Ted Jones, Real Estate Research Center; Joel Kan, Mortgage Bankers Association; Maggie Kasperski, National Association of Realtors; Cathy Keary, Merrill Lynch; Carolyn Kemp, Mortgage

Bankers Association; Sam Khater, National Association of Realtors; Alfred King, Federal National Mortgage Association (Fannie Mae); Andrew Kochera, National Association of Home Builders; Doug Krug, Norwest; Jan Kruse, National Consumer Law Center; Mindy La Branche, National Council of State Housing Agencies; Toni Langkau, New York State Housing Authority; Sarah Lawler, National Council of State Housing Agencies; Sandy Levy, Universal Lending; John Lewis, G.E. Capital; William Lloyd, Norwest Mortgage; Dick Manuel, U.S. Department of Housing and Urban Development; Howard Marder, New York State Housing Authority; Greg Martin, Draper and Kramer; Laura Maxwell, Deloitte & Touche; Daniel McCue, Joint Center for Housing Studies at Harvard University; Ken McKinnon, U.S. Department of Veterans Affairs; Jason Menke, Wells Fargo; Ed Mierzwinski, U.S. Public Interest Research Group (PIRG); Walter Molony, National Association of Realtors; Paul Mondor, Mortgage Bankers Association; Katie Monfre, Mortgage Guaranty Insurance Corporation; Larry Montague, Deloitte & Touche; Trish Morris, National Association of Realtors; Eileen Neely, Federal National Mortgage Association (Fannie Mae); Bonnie O'Dell, Federal National Mortgage Association (Fannie Mae); David Olson, Wholesale Access; Martin O'Malley, Stratis Financial Corporation; Forrest Pafenberg, National Association of Realtors; Wendy Peca, Chicago Title and Trust; Sharon Peters, Institute of Real Estate Management; Andrew Pizor, National Consumer Law Center; Julie Reeves, National Council of State Housing Agencies; Cheryl Regan, Federal Home Loan Mortgage Corporation (Freddie Mac); Sharon Ridenour, Norwest Mortgage; Vicki Riedel, Mortgage Bankers Association; Douglas Robinson, Federal Home Loan Mortgage Corporation (Freddie Mac); Nicole Robinson, Homeownership Preservation Foundation; Sam Rogers, Center for Responsible Lending; Molly Rohal, Pew Research Center; Marcia Rosen, National Housing Law Project; Michelle Sabolich, Atomic Public Relations; Connie St. John, Bank of America; Margot Saunders, National Consumer Law Center; Michael Schlerf, Mortgage Bankers Association; Jay Shackford, National Association of Home Builders; Christine Seltz, Hewitt Associates; Adrian Skiles, Atlanta Mortgage Group; Brian Sullivan, U.S. Department of Housing and Urban Development;

Jacqueline Susmann, U.S. Department of Agriculture; Dave Totaro, Dime Savings Bank; Rick Trilsch, Florida Public Interest Research Group (PIRG); John Tuccillo, National Association of Realtors; Robert Van Order, Federal Home Loan Mortgage Corporation (Freddie Mac); Robert Van Raaphorst, Mortgage Bankers Association; Jesse Van Tol, National Community Reinvestment Coalition; Bob Visini, LoanPerformance; John H. Vogel, Tuck School of Business at Dartmouth College; Andrea Waas, National Association of Mortgage Brokers; Susan M. Wachter, The Wharton School, University of Pennsylvania; Ginny Walker, RealtyTrac.com; Margery Wasserman, National Association of Personal Financial Advisors; Sabrina White, Merrill Lynch; William White, U.S. Department of Veterans Affairs; George Wilson, Department of Housing and Urban Development; Susan E. Woodward, Sand Hill Econometrics; Lemar C. Wooley, U.S. Department of Housing and Urban Development; Jean Wussow, National Association of Realtors; Kris Yamamoto, Countrywide Funding Corporation; Catherine Zimring, Countrywide Funding Corporation.

Chapter 8: Insurance: What You Need and What You Don't

Laura Adams, InsuranceQuotes.com; Roy Assad, RBA Insurance Strategies; Rich Bailey, UnumProvident; Bob Barney, Compulife; Michael Barry, Insurance Information Institute; Kathy Bell, Progressive Auto Insurance; Kip Biggs, State Farm Insurance Company; Birny Birnbaum, Consumers Union and the Center for Economic Justice; Bob Bland, Quotesmith; Phyllis Bonfield, American Society of Chartered Life Underwriters; Joseph Bosnack, Sr., Arthur Rothlein Agency; Ann H. Brockmeyer, Hartmann & Associates; Steve Brostoff, American Council of Life Insurers; Bruce Bruscia, InterWest Insurance Services; Karen Burger, American Institute for Chartered Property Casualty Underwriters; Anthony Burke, Internal Revenue Service; John Calagna, New York State Department of Insurance; Brenda Cargile, Federal Crime Insurance Program; Dee Caruso, Illinois Department of Insurance; Paul Cholette, Blue Cross and Blue Shield Association; Diane Coffey, American Council of Life Insurers; Mark Connor, U.S. Department of Labor; Richard Coorsh, Health Insurance Association of America; Sam Cunningham, Anderson & Anderson Insurance Brokers; Glenn Daily, fee-only insurance consultant; Gloria Della, Employee Benefits Security Administration; Chris d'Eon, InsureWell; Dan Devine, Employee Benefit Research Institute; Jack Dolan, American Council of Life Insurers; Bill Dommasch, GEICO; Henry Dowdle, Provident Life and Accident Insurance Company; Pam Drellow, Blue Cross and Blue Shield Association; Sande Drew, eHealth; Rob Eddy, National Association of Insurance and Financial Advisors; Andrew Ede, Massachusetts Mutual Life Insurance Company; Susan Farmer, American Society of Chartered Life Underwriters; Terrence Fergus, KPMG Peat Marwick; Mary Fortune, Unum; LaToya Gardner, Allstate Insurance Company; Scott Garland, State Farm Insurance Company; Anne Getz, Moody's Investors Services; Terence Gordon, Avis Rent A Car System; Gene Grabowski, American Council of Life Insurers; Ed Graves, The American College; Paul Gribbons, Massachusetts Mutual Life Insurance Company; Don Haas, Haas Financial Services; Karen Hamilton, American Institute for Chartered Property Casualty Underwriters; Ed Hansen, Mercer & Associates; Lemore Hecht, MetLife; Susan Hendrick, Federal Emergency Management Agency; Judith Hill, The American College; Ric Hill, 20th Century Insurance Company; Katherine Hoffman, National Association of Professional Insurance Agents; Kevin Hofmockel, American Academy of Estate Planning Attorneys; Erin Holve, AcademyHealth; Charles Horne, Amica Mutual Insurance Company; James Hunt, Consumer Federation of America; Robert Hunter, Consumer Federation of America; Ted Huntington, Professional Insurance Agents of California and Nevada; Amy Ingram, TermQuote; Kenneth Ingram, TermQuote; Matthew J. Jachelski, Financial Solutions Group; Linda Jackson, U.S. Department of Labor; William Jarrett, Social Security Administration; Donald Jayne, Executive Financial Systems; Amy Jeter, Kaiser Family Foundation; James Johnson, Unum; Chuck Jones, ChoicePoint Asset Company; Katherine Jones, National Association of Insurance Commissioners; Stuart Kantor, Urban Institute; Peter Katt, independent life insurance advisor; Susan Keller, Golden Eagle Insurance; Kate Kennedy, Society for Human Resource Management; Peter Kensicki, Eastern

Kentucky University; Chris Ketchum, American Institute for Chartered Property Casualty Underwriters; Al Killeffer, MetLife; Rick Koski, Buck Consultants; Amy Kraus, Mutual of Omaha Insurance Company; Randy Lamm, Allstate Insurance Company; Bruce Lee, Mercer & Associates; Arlene Lilly, American Council of Life Insurers; Elliot Lipson, independent insurance consultant; Dick Luedke, State Farm Insurance Company; Adam Lyons, TheZebra.com; Jim Marks, Society of Chartered Property Casualty Underwriters; Greg Marsh, GEICO; Brandi Marth, Fireman's Fund Insurance Company; Kristi Martineau, InsureWell; Robert Marvin, Internal Revenue Service; Judith Maurer, Low Load Insurance Services; Keith Maurer, Low Load Insurance Services; Mike Mayers, Beall Garner Screen & Geare Company; Larry Mayewski, A. M. Best Company; Ken McDonnell, Employee Benefit Research Institute; Wayne McHargue, American United Life Insurance Company; Jennifer McInnis, Amica Mutual Insurance Company; Annalise McKean-Marcus, Hertz Corporation; Kathy Melley, Community Catalyst; Robert Miller, New York Life Insurance Company; Al Minor, Health Insurance Association of America; Tom Monson, State Farm Insurance Company; Rhonda Moritz, A. M. Best Company; Todd Muller, Independent Insurance Agents of America; Tim Murphy, Northwestern Mutual Life Insurance Company; Nan Nases, Illinois Department of Insurance; Haig Neville, Haig Neville Associates; Eric Nordman, National Association of Insurance Commissioners; Mike Norton, Unum; Donald Oakes, Society of Chartered Property Casualty Underwriters; Mike Odom, Blue Shield of California; Bill O'Neill, Standard & Poor's; Kendal-Leigh O'Neill, Time Warner; John Paganelli, First Transamerica Life Insurance Company; Jerry Parsons, State Farm Insurance Company; Carolyn Pemberton, Employee Benefit Research Institute; Nancy Peskin, Metropolitan Life Insurance Company; Chris Petrocelli, Petrocelli Group; Irving Pfeffer, insurance consultant; Tim Pfeifer, consulting actuary; Jerome Phillip, Mutual of Omaha Insurance Company; Stephanie Poe, Mercer & Associates; Mark Prindle, Risk Management Solutions; Lee Procida, Braithwaite Communications; Nate Purpura, eHealth; Usha Ranji, Kaiser Family Foundation; Diana Reace, Hewitt Associates; Donna Reichle, National Automobile Dealers Association; Andrea Riggs, GetInsured.com; John Roman,

American Association of Preferred Provider Organizations; Ted Rossman, Bankrate.com; Fred Rumack, Buck Consultants; Walter Runkle, Consumer Credit Insurance Association; Jeanne Salvatore, Insurance Information Institute; Dennis M. Sandoval, American Academy of Estate Planning Attorneys; Bob Sasser, State Farm Insurance Company; Paul Schattenberg, USAA; Tracy Schauer, IDEA; David Seldin, Blue Shield of California; Iris Shaffer, Blue Cross and Blue Shield of Illinois; Craig P. Shanley, Amica Mutual Insurance Company; Tracy Sherman, Unum; Harold Skipper, Department of Risk Management & Insurance Research, Georgia State University; Judy Snelson, Allied Insurance Agencies of America; Camille Sorosiak, American Hospital Association; Steve Stark, SelectQuote; Peter Starratt, GetInsured.com; Dale Stephenson, National Conference of Insurance Guaranty Funds; Morey Stettner, insurance consultant; Mark Stevens, Federal Emergency Management Agency; Dottye Stewart, Wholesale Insurance Network; Jennie Storey, Provident Life and Accident Insurance Company; Ron Sunderman, Skogman Carlson Insurance; Phil Supple, State Farm Insurance Company; Catherine Theroux, LIMRA; Doug Tillett, National Association of Life Underwriters; Des Toups, Insurance.com; Julie Vokracka, American Express; Billy Watson, Anderson & Watson; Steven Weisbart, Insurance Information Institute; Lisa Wetherby, Society of Financial Service Professionals; Don White, Group Health Association of America; Eric Wiening, American Institute for Chartered Property & Casualty Underwriters; Rolf Winch, Lifetime Financial Partners; Scott Witt, Witt Actuarial Services; Jim Woods, Lowest Premium Insurance Services; Loretta Worters, Insurance Information Institute; Josh Wozman, Towers Watson; Sara Woznicki, Compare.com; Gay Yellen, Ameritas Life Insurance Company; Mark Zagaroli, State Farm Insurance Company; John Zarubnicky, First Transamerica Life Insurance Company; Robert Zirkelbach, America's Health Insurance Plans.

Chapter 9: How to Make Your Life Less Taxing

Nancy Anderson, H&R Block; John Battaglia, Deloitte & Touche; Henri Bersoux, Ernst & Young; Andrea Bierstein, Kirby McInerney

& Squire; Robert Blodgett, Intuit; Richard Borean, Tax Foundation; Sarah Bulgatz, Charles Schwab; Anthony Burke, Internal Revenue Service; Joan Carroll, Coopers & Lybrand; William Church, Ernst & Young; Matthew Cimento, American Bar Association; John Collins, Investment Company Institute; Nic Corpora, Intuit; Beth Dozier, Free File Alliance; Gary DuBoff, Ernst & Young; Ed Emerman, A. Foster Higgins & Company; Wilson Fadely, Internal Revenue Service; David Fridling, Towers Perrin; Lewis Gatch, Gatch Law Offices; Jerry Gattegno, Deloitte Tax; Sam Gilford, Consumer Financial Protection Bureau; Stephen Gold, Tax Foundation; Steven Gold, Center for the Study of the States; Jeffrey Gotlinger, Ernst & Young; Nadine Habousha, Arthur Andersen; Tom Hakala, KPMG Peat Marwick; David Hochstim, Bear Stearns; Ken Hubenak, Internal Revenue Service; Jay Hyde, American Institute of CPAs; Anjali Jariwala, FIT Advisors; Malin Jennings, Investment Company Institute; Michael Keaton, American Moving & Storage Association; Judy Keisling, H&R Block; Kate Kennedy, Society for Human Resources Management; Sidney Kess, CPA; Stuart Kessler, Goldstein Golub Kessler & Company; Gene King, H&R Block; Roger Kirby, Kirby McInerney & Squire; John Koegel, Grant Thornton; Melissa Labant, American Institute of CPAs; Dina Lee, Ernst & Young; Terry Lemons, Internal Revenue Service; L. Harold Levinson, Vanderbilt University; Glenn Liebman, Ernst & Young; Norm Magnuson, Associated Credit Bureaus; Tom Margenau, Social Security Administration; Brian Mattes, Vanguard; Daniel D. Morris, Morris + D'Angelo; Marilyn Morrison, Fidelity Investments; Colette Murphy, Ernst & Young; Yadira Nadal, Internal Revenue Service; Tracy Nelson, Paychex; Tom Ochsenschlager, Grant Thornton; Maggie O'Donovan-Bolton, Coopers & Lybrand; Glenn Pape, Ayco Company; Jodi Patterson, Internal Revenue Service; Ira Pilchen, American Bar Association; Kyle Pomerleau, Tax Foundation; Sylvia Pozarnsky, Ernst & Young; Todd Ransom, H&R Block; Ellen Ringel, PricewaterhouseCoopers; Diane Rivers, tax attorney; Don Roberts, Internal Revenue Service; Jeff Saccacio, Coopers & Lybrand; Sheri Sankner, BDO Seidman; Bertram Schaeffer, Ernst & Young; Martin Shenkman, tax attorney; Susan Stawick, Internal Revenue Service; Ronald Stone, Stone & Associates; Richard Stricof, BDO Seidman; Peter L. Tashman, CPA; Michael Townsend, American Bankers Association; Susan

Van Alstyne, H&R Block; James E. Velten, Coopers & Lybrand; Mary Vogel, H&R Block; Sidney Weinman, Research Institute of America; John Whitham, American College of Financial Services; Craig Wolman, Ernst & Young; Paul Yurachek, Gurtz & Associates; John Ziegelbauer, Grant Thornton.

Chapter 10: Making the Most of Military Benefits

Edward Early, Navy Office of Information; Terry Howell, Military .com; Cynthia Olson, Iraq and Afghanistan Veterans of America; Egan Reich, U.S. Department of Labor; Matt Ross, Iraq and Afghanistan Veterans of America; Mark Szymanski, Iraq and Afghanistan Veterans of America; Jesus Uranga, Navy Office of Information.

INDEX

ABOUT THE AUTHOR

Beth Kobliner is a personal finance commentator and journalist. She is also the author of a guide for parents, *Make Your Kid a Money Genius (Even If You're Not)*. She was selected by President Obama to serve on the President's Advisory Council on Financial Capability for Young Americans, dedicated to increasing the financial know-how of kids of all ages and economic backgrounds. A former staff writer at *Money* magazine, Beth has contributed to the *New York Times* and the *Wall Street Journal* and has appeared on CNN, MSNBC, *Today*, *Sesame Street*, and NPR. She began her career researching and writing more than one hundred columns for the personal finance pioneer Sylvia Porter, whose syndicated column appeared in over 150 newspapers nationwide. Beth graduated from Brown University and lives with her family in New York City.